A multi-locus analysis of Arabic negation

T0322710

Edinburgh Studies in Theoretical Linguistics

Series Editors: Nikolas Gisborne, University of Edinburgh and Andrew Hippisley, University of Kentucky

Books in the series address the core sub-disciplines of linguistics – phonology, morphology, syntax, semantics and pragmatics – and their interfaces, with a particular focus on novel data from various sources and their challenges to linguistic theorising.

Series Editors
Nikolas Gisborne is Professor of Linguistics at the University of Edinburgh.

Andrew Hippisley is Professor of Linguistics and Linguistics Programme Director at the University of Kentucky.

Editorial Board
Umberto Ansaldo, University of Hong Kong
Balthasar Bickel, Universität Zürich
Olivier Bonami, Université Paris Diderot
Heinz Giegerich, University of Edinburgh
Jen Hay, University of Canterbury
Stefan Müller, Humboldt-Universität zu Berlin
Mitsuhiko Ota, University of Edinburgh
Robert Truswell, University of Edinburgh
David Willis, University of Cambridge
Alan Yu, University of Chicago

Visit the Edinburgh Studies in Theoretical Linguistics website at www.edinburghuniversitypress.com/series/esitl

A multi-locus analysis of Arabic negation

Micro-variation in Southern Levantine, Gulf, and Standard Arabic

Ahmad Alqassas

EDINBURGH
University Press

Edinburgh University Press is one of the leading university presses
in the UK. We publish academic books and journals in our selected
subject areas across the humanities and social sciences, combining
cutting-edge scholarship with high editorial and production values to
produce academic works of lasting importance. For more information
visit our website: edinburghuniversitypress.com

First published in hardback by Edinburgh University Press 2019

Edinburgh University Press Ltd
The Tun – Holyrood Road, 12(2f) Jackson's Entry, Edinburgh EH8 8PJ

Typeset in 10/12 pt Sabon by
Servis Filmsetting Ltd, Stockport Cheshire,
and printed and bound by CPI Group (UK) Ltd,
Croydon, CR0 4YY

A CIP record for this book is available from the British Library

ISBN 978 1 4744 3314 3 (hardback)
ISBN 978 1 4744 3315 0 (paperback)
ISBN 978 1 4744 3316 7 (webready PDF)
ISBN 978 1 4744 3317 4 (epub)

Contents

List of illustrations

Figures

Tables

Acknowledgments

This monograph is largely based on research I have carried out since joining Georgetown University in 2013. Some of the ideas in this monograph originated in my dissertation research on negation in Jordanian Arabic and I thank my dissertation advisor, Steven Franks, and my reader, Barbara Vance, for their support, encouragement, and helpful comments.

Nonetheless, these ideas have since been significantly revised as my project expanded in its empirical breadth and theoretical depth. Since 2013, the results of this research project have been presented at various conferences such as the 28th, 29th and 30th meetings of the Annual Symposium on Arabic Linguistics at the University of Florida, the Universty of Wisconsin-Milwaukee and Stony Brook University, respectively, the Linguistics in the Gulf conference at Qatar University and the Georgetown University Roundtable on Linguistics. The research I presented at the various conferences has benefitted from insights, questions, and comments I received from many members of the audiences. I especially thank Abbas Benmamoun, Youssef Haddad, Perter Hallman, Hamid Ouali, Usama Soltan, Ali Idrissi, Fassi Fehri, Mohammad Mohammad, and many others who attended my talks on this project.

Thanks are also due to Geogretown University for the support I received from the faculty research grants and conference funds associated with this project. The invaluable resources and conference travel would not have been possible without this funding.

I also wish to thank the anonymous reviewers of this monograph and papers related to it for their deep insights and comments on the various proposals and analyses in this book. Thanks are also due to the native speakers who gave me their grammatical judgments on data from the various Arabic dialects.

I also thank the editors of the series, Nikolas Gisborne and Andrew Hippisley, for their time and effort in processing this project, securing the invaluable reviews from experts in the field and enthusiastically supporting this project. I thank the team at Edinburgh University Press for their support and professional help in processing the project, especially my commissioning editor, Laura Williamson. I thank her for doing a great job throughout the process.

This project has taken a significant amount of time and effort which would not have been possible without the support of my family. I thank my family and I dedicate this book to them.

List of abbreviations

1	first person
2	second person
3	third person
ACC	accusative
adj	adjective
adv	adverb
AGR	agreement morphology
AP	active participle
ASP	aspect
COMP	complementizer
conj	conjunction
COP	copula
CP	complementizer phrase
DEF	definite
DEM	demonstrative
DET	determiner
DP	determiner phrase
F	feminine
FocP	focus phrase
FP	functional projection
FUT	future
GEN	genitive
IMP	imperative
IMPR	imprecative
IND	indicative
INDEF	indefinite
IP	inflection phrase
IPFV	imperfective
JUSS	jussive
M	masculine
NCI	Negative Concord Item
NEG	negative
NegP	negation phrase

NOM	nominative
NP	noun phrase
NPI	Negative Polarity Item
NSI	Negative Sensitive Item
PAR	particle
PASS	passive
PF	phonetic form
PFV	perfective
PL	plural
pp	prepositional phrase
PREP	preposition
PROG	progressive
PRON	pronoun
SBJV	subjunctive
SG	singular
Spec	specifier
TNS	Tense morphology
TP	tense phrase
VP	verb phrase

Introduction

This comparative study is mainly concerned with the syntax of negation in Arabic. The principal aim is to characterize the properties of negation that are particular to different varieties of Arabic and the properties they share. The book primarily discusses negation in three varieties of Arabic – Southern Levantine, Gulf, and Standard Arabic. Egyptian Arabic (EA)is discussed in this book but it is limited to the background literature and the discussion in Chapter 5, where I show how the distribution of negation strategies in EA contrasts with Jordanian Arabic (JA). The Southern Levantine data is primarily from the dialect spoken in the Jordanian Houran, the author's native variety. The Gulf and Standard Arabic data is drawn from grammar books and scholarly studies, and complemented with novel data from the author's native dialect (including data from older speakers of this dialect), native speakers of Gulf Arabic (GA) and a corpus study of negation in classical and modern Standard Arabic. The corpus study is a syntactic analysis of negation in the Quran (around 86,000 words) and Levantine literature (around 86,000 words). Though the study is based on data from three varieties, the results largely represent the range of possible variations in the expression of negation in Arabic and other languages, and the interaction between negation and other elements of the clause structure such as tense, aspect, agreement, adverbs, adjuncts, and negative polarity/concord. Southern Levantine Arabic has preverbal and postverbal negative markers, GA only has preverbal negative markers, and Standard Arabic has preverbal negative markers that are tensed and others that carry agreement inflections.

Another advantage of considering these related varieties of Arabic is that they make it possible to do a micro-variation analysis that allows us to investigate negation in a somewhat controlled context (cf. Zanuttini 1997a for this methodological rationale in studying negation in Romance). Having such a controlled context is especially helpful in running a battery of tests to probe the structure of negation and related categories in Arabic. This is particularly useful because Arabic syntax is known for its flexibility and tolerance for a wide range of variation within and across the dialects. This is one of the main reasons that there are still either lengthy debates on issues like the position of subjects in the syntactic structure, the syntax of negative polarity/concord, and the basic word order, or very few studies on issues like the syntax of adverbs. Studying negation in a controlled context can lead to a better investigation of negation by avoiding variables external to negation, and can even give us insights into the syntax of those controversial categories related to negation.

The central thesis of this study is that negation as a functional category (NegP) in generative linguistics can occupy a position below or above the tense phrase (TP), and that there are syntactic, semantic/pragmatic, and morphosyntactic effects for these positions. These positions manifest a wide range of negation patterns, some particular to and some shared between the different varieties under investigation. It is worth noting that while this monograph challenges the parametric approach to the syntax of negation in particular, there is a growing body of literature that challenges the idea that universal grammar is parametrized (cf. Lightfoot 2017 and references therein). Lightfoot (2017) argues that universal grammar is open and that there are no parameters that children use to evaluate their internal grammar (I-Language) during their language acquisition process. Instead, children use universal grammar to PARSE their linguistic environment (E-Language) and DISCOVER their I-Language. In addition to the syntactic, semantic and morphosyntactic evidence, this book advances language change arguments against parametrizing negation based on evidence from a change-in-progress in JA negation.

The syntactic effects of placing negation below and above TP in JA are partially discussed in a (2015) journal article I published in *Lingua*. The full range of syntactic effects in JA as well as novel data from GA and Standard Arabic (SA) are included in this book. The semantic effects of this proposal present novel data and analysis for JA, GA and SA. Part of the JA data and a few ideas incorporated in the analysis are from my unpublished Ph.D. dissertation at Indiana University, Bloomington. These ideas have since been revised in my research conducted and presented after year 2013. Recent research included data on SA, GA, and EA and expanded in its theoretical depth by including research on tense, aspect, mood/modality, semantic scope of negation, Negative Polarity Items, Negative Concord Items, and language change in JA negation.

Issues in the syntax of sentential negation

1.1 Negative markers and clausal structure

The three major categories of negative markers found in Arabic are single negation, bipartite negation and enclitic negation. This chapter introduces these three categories in a descriptive manner, making minimal theoretical reference only when necessary. The distinctions made between these categories are relevant to the organization of the book and its discussion of empirical and theoretical issues. Contrasts in the distribution of these negative markers among the three varieties of Arabic under investigation in this book clearly show that negation in Arabic can occupy various syntactic positions, but that there are word order restrictions that regulate these occurrences.

1.1.1 Single negation

The three Arabic varieties under investigation have negative markers that precede the verb. Jordanian Arabic (JA), Standard Arabic (SA) and Qatari Arabic (QA) have the negative marker *maa*. Crucially, negative markers do not have to be adjacent to the verb in any of the three varieties. It is widely assumed that negative markers have to be adjacent to the verb and that the preverbal negative marker *maa* is a proclitic attached to the verb. Consider the following examples where adverbs and definite subjects, for example, cannot intervene between the negative marker and the verb.

(1) a. maa (*Zeid) (*fiʕlan) bi-saafir   (JA)
         NEG (*Zeid) (*really) ASP-travel.3MSG.IPFV
         (Zeid) (fiʕlan) kul   yoom
         (Zeid) (really) every day
         'Zeid doesn't really travel every day.'

     b. ma   (*Zeid) (*fiʕlan) y-saafir   (QA)
         NEG (*Zeid) (*really) ASP-travel.3MSG.IPFV
         (Zeid) (fiʕlan) kul   yoom
         (Zeid) (really) every day
         'Zeid doesn't really travel every day.'

c. la   (*Zaydun) (*bilfiʕli) yusaafiru   (Zaydun) (bilfiʕli) (SA)
    NEG   (*Zeid)   (*really) travel.3MSG.IPFV (Zeid)   (really)
    kulla yawm
    every day
    'Zeid doesn't really travel every day.'

Nonetheless, indefinite subjects can intervene between the negative marker and the verb.

(2) a. ma   ħada   bi-saafir   kul   yoom   (JA)
         NEG   one   ASP-travel.3MSG.IPFV   every day
         'No one travels every day.'

     b. ma   ħadd   y-saafir   kul   yoom   (QA)
         NEG   one   ASP-travel.3MSG.IPFV   every day
         'No one travels every day.'

     c. la   ʔahad-a   yusaafiru   kulla yawm   (SA)
         NEG   one   travel.3MSG.IPFV   every day
         'No one travels every day.'

Interestingly, adverbs can also intervene between the negative marker and the verb in such contexts:

(3) a. ma   ħada   fiʕlan   bi-saafir   kul   yoom   (JA)
         NEG   one   really ASP-travel.3MSG.IPFV every day
         'No one really travels every day.'

     b. ma   ħadd   fiʕlan   y-saafir   kul   yoom   (QA)
         NEG   one   really ASP-travel.3MSG.IPFV every day
         'No one really travels every day.'

     c. la   ʔahad-a   fiʕlan   yusaafiru   kulla yawm   (SA)
         NEG   one   really travel.3MSG.IPFV every day
         'No one really travels every day.'

Moreover, there are contexts in which certain adverbs can intervene between *maa* and the verb even in the absence of an indefinite subject:

(4) a. wallah   maa   b-yoom   bisaamħ-ak   (JA)
         by-God   NEG   in-day   forgive.3MSG.IPFV-you
         'He will not forgive you in any day.' = 'He will never forgive you.'
         (adapted from Alqassas 2015: 114)

     b. ʕumr-o   maa   b-yoom   bisaamħ-ak   (JA)
         NPI-ever-his NEG   in-day   forgive.3MSG.IPFV-you
         'He will not forgive you in any day.' = 'He will never forgive you.'

c. maa   gad   fi-sˤsˤaf   kallamt-a   (QA)
    NEG   ever   in class   talk.1SG.PFV-him
    'I've never talked to him in class.'

It is important to note that the negative markers in all of the above examples are sentential, i.e., they scope over the whole sentence including the quantifier *kull* 'all' and thus we get the reading not>all in examples (3)a–c. This contrasts with the markers *miš*, *mub*, and *ma* in JA, QA and SA respectively, which are markers of constituent negation and can only scope over the constituent they precede. When these markers precede *kull* 'all' we also get the reading not>all. However unlike markers of sentential negation, these negatives cannot scope over the NPI *ħada* 'anyone', hence the ungrammaticality in the following examples:

(5) a. miš   kul   yoom   bi-saafir   (*ħada)   (JA)
         NEG   every day   ASP-travel.3MSG.IPFV   NPI-one
         'Intended reading: *not everyday anyone travels'

     b. mub   kul   yoom   y-saafir   (*ħadd)   (QA)
         NEG   every day   ASP-travel.3MSG.IPFV   NPI-one
         'Intended reading: *not everyday anyone travels'

     c. ma   kulla yawm   yusaafiru   (*ʔahadun)   (SA)
         NEG   every day   travel.3MSG.IPFV   NPI-one
         'Intended reading: *not everyday anyone travels'

Note that *ma* in SA can also function as a marker of sentential negation. In such a case, indefinite nouns can intervene between the negative marker and the verb. Adverbs can also intervene, as seen in the example below:[1]

(6) a. maa   (*bilfiʕli)   yusaafiru   ʔahad-un   (bilfiʕli)   (SA)
         NEG   really   travel.3MSG.IPFV   one   really
         kulla   yawmin
         every   day
         'No one really travels every day.'

     b. maa   ʔahadun   fiʕlan   yusaafiru   kulla   yawm   (SA)
         NEG   one   really   travel.3MSG.IPFV   every   day
         'No one really travels every day.'

Unlike the other Arabic varieties, SA has the tensed negative markers *lam* and *lan*. *Lam*, a negative marker with a past tense interpretation, always precedes imperfective verbs marked with a jussive marker. *Lan*, a negative marker with a future tense interpretation, always precedes imperfective verbs marked with a subjunctive marker.

(7) a. lam   yusaafir-ø   ?ahadun   (SA)
        NEG.past travel.3MSG.PFV-JUSS   NPI-one
        'No one traveled.'

    b. lan   yusaafir-a   ?ahadun   (SA)
        NEG. FUT buy.3MSG-SBJV   NPI-one
        'No one will travel.'

With these markers, nothing can intervene between the negative marker and the verb:

(8) a. lam   (*?ahadun)   yusaafir-ø   (SA)
        NEG.past NPI-one   travel.3MSG-JUSS.
        'No one traveled.'

    b. lan   (*?ahad-un) yusaafir-a   (SA)
        NEG. FUT NPI-one   travel.3MSG-SBJV.
        'No one will travel.'

All three varieties use the marker *laa* preceding the imperfective verb to form negative imperatives:

(9) a. laa   t-saafir   (JA)
        NEG.IMP 2-travel.IMP
        'Don't travel.'

    b. laa   t-saafir   (QA)
        NEG.IMP 2-travel.IMP
        'Don't travel.'

    c. laa   tu-saafir   (SA)
        NEG.IMP 2-travel.IMP
        'Don't travel.'

SA also has complex tense constructions that involve the use of the verbal copula *kwn* and a lexical verb. Both the verbal copula and the lexical verb can be in the perfective or imperfective form, yielding four possible combinations each with its own aspecto-temporal interpretation. The negative marker *maa* can negate the perfective copula, while *laa* can negate the imperfective copula:

(10) a. maa   kaana   yadrusu   (SA)
         NEG   COP.PFV   study.3MSG.IPFV
         'He was not studying.'

b. maa   kaana   darasa   (SA)
    NEG   COP.PFV   study.3MSG.PFV
    'He had not studied.'

c. laa   yakuunu   yadrusu   (SA)
    NEG   COP.IPFV   study.3MSG.IPFV
    'He will not be studying.'

d. laa   yakuunu   darasa   (SA)
    NEG   COP.IPFV   study.3MSG.PFV
    He will not have studied.'

It is also possible in SA to negate the lexical verb directly by inserting the
negative marker between the copula and the lexical verb.

(11) a. kaana   laa   yadrusu   (SA)
          COP.PFV   NEG   study.3MSG.IPFV
          'He was not studying.'

      b. kaana   lam   yadrus   (SA)
          COP.PFV   NEG.past   study.3MSG.IPFV
          'He had not studied.'

      c. yakuunu   laa   yadrusu   (SA)
          COP.IPFV   NEG   study.3MSG.IPFV
          'He will not be studying.'

      d. yakuunu   lam   yadrus   (SA)
          COP.IPFV   NEG.past   study.3MSG.IPFV
          'He will not have studied.'

JA and QA have similar complex tense constructions which allow the
negative marker *maa* to precede the verbal copula or follow it:

(12) a. (maa)   kaan   (maa)   yilʕab   (JA)
          NEG   COP.PFV   NEG   play.3MSG.IPFV
          'He was not playing.'

      b. (maa)   kaan   (maa)   liʕib   (JA)
          NEG   COP.PFV   NEG   play.3MSG.PFV
          'He had not played.'

      c. (maa)   b-ykuun   (maa)   yilʕab   (JA)
          NEG   ASP-COP.IPFV   NEG   play.3MSG.IPFV
          'He will not be playing.'

      d. (maa)   b-ykuun   (maa)   liʕib   (JA)
          NEG   ASP-COP.IPFV   NEG   play.3MSG.PFV
          'He will not have played.'

(13) a. (maa)   kaan   (maa)   yilʕab   (QA)
        NEG   COP.PFV   NEG   play.3MSG.IPFV
        'He was not playing.'

    b. (maa)   kaan   (maa)   liʕab   (QA)
        NEG   COP.PFV   NEG   play.3MSG.PFV
        'He had not played.'

    c. (maa)   ykuun   (maa)   yilʕab   (QA)
        NEG   COP.IPFV NEG   play.3MSG.IPFV
        'He will not be playing.'

    d. (maa)   ykuun   (maa)   liʕab   (QA)
        NEG   COP.IPFV NEG   play.3MSG.PFV
        'He will not have played.'

In SA, *maa* can precede subjects of verbal sentences, while *laa* cannot:

(14) a. maa   ʔana   qul-tu   haaða   (SA)
        NEG   I   say.1SG.PFV   this
        'I did not say this.'   (Fassi Fehri 1993: 165)

    b. maa/*laa   ʔana   ʔaquulu   haaða   (SA)
        NEG/*NEG   I   say.1SG.PFV   this
        'I do not say this.'

1.1.2 *Bipartite negation*

Bipartite negation in JA involves the use of the proclitic *ma-* and the enclitic *-š* on the verb. The term 'continuous negation' is sometimes used to refer to this type of negation. In such contexts nothing can intervene between *ma* and the verb.

(15) a. ma-basaamiħ-k-iš   (JA)
        NEG-forgive.1SG.IPFV-you-NEG
        'I will not forgive you.'

    b. *ma   b-yoom   basaamiħ-k-iš   (JA)
        NEG   in-day   forgive.1SG.IPFV-you-NEG
        'I will not forgive you in any day.' (Alqassas 2015: 114)

Bipartite negation is the canonical form of negation in the JA variety spoken in the Jordanian Houran. It can be used with imperfective verbs, perfective verbs, the pseudo-verb *badd* 'want', and some non-verbal predicates, for example prepositional predicates expressing possessive relationships. However, as will be discussed further in later chapters,

bipartite negation in JA is not possible in various syntactically and pragmatically marked contexts.

(16) a.   ma-ruħt-iš   (JA)
           NEG-go.1SG.PFV-NEG
           'I did not go.'

      b.   ma-badd-ii-š   ʔaruuħ   (JA)
           NEG-want-I-NEG   go.1SG.IPFV
           'I do not want to go.'

      c.   ma-maʕ-naa-š   masˤaari   (JA)
           NEG-have-us -NEG money
           'We do not have money.'

      d.   ma-fii-naa-š   ħeel   (JA)
           NEG-in-us-NEG strength
           'We do not have the strength.'

In complex tense constructions, bipartite negation can appear on the
verbal copula or the lexical verb:

(17) a.   ma-kaan-iš   yilʕab   (JA)
           NEG-COP.PFV-NEG   play.3MSG.IPFV
           'He was not playing.'

      b.   ma-kaan-iš   liʕib   (JA)
           NEG-COP.PFV-NEG   play.3MSG.PFV
           'He had not played.'

      c.   ma-b-ykuun-iš   yilʕab   (JA)
           NEG-ASP-COP.IPFV-NEG   play.3MSG.IPFV
           'He will not be playing.'

      d.   ma-b-ykuun-iš   liʕib   (JA)
           NEG-ASP-COP.IPFV-NEG   play.3MSG.PFV
           'He will not have played.'

(18) a.   kaan   ma-yilʕab-iš   (JA)
           COP.PFV   NEG-play.3MSG.IPFV-NEG
           'He was not playing.'

      b.   kaan   ma-liʕb-iš   (JA)
           COP.PFV   NEG-play.3MSG.PFV-NEG
           'He had not played.'

      c.   ma-b-ykuun-iš   ma-yilʕab-iš   (JA)
           NEG-ASP-COP.IPFV-NEG   NEG-play.3MSG.IPFV-NEG
           'He will not be playing.'

    d. b-ykuun   ma-liʕb-iš   (JA)
        ASP-COP.IPFV NEG-play.3MSG.PFV-NEG
        'He will not have played.'

1.1.3 Enclitic negation (postverbal negation)

Unlike QA and SA, JA exhibits an enclitic negative marker that is postverbal. This marker follows the verb or non-verbal predicate. This negation strategy is possible with imperfective verbs prefixed with the aspectual marker *b-*, with labial-initial possessive prepositions and the pseudo-verb *badd* 'want', and with imperative verbs:

(19) a. b-aʕrif-iš   (JA)
         ASP-know.1SG.IPFV-NEG
         'I don't know.'

      b. maʕ-naa-š   masʕaari   (JA)
         have-us-NEG   money
         'We do not have money.'

      c. fii-naa-š   ħeel   (JA)
         in-us-NEG   strength
         'We do not have the strength.'

      d. bad-naa-š   nruuħ   (JA)
         want.IPFV-we-NEG go.1PL.IPFV
         'We do not want to go.'

      e. truuħ-iš   (JA)
         go.2MSG.IMP-NEG
         'Don't go.'

Although the verb form in negative imperatives resembles the subjunctive verb form, it is not possible to negate a subjective verb using the postverbal marker by itself:

(20) mišan   *(ma)-truuħ-iš   (JA)
        COMP   *(NEG)-sleep.2MSG.IPFV-NEG
        'So that you don't sleep.'

Likewise, in complex tense constructions it is not possible to use enclitic negation by itself to directly negate the imperfective lexical verb. The lexical verb has to be prefixed by either the negative marker *ma-* or the aspectual prefix *b-*:

(21) a. kaan   *(ma)-yilʕab-iš   (JA)
          COP.PFV   NEG-play.3MSG.IPFV-NEG
          'He was not playing.'

      b. kaan   *(b)-yilʕab-iš   (JA)
          COP.PFV   NEG-play.3MSG.IPFV-NEG
          'He was not playing.'

1.1.4 *Negation of non-verbal predicates*

Arabic is known for having so-called verbless sentences, which consist of
a subject and a non-verbal predicate such as the nominal predicate below.
These sentences are negated using *miš*, *mub*, and *laysa* in JA, QA, and SA,
respectively:

(22) a. inta   miš   muhandis   (JA)
          you   NEG   engineer
          'You are not an engineer.'

      b. inta   mub   muhandis   (QA)
          you   NEG   engineer
          'You are not an engineer.'

      c. anta   lasta muhandisan   (SA)
          you   NEG   engineer
          'You are not an engineer.'

These negative markers can also negate adjectival and prepositional
predicates:

(23) a. inta   miš   zaʕlaan   (JA)
          you   NEG   upset
          'You are not upset.'

      b. inta   mub   zaʕlaan   (QA)
          you   NEG   upset
          'You are not upset.'

      c. anta   lasta ħazinan   (SA)
          you   NEG   sad
          'You are not sad.'

(24) a. es-sayyaara   miš   ʕind-o   (JA)
          DEF-car   NEG   have-him
          'The car is not with him.'

b. es-sayyaara   mub   ʕind-uh   (QA)
   DEF-car   NEG   have-him
   'The car is not with him.'

c. as-sayyaaratu   laysat   ʕinda-hu   (SA)
   DEF-car   NEG   have-him
   'The car is not with him.'

Verbless sentences with a past tense interpretation use the verbal copula *kwn* and can be negated by bipartite negation in JA, *maa* in QA, and *lam* in SA:

(25) a. es-sayyaara   ma-kaanat-iš   ʕind-o   (JA)
        DEF-car   NEG-COP.3FSG.PFV-NEG   have-him
        'The car was not with him.'

     b. es-sayyaara   maa   kaanat   ʕind-uh   (QA)
        DEF-car   NEG   COP.3FSG.PFV   have-him
        'The car was not with him.'

     c. as-sayyaaratu   lam   takun   ʕinda-hu   (SA)
        DEF-car   NEG.past COP.3FSG.IPFV   have-him
        'The car was not with him.'

The two negatives *maa* and *laa* contrast in compatibility with verbless sentences. *Maa* can precede subjects of verbless sentences, while *laa* cannot:

(26) a. maa   Muħammad-un   kaatib-un   (SA)
        NEG   Mohammad-NOM   writer-NOM
        'Mohammad is not a writer.' (Aoun et al. 2010: 116–17)

     b. *laa   Muħammad-un   kaatib-un   (SA)
        NEG   Mohammad-NOM   writer-NOM

1.1.5 *Negation and subordination*

The type of negative markers which can occur in subordinate clauses and their subject-verb word order vary in JA and SA. In JA, only single negation can occur in the clausal complement of adjectival predicates, such as *maliiħ* 'it is good/fortunately,' and when expressing purpose subordination:

(27) maliiħ   maa   rasab-(*iš)   l-walad   (JA)
     Good   NEG   fail.2MSG.PFV-(*NEG)   DEF-boy
     'It is good that you didn't fail.'

Here, *maa* functions not only as a negative expression but also as a connector of two clauses. The first clause has the adjective *maliiħ* 'it is good/ fortunately,' which is the predicate of a copular sentence. The subject of this sentence is silent (Arabic is pro-drop), and the copula is null because the present tense copula is usually covert. The second clause is the verb phrase *rasab l-walad*. In such a construction, it is possible for the subject to intervene between negation and the verb:

(28) maliiħ   maa   (l-walad)   rasab   (l-walad)   (JA)
      Good   NEG   DEF-boy   fail.2MSG.PFV   DEF-boy
      'It is good that the boy didn't fail.'

The following example gives evidence for the use of *laa* as a negative complementizer in JA. As can be seen in the English translation, *laa* functions as a complementizer to express *purpose*. Example (29) a and b show that in this case bipartite negation is not possible. Instead, single negation using *laa* allows the subject to intervene between negation and the verb.

(29) a. ʔilbas   dʒakeet   laa   yidʒmad-(*iš)   dʒism-ak   (JA)
          wear   jacket   NEG   freeze.3MSG.IPFV-(*NEG)   body-your
          'Wear a jacket so that your body doesn't freeze.'

      b. ʔilbas   dʒakeet   *laa*   (dʒism-ak)   yidʒmad   (dʒism-ak) (JA)
          wear   jacket   NEG   body-your   freeze.3MSG.IPFV   body-your
          'Wear a jacket so that your body doesn't freeze.'

The marker *maa* also interacts with the superlative adjective *ʔaħsan*. This adjective can be used along with *maa* to form a negative complementizer *ʔaħsan maa* which corresponds to the English 'so that.' Bipartite negation is not possible in this context, and the subject can intervene between negation and the verb.

(30) a. ʔilbas   dʒakeet   ʔaħsan   maa   tidʒmad-(*š)   (JA)
          wear   jacket   COMP   NEG   freeze.2MSG.IPFV-NEG
          'Wear a jacket so that you don't freeze.'

      b. ʔilbas   dʒakeet   ʔaħsan   maa   (dʒsm-ak)
          wear   jacket   COMP   NEG   body-your
          yidʒmad   (dʒism-ak)   (JA)
          freeze.3MSG.IPFV   body-your
          'Wear a jacket so that you don't freeze.'

In SA, *maa* and *laa* contrast in compatibility with nonfinite verbs that occur after the complementizer *ʔan*. While *laa* can follow the complementizer *ʔan*, *maa* cannot.

(31) a. ʔuriid-u   ʔan   laa   tadxul-a   (SA)
          I-want-IND   that   NEG   enter.2MSG.IPFV-ACC
          'I want you not to enter.' (Fassi Fehri 1993: 172)

      b. *ʔuriid-u   ʔan   maa   tadxul-a   (SA)
          I-want-IND   that   NEG   enter.2MSG.IPFV-ACC

The empirical generalizations, word order restrictions and distribution of the negation strategies presented are discussed in Chapter 2 and Chapter 5.

1.2 Negation, rhetorical questions, and oath words

Rhetorical questions in JA show another environment in which the use of *ma-* is the only possibility. In the examples below, the speaker is not asking for information but rather making a statement, asserting that the items should have been brought. The use of the negative marker -*š* is ungrammatical when the question is rhetorical.

(32) leeš   inbaariħ   ma-dʒaab-hin-(*iš)!   (JA)
       why   yesterday   NEG-bring.PFV-them.fem-(*NEG)
       'Why didn't he bring them yesterday!'
       (Rhetorical: implying he should have brought them)

(33) miin   ma-dʒaab-hin-(*iš)!   (JA)
       who   NEG-bring.PFV-them.fem-*(NEG)
       'Who could bring them!'
       (Rhetorical: implying no one could bring them)

Another context where *ma* is the only possible negative marker is in sentences with oath words. Sentences with oath words such as *wallah* 'by God' and *inšaallah* 'God willing' do not allow the use of the negative marker -*š*. In these cases the negative marker *ma* has to be used by itself.

(34) wallah   ma-ba-saaʕd-ak-(*iš)   (JA)
       by God   NEG-ASP-help.1SG-you-(*NEG)
       'By God, I will not help you.'

(35) inšaallah   ma-bi-rsub-(*iš)   (JA)
       god willing   NEG-ASP-fail.3MSG-(*NEG)
       'God willing, He will not fail.'

The interaction between the different types of negation, mood, and modality in these various contexts is discussed in Chapter 3.

1.3 Distribution of Negative Sensitive Items

There are certain types of Negative Sensitive Items (NSIs) that interact with negation in interesting ways. The two main categories of NSIs discussed in this book are Negative Polarity Items (NPIs) and Negative Concord Items (NCIs).[2] The temporal adverbs *ʕumr* in JA and *gad* in QA require the presence of negation and allow prepositional adverbs to intervene. JA also displays sensitivity to the type of negation that can co-occur with *ʕumr*. Specifically, single negation is allowed while bipartite negation is not.

(36) a. ʕumr-o   bi-sˤsˤaf   *(ma)-ħaka   maʕ-i   (JA)
         NPI-ever-his   in-class   NEG-talk.3MSG.PFV   with-me
         'He has never talked to me in class.'

      b. *(maa)   gad   fi-sˤsˤaf   ʔaħmad   kallam-a   (QA)
         NEG   ever   in class   Ahmad   talk.3MSG.PFV-him
         'Ahmad has never talked to him in class.'

      c. *ʕumr-o   ma-zaar-iš   el-batra   (JA)
         NPI-ever-his   NEG-visit.3MSG.PFV-NEG   DEF-Petra
         'He has never visited Petra.'

SA has the temporal adverb *baʕd* 'yet' which must co-occur with negation and can also intervene between negation and the verb:

(37) *(lamma)   baʕd   yaħdʕur   (SA)
      NEG   yet   arrive.3MSG.IPFV
      'He has not yet arrived.'

Another interesting item is *wala* in JA, which can combine with the indefinite noun *ħada* 'one' to form the NSI *wala-ħada* 'anyone/no one'. This NSI must co-occur with negation when postverbal and stands by itself when preverbal:

(38) a. ma-zaar-ni-š   wala-ħada   (JA)
         NEG-visit.3MSG.PFV-me-NEG   no-one
         'No one visited me.'

      b. wala-ħada   zaar-ni   (JA)
         no-one   visit.3MSG.PFV-me
         'No one visited me.'

Issues relating to how these NSIs establish their dependency with negation are discussed in Chapter 4. Chapter 4 also discusses how the different types of negation influence the dependency relations with the NSIs.

1.4 Jespersen's Cycle

The present synchronic study gives us two important findings in support of Lucas's (2009, 2010) Jespersen's Cycle reconstruction of -*š* as an NPI adverb *šay?/?iši* 'at all'.[3] The three stages of Jespersen's Cycle are as follows:

In stage I, negation is expressed by one element.

    (39)   maa   b-aʕrif   (JA)
            NEG   ASP-know.1SG.IPFV
            'I don't know'.

In stage II, this element weakens, and a new element is introduced to reinforce the first element.

    (40)   ma-b-aʕrif-iš   (JA)
            NEG-ASP-know.1SG.IPFV-NEG
            'I don't know.'

In stage III, the first element is dropped and the new element becomes the only marker of negation.

    (41)   b-aʕrif-iš   (JA)
            ASP-know.1SG.IPFV-NEG
            'I don't know.'

The three major categories of negation (single, bipartite, and enclitic) can represent the three stages of the cycle (I, II, and III, respectively). They co-exist synchronically but in different syntactic and pragmatic contexts (see Chapters 2, 3, and 4 for a more detailed analysis).

Second, the incompatibility between single negation and -*š* reveals the inner workings of the cycle. Being syntactically adjacent to the verb, the lower marker *ma* weakens morphologically, hence the need for *?iši/-š* as a reinforcer. However, since *maa* is higher and not adjacent to the verb, we do not expect it to weaken or give rise to the need for -*š*, resulting in the incompatibility between single negation and -*š*. These issues are discussed further in Chapter 6.

The availability of the three stages of negation in JA bears on a key syntactic issue in this book, namely whether negation has a fixed- or multi-locus in the syntactic structure of the I-Language of a speaker. Chapter 6 presents evidence that the I-Language of JA speakers has multiple positions for negation and that phonological and syntactic factors conspire to nurture this diversity.

1.5 Organization of the book

The word order restrictions mentioned in section 1.1, along with some other word order restrictions such as negative complementizers, figure prominently in Chapter 2's generative syntactic analysis of negation. The central thesis is that negation can occupy multiple positions in the syntactic structure, departing from the standard claim that negation has a fixed position (Ouhalla 1990, 1991; Benmamoun 1992, 1997, 2000; Shlonsky 1997; Mohammad 2000; Hoyt 2007; Soltan 2007, 2012, among others).

This chapter has also presented other word order restrictions which concern the interaction between negation on the one hand and time adverbials and presupposition on the other hand. Chapter 3 puts forward an analysis of these word order restrictions restrictions and their corollary semantic effects. The interaction between NSIs and negation is discussed in Chapter 4, which shows that the multi-locus analysis has direct implications for theories of NPI and NCI syntactic licensing. Word order restrictions involving the non-discontinuous (independent) versus discontinuous negation markers are analyzed in Chapter 5. The analysis shows that the multi-locus analysis of negation makes it possible to predict the distribution of the various negation strategies in colloquial and Standard Arabic. The chapter also has implications for whether head movement is a movement that takes place in the syntax proper or post-syntactically at the phonetic form (PF) component. Chapter 6 discusses the implications of the multi-locus analysis from a diachronic perspective by recasting the results of the multi-locus analysis in view of the Jespersen Cycle of negation and by taking into account a current change-in-progress in JA. A general summary and conclusion, with a brief discussion of some residual issues, is the focus of Chapter 7.

Notes

1. Note that when *ma* precedes preposed noun phrases (NPs) or prepositional phrases (PPs), the scope of negation is not sentential and only the NP or PP is negated (i.e., constituent negation).

   (i) maa RIWAAYAT-AN ʔallafat   Zaynabu (bal qasiidat-an)   (SA)
        NEG novel-ACC   write.3FSG.PFV Zaynab   (but poem-ACC)
        'It is not a novel that Zaynab has written (but a poem).' (Ouhalla 1993: 277)

(ii)   maa BI-S-SIKKIN-I   dʒaraħa   xaalid-un   bakr-an   (SA)
       NEG with-the-knife.GEN wound.3MSG.PFV Khalid-NOM Bakr-ACC
       'It was not with a knife that Khalid wounded Bakr.' (Moutaouakil 1993: 81)

2. The key difference between these two categories is that NPIs cannot be used as fragment answers without negation and they can occur in non-negative contexts such as interrogative and conditional contexts. NCIs display the opposite behavior.

3. Contra Wilmsen's 2014 reconstruction of -š as an interrogative pronoun.

Locus of negation in syntactic structure

2.1 Position of negation in the hierarchical structure[1]

The literature on the locus of negation in syntactic structure focuses primarily on the position of negation relative to the spine of the clause, the Inflectional Phrase (IP/TP), and whether the negation phrase (NegP) follows or precedes TP. Of particular debate is whether or not the locus of NegP is a parametric choice whereby the Individual/Internal Language (I-Language) of the speaker has the locus of NegP set to one of the two options available in universal grammar (UG). The alternative view is that NegP can project below or above TP and can have multiple positions within the structure, each with different syntactic and semantic effects. This chapter discusses both views and proposes a multi-locus analysis for negation in Arabic. After a discussion of these two views, I discuss key issues in the syntax of subjects, verb movement, and tense and aspect in Arabic. These topics are intimately related to the syntax of negation and the analyses presented in this and the subsequent chapters of this book. I then present the multi-locus analysis, advancing empirical and theoretical arguments from key word order generalizations involving adverbs, subjects, complementizers, and the verbal copula.

The parametric view (Ouhalla 1991) holds that all languages have NegP but differ in whether the NegP projection is on top of TP or on top of the verb phrase (VP). Under this proposal, NegP selects TP in languages whose tense and agreement morphemes are closer than the negative morpheme to the verb, while NegP selects VP in languages whose negative morpheme is closer to the verb than are the tense and agreement morphemes.[2]

Ouhalla's arguments are based on facts from languages such as Turkish and Berber, illustrated in (1)a and (1)b, respectively. The following is an illustration (Ouhalla 1990: 136–37):

(1) a. john elmayi ser-me-di-o   (Turkish)
         John apples like-NEG-past(TNS)-3s(AGR)
         'John does not like apples.'

b. ur-y-sgh   moha   tadda   (Berber)
    NEG-3MSG-bought   Moh   House
    'Moha has not bought a house.'

In Turkish, negation appears closer to the verb than agreement morphology (AGR) and Tense morphology (TNS), while in Berber negation
appears outside AGR and TNS. Accordingly, Ouhalla proposes the NEG
parameter in (2) and illustrated in (3):

(2)   The NEG parameter: (Ouhalla 1990: 194)
      a. NEG   selects VP
      b. NEG   selects TP

(3)   a.   b.

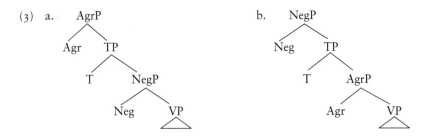

In Arabic, negation morphemes are in fact not closer to the verb than
tense and agreement morphemes because *ma* in all varieties (and *-š* in
JA) appear external to the verbal complex, which has AGR as in (4)a and
sometimes object clitics as in (4)b:

(4)   a. ma-b-aʕirf-iš   (JA)
          NEG-ASP-know.1SG.IPFV-NEG
          'I don't know.'

      b. ma-b-aʕirf-huu-š   (JA)
          NEG-ASP-know.1SG.IPFV-him-NEG
          'I don't know him.'

      c. ma   y-saafir   kul   yoom   (QA)
          NEG ASP-travel.3MSG.IPFV   every day
          'He does not travel every day.'

      d. ma   yusaafiru   kulla yawm   (SA)
          NEG travel.3MSG.IPFV   every day
          'He does not travel every day.'

Since tense and agreement in Arabic are closer to the verb than negation is, under Ouhalla's proposal we would expect NegP to be higher

than tense. However, most analyses of negation in Arabic dialects place NegP below TP (cf. Aoun et al. 2010 for a number of Arabic dialects including Moroccan and LA; Benmamoun 2000 and Ouhalla 1991, 1993, for Palestinian Arabic (PA)). There are at least two main reasons for advancing the analysis that NegP is below TP. First, the adjacency between negation and the verb is particularly clear from the proclitic status of the negative marker *ma* in the Arabic dialects. With bipartite negation, the markers *ma* and *-š* appear as a discontinuous marker on either side of the verb. With adjectival and nominal predicates, bipartite negation appears as a non-discontinous marker *miš*:

(5) a. inta miš muhandis   (JA)
         you   NEG engineer
         'You are not an engineer.'

     b. inta mub muhandis   (QA)
         you   NEG engineer
         'You are not an engineer.'

By allowing negation to project under TP, it is possible to reduce the distribution of discontinuous and non-discontinous negation to whether or not the predicate undergoes movement to NegP (cf. Benmamoun 2000 and Aoun et al. 2010 for this analysis). The assumption is that the verb, unlike adjectival and nominal predicates, undergoes V-to-T movement and merges with negation on its way up to T.

(6) a.   b.

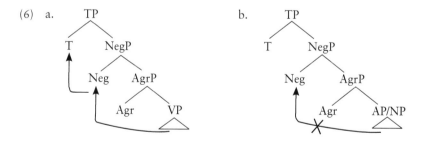

This is because the verb has to merge with negation, and movement of the verb to tense can explain the obligatoriness of verb movement to negation. In other words, the verb has to merge with negation because it cannot move to T without incorporating with the head NegP due to the Head Movement Constraint. When nothing merges with negation, as in the case of adjectival and nominal predicates, the result is the independent morpheme *miš*. Therefore, if NegP is above T, it would be unclear how and when the verb merges with negation.

The second motivation for analyzing NegP below TP comes from SA. Recall that SA has the tensed negative markers *lam* and *lan* expressing past and future tense, respectively:

(7) a. lam   yusaafir-ø   ?ahadun   (SA)
         NEG.past   travel.3MSG.IPFV-JUSS NPI-one
         'No one traveled.'

     b. lan   yusaafir-a   ?ahadun   (SA)
         NEG.FUT   travel.3MSG.IPFV-SBJV NPI-one
         'No one will travel.'

The fact that negation intercepts tense – and the verb fails to express tense – motivates placing NegP between TP and VP (cf. Ouhalla 1993 for this proposal). Thus a verb in SA does not undergo V-to-T movement and negation carries the tense of the clause.

(8) a.

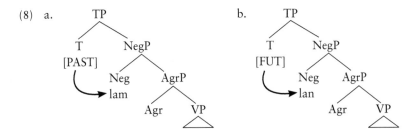

Ouhalla's proposal for parameterizing NegP position based on the distribution of AGR is not followed in various analyses of negation in Arabic (cf. Benmamoun 1997, 2000; Aoun et al. 2010, among others). There are other analyses that place NegP on top of TP in Arabic (Fassi Fehri 1993; Shlonsky 1997; Soltan 2007; Benmamoun et al. 2013). Benmamoun et al. (2013) advance various pieces of evidence that can be classified into three main arguments in support of such an analysis. The first argument appeals to Soltan's (2007) analysis of the future marker *ħa-* in EA as a tense marker occupying the tense head, an analysis extended to the MA future marker *ɣadi*.

(9) a. ħa-yištaɣal-u   lamma   yiʕraf-u   (EA)
         FUT-work-3MPL   when   can-3MPL
         'They will work when they can.' (Benmamoun et al. 2013: 97)

     b. ma-ɣadi-š   yqra   (MA)
         NEG-going.FUT-NEG   read.3MSG
         'He is not going to read/will not read.' (Benmamoun et al. 2013: 95)

However, I argue that the future marker is an aspectual model lower than TP (cf. Section 2.2.3, arguing that both negation and the future marker can be below TP).

The second argument for a parametric view of negation comes from negative markers that precede the subject of the sentence. Benmamoun et al. (2013) show that the negative marker *laa* in SA can assign accusative case to the subject. Consider the following example whereby the negative marker *laa* can assign accusative case to the subject of a verbless sentence (cf. Al-Naadirii 2009):[3]

(10) laa   mudarris-iin   ɣaaʔib-uun   (SA)
      NEG   teachers-MPL.ACC   absent-MPL.NOM
      'No teachers are absent.'

The argument is that negation in this case behaves on a PAR with complementizers in Arabic, suggesting that, like CP, negation is above TP. Another case where negation precedes the subject is the use of the non-discontinous marker *miš* in the context of a verbal predicate (examples in (11) are from Benmamoun et al. 2013: 103):

(11) a. muu   gilṭ   ᵾhwa   raaħ   (Kuwaiti)
          NEG   say.2MSG.PFV he   leave.3MSG.PFV
          'Didn't you say that he left?' (native Speaker)

      b. miš   kunti   fi-l-beyt?   (LA)
          NEG   be.2FSG.PFV in-DEF-house
          'Weren't you in the house?' (native speaker)

      c. maši   kunti   f-d-dar?   (MA)
          NEG   be.2FSG.PFV in-DEF-house
          'Weren't you in the house?' (native speaker)

      d. miš   gibti   badla?   (EA)
          NEG   get.2FSG.PFV suit
          'Didn't you get a suit?' (Brustad 2000)

While this argument may be legitimate grounds for analyzing negation as above TP within a specified context, I take issue with using this argument as evidence that negation, both within a single dialect and across dialects in Arabic, is above TP across the board. Later I argue for a multi-locus analysis of negation that allows for negation to project both below and above TP. The specific cases in (11) are analyzed as special cases where the negative projection above TP is associated with a presuppositional interpretation.

The third major argument in Benmamoun et al. (2013) comes from the distribution of Negative Polarity Items (NPIs) with respect to negation.

Roughly speaking, NPIs are polarity items that are licensed by negation. In a negative declarative statement, the NPI is arguably licensed either under c-command by negation or by occupying the Spec/NegP position (Benmamoun 1997, 2006). The authors show that the NPI *ħatta* in MA can occupy the subject position that precedes the verb and negation. The authors contend that allowing negation to project above TP gives a straightforward analysis of the position of the subject NPI. That is to say, the NPI can occupy the Spec/NegP position and be licensed under the specifier-head (Spec-Head) relation.

(12)   ħətta   wəld   ma-qra   lə-ktab   (MA)
       any   boy   NEG-read.3MSG.PFV   DEF-book
       'No boy read the book.' (Benmamoun et al. 2013: 102)

The NPI *ʕəmmər/ʕmr* can also occupy a position preceding negation and a past tense verb. Assuming that past tense verbs undergo V-to-T movement (Benmamoun 2000), the NPI can only be licensed if negation is above TP. Benmaoun et al. also contend that the mere fact that the NPI can merge with negation in Levantine Arabic is evidence that negation is above TP.

(13)   a.   ʕəmmər   ma-ža   (MA)
            never   NEG-come.3MSG.PFV
            'He never came.' (Benmamoun et al. 2013: 105)
       b.   maa-ʕumri-š   smaʕt-ha   (LA)
            NEG-never-NEG   hear.1SG.PFV-it
            'I never heard it.' (Benmamoun et al. 2013: 106)

Later I argue that while these cases do lend credence to analyzing negation above TP, they do not establish a legitimate ground for analyzing negation above TP across the board within and across the dialects' complex negation strategies. These cases represent the special syntactic and semantic effects correlated with the marked locus of negation above TP.

Crucially, all of these analyses for Arabic negation assume the parametric view irrespective of AGR distribution. The position of negation under these analyses is unilocus. The locus of negation is below TP in some analyses and above it in the other analyses. Nonetheless, there are at least three counter-arguments for the idea that the position of negation is parameterized. Zeijlstra (2004) advances two arguments (and cites a third one from Zanuttini 1998, 2001) against a fixed position of NegP on top of TP. Zeijlstra's first criticism is founded in the unclear status of the negative markers in (1) above, that is, whether they are affixes or clitics attached to the finite verb. Second, Zeijlstra suggests that, contrary to facts from Czech, a language which has NegP on top of TP should license subject NPIs even if the negative marker appears to the right of this NPI. Third, Zeijlstra appeals to Zanuttini's (1998, 2001) conclusion that negation can have more than two positions, suggesting that negation is not parameterized.

Zeijlstra shows that the contrast in the position of negation cannot be established in the absence of a clear analysis for the status of the negative morpheme in Berber. In other words, the negative morpheme in Berber could be head-adjoined to the verbal complex as in (14) or an affix attached to the finite verb as in (14)b (cf. representations below from Zeijlstra (2004: 177)):

(14) a. $[[_{Neg0}\ ur]\ [_{V0}\ ad\text{-}y\text{-}xdel\ ]]$
      b. $[[_{V0}\ ur\text{-}ad\text{-}y\text{-}xdel_{[uNEG]}\ ]]$

Second, following Ouhalla's proposal, Czech should be analyzed as a language with NegP on top of TP since, as in (15)b, the negative marker is external to the verb and tense and agreement show up as inflections which are part of the verb *dal* 'pay'. Zeijlstra argues that if NegP is on top of TP in this language, the negative operator should be able to license the NPI subject since this operator is in a position higher than Spec/TP (the subject position), even though the negative marker appears to the right of the NPI subject. This is expected since the standard analysis for licensing of the NPI assumes that the negative marker has to c-command it. However, this expectation is empirically challenged by the ungrammaticality of (15)a. On the other hand, the NPI object can appear to the left of the negative marker since it arguably originates in a position lower than the negative marker as in (15)b:

(15) a. *Petnik   by   za   to   nebyl   dan   (Czech)
          nickel   would   for   it   NEG.be   given
          'A single cent wouldn't be paid for it.'

      b. Petnik   by   za   to   nedal   (Czech)
          nickel.NPI would   for   it   NEG.pay.3s
          'He wouldn't pay a single cent for it.'

Third, Zeijlstra suggests that Ouhalla's proposal of a parameterized position for NegP can be challenged by Zanuttini's (1998, 2001) conclusion that NegP can have more than two positions. Zanuttini suggests four different positions for NegP in Romance dialects by considering the distribution of adverbs as in (16) (cf. Zeijlstra 2004: 178):[4]

(16) [NegP1 [TP1 [NegP2 [TP2 [NegP3 [AspP PFV [Asp GEN/PROG [NegP4]]]]]]]]

Notice that the parametric view predicts that the chance of there being languages with NegP on top of *v*P is similar to that where NegP is on top of TP. However, given the counter-arguments to the parametric view, there are advantages to a non-parametric view which analyzes the canonical position for NegP as on top of *v*P. The most obvious advantage of analyzsing negation lower than TP is that it provides a straightforward explanation for the blocking effect negation has on the verb and tense phrases. The merger between negation and the verb can be reduced to V-to-T verb movement, whereby the verb has to move to the intervening negative head on its way up to the tense phrase (cf. Benmamoun's 2000 analysis for Arabic). This can also explain the do-support in English negative sentences as a necessary last resort mechanism when negation blocks lowering of the tense affix from its position under the tense head to the main verb (cf. Radford 1997). There is another major advantage to analyzing the canonical position of negation under the tense head. Specifically, we can probe the special syntactic and semantic effects that the position of negation above the tense phrase can have, thus deepening our understanding of the syntax of negation and linguistic theory in general. All of this is possible with a non-parametric view of negation.

By analyzing the locus of negation above TP as a non-canonical (marked) position, we can probe the markedness effects that this higher position exhibits. In other words, these effects become very clear in a language that has different negative markers which are mutually exclusive in certain contexts. Consider the Bengali examples from Ramchand (2001, 2002), who holds the view that a certain language may opt for any position of NegP. Ramchand shows that Bengali has two different negative markers, *ni* and *na*. Ramchand proposes that *na* binds the event variable, and *ni* binds the time variable. She shows that only *ni* can license the NPI adverb *kokhono* 'ever' as in the contrast below. This negative marker happens to be the marked one, as Zeijlstra reports from Ramchand.

(17) a. Ami kokhono an   khai ni   (Bengali)
          I   ever   mangoes   ate NEG
          'I never ate mangoes.'

      b. *Ami kokhono an   khai na   (Bengali)
          I   ever   mangoes   ate NEG
          'I never ate mangoes.'

Under this approach, the variation in position of NegP is not due to a syntactic parameter determining whether NegP selects TP or VP, but rather to the syntactic and semantic properties of negation (Zeijlstra

2004; Ramchand 2001, 2002; Zannuttini 1997a, 1997b; Alqassas 2015). The semantic properties of negation differ in terms of whether the negative marker binds an event variable (vP) or a time variable (TP). In such an analysis, negation which binds an event variable is assumed to be the most common (following Acquaviva 1997; Giannakidou 1999; Zeijlstra 2004).

Along the same lines, Zeijlstra (2004) follows Ramchand (2001, 2002) and suggests that the main reason for the variation in the position of NegP is syntactic, as in the Hindi example below, and that subtle but not salient differences in interpretation can result from variation of the position of NegP. According to Zeijlstra, analyzing NegP on top of TP in the example below yields a straightforward explanation for why the NPI subject can appear to the left of the negative marker. The NPI subject cannot be licensed by a negative lower than TP, assuming that the NPI can only be licensed under either the Spec-Head relationship or the c-command configuration. Projecting NegP above TP allows the subject NPI to be licensed under c-command by negation.

(18) Koi-bhii   nahii   aayaa   (Hindi)
      Anybody   NEG   came
      'Nobody came.' (Zeijlstra 2004)

Accordingly, we see that this system attributes the position of NegP on top of TP to syntactic and semantic reasons like scoping over time variables and licensing polarity items. Moreover, this analysis predicts that an element can have more than one position in the same language for semantic or pragmatic reasons. This approach stands in sharp contrast to one that views the position of an element to be parametric. This is because both positions of NegP can be found in the same language.[5] In Chapters 3 and 4, I show the special syntactic and semantic contexts in which there is evidence that negation is higher than TP.

We have thus far reviewed two approaches to determining the position of NegP. The first depends on word order and the position of bound morphemes within the verbal complex (Pollock 1989; Ouhalla 1990, among others),[6] while the second is based on the syntactic and semantic properties of the negative markers such as negative scope and NPI licensing (Zannuttini 1997; Ramchand 2001, 2002; Zeijlstra 2004, 2008).[7]

2.2 The syntax of subjects, verb movement, and tense/aspect

This section presents key issues relating to the clause structure of negative sentences. The position of preverbal subjects, verb movement to tense and the syntax of tense, aspect and phi-agreement will all be discussed. While these issues are controversial in the literature, this chapter uses empirical and theoretical arguments to take a stand on their analysis. In particular, preverbal subjects in the dialects and in SA exhibit micro-variation in their position in Spec-TP and Spec-CP, and the position of negation relative to the preverbal subject will be part of the battery of tests deployed in the multi-locus analysis of negation. Regarding verb movement, I follow Benmamoun (2000) in that perfective verbs undergo V-to-T movement while imperfective verbs do not. The analysis in this monograph and particularly in Chapter 5 appeals to this claim. The syntax of tense, aspect, and AGR is of particular relevance to negation, because all of these syntactic categories interact with both the verb and with each other. The nature of this interaction will become clear as we go through the analyses developed in the subsequent chapters. Descriptively speaking, the interaction among these categories involves word order restrictions, semantic ambiguities, and co-occurrence restrictions. The theoretical relevance of these various aspects of interaction has consequences for the locus and licensing of these syntactic categories in the clause structure, the scope of negation over tense, events and Negative Sensitive Items (NSIs), and the nature of head movement in linguistic theory.

2.2.1 *The position of the preverbal subject*

Preverbal subjects have been the topic of much discussion in the research on Arabic syntax. This section briefly discusses the standard analyses of subject-verb word order in Arabic.

Arabic allows both verb-subject (VS) and subject-verb (SV) word orders:

(19) a. ʔakal-uu   li-wlaad   (JA)
          eat.PFV-3MPL   DEF-kids
          'The kids ate.'

      b. li-wlaad   ʔakal-uu   (JA)
          DEF-kids   eat.PFV-3MPL
          'The kids ate.'

While the status of postverbal subjects is generally not controversial, there is a debate in the literature regarding the status of preverbal subjects in Arabic. It is generally assumed that postverbal subjects stay inside the thematic domain in the VP projection, in line with the internal subject hypothesis (Kitagawa 1986; Kuroda 1988; Sportiche 1988; Koopman and Sportiche 1991; McCloskey 1997). In contrast, it is generally assumed that preverbal subjects do not stay in the VP domain. There are various arguments showing conflicting evidence as to whether the external argument in subject-verb word order is a true subject in Spec-TP or a left dislocated NP, that is to say a topic in Spec-CP (Aoun et al. 2010). Since the status of SV word order is controversial, it is helpful to highlight key distributional contrasts and steer away from the controversial claims simply in order to provide background knowledge with respect to an analysis of negation. There are striking contrasts in the distribution of SV word order in colloquial Arabic and SA. First, the preverbal subject can follow sentential negation if it is an indefinite NP:

(20) a. ma   ħada   bi-saafir   kul   yoom   (JA)
        NEG   one   ASP-travel.3MSG.IPFV   every   day
        'No one travels every day.'

     b. ma   ħadd   ysaafir   kul   yoom   (QA)
        NEG   one   travel.3MSG.IPFV   every   day
        'No one travels every day.'

     c. la   ʔahad-a   yusaafiru   kulla   yawm   (SA)
        NEG   one   travel.3MSG.IPFV   every   day
        'No one travels every day.'

(21) a. ma   (*Zeid) bi-saafir   (Zeid) kul   yoom   (JA)
        NEG   Zeid   ASP-travel.3MSG.IPFV   Zeid   every   day
        'Zeid does not travel every day.'

     b. ma   (*Zeid) ysaafir   (Zeid) kul   yoom   (QA)
        NEG   Zeid   travel.3MSG.IPFV   Zeid   every   day
        'Zeid does not travel every day.'

     c. la   (*Zayd) yusaafiru   (Zayd) kulla   yawm   (SA)
        NEG   Zayd   travel.3MSG.IPFV   Zayd   every   day
        'Zayd does not travel every day.'

Second, the preverbal subject can follow question words in colloquial Arabic but not in SA:

(22) a. wein   (Zeid)   saafar   (Zeid)   (JA)
        where   Zeid   travel.3MSG.PFV   Zeid
        'Where did Zeid travel?'

     b. ʔyana   (*Zeid) saafar   (Zeid)   (SA)
        where   Zeid   travel.3MSG.PFV   Zeid
        'Where did Zeid travel?'

Third, the preverbal subject in colloquial Arabic can intervene between the complementizer and the verb. This is not possible in SA.

(23) a. ʕašaan   (Zeid) yindʒaħ   (Zeid)   (JA)
          so that   Zeid   succeed.3MSG.IPFV Zeid
          'So that Zeid succeed.'

      b. likay   (*Zayd) yandʒaħ   (Zayd)   (SA)
          so that   Zayd   succeed.3MSG.IPFV Zayd
          'So that Zeid succeed.'

This is relevant to the micro-variation in the position of preverbal subjects relative to the negative marker *maa*. The micro-variation can be seen
in JA and QA where the sentential negative marker *maa* can precede the
definite preverbal subject, but not in SA. These empirical facts suggest
that the definite preverbal subject in SA occupies a position higher than
its counterpart in JA and QA. This in turn leads us to predict that the definite preverbal subject in JA and QA should be able to intervene between
the verb and the negative marker that is located above TP. Looking at the
special cases where negation can occupy a position above TP, we find evidence that the definite preverbal subject can intervene between the verb
and the marker *maa*:

(24) a. ʕumr-o   maa b-yoom   ʕumar bisaamħ-ak   (JA)
          NPI-ever-his NEG in-day   Omar   forgive.3MSG.IPFV-you
          'Omar will not forgive you in any day.' = 'He will never forgive you.'

      b. maa gad   fi-sˤsˤaf   ʕumar kallam-a   (QA)
          NEG ever in class   Omar   talk.3MSG.PFV-him
          'Omar has never talked to him in class.'

By the same logic, if the definite preverbal subject in SA occupies a position higher than its counterpart in JA and QA, which is to say in the complementizer phrase (CP) layer, the prediction is that the definite preverbal
subject cannot intervene between the negative marker *maa* and the verb.
This prediction is borne out:

(25) ma   (*ʕumaru) y-zuuru   (ʕumaru) ʔaħadan   (SA)
      NEG   Omar   ASP-visit.3MSG.IPFV Omar   NPI-one
      laylan
      at night
      'Omar does not visit anyone at night.'

I show that when preceding the preverbal subject, *maa* in JA and QA can
have a sentential interpretation, whereas in SA it can only have a contrastive focus interpretation and fails to have a sentential interpretation that
can license NPIs. These empirical facts can be captured under a multi-locus
analysis of negation but cannot be captured under a unilocus analysis.

Crucially, while the definite preverbal subject can intervene between negation and the verb only in particular contexts where negation is arguably higher than tense, the indefinite preverbal subject can intervene between negation and the verb in any context:

(26) a. maa   ħada/waaħad/ʔinsaan/walad   saaʕad-ni   (JA)
          NEG   anyone/one/human/a boy   help.3MSG.PFV-me
          'No one/human/boy helped me.'

      b. *ħada/*waaħad/*ʔinsaan/*walad   maa   saaʕad-ni   (JA)
          anyone/one/human/a boy   NEG   help.3MSG.PFV-me

(27) a. ʔaħmad/l-walad   maa   saaʕad–ni   (JA)
          Ahmad/DEF-boy   NEG   help.3MSG.PFV-me
          'Ahmad/the boy did not help me.'

      b. maa   *ʔaħmad/*l-walad   saaʕad–ni   (JA)
          NEG   Ahmad/DEF-boy   help.3MSG.PFV-me

Therefore, I claim preverbal definite noun phrases are topics in Spec-CP when they cannot intervene between negation and the verb. However, preverbal indefinite noun phrases, which can intervene between negation and the verb, are subjects in Spec-TP. I treat the position of the preverbal noun phrase relative to the negative marker as a test for deciding whether it is a subject or a topic. Preverbal noun phrases which can intervene between the negative marker and the verb are subjects in Spec-TP, but those which cannot are topics in Spec-TP.

2.2.2 *Verb movement*

The literature on the syntax of verb movement in Arabic largely assumes that perfective verbs undergo V-to-T movement, while imperfective verbs do not (Benmamoun 2000; Aoun et al. 2010; Soltan 2012; Alqassas 2015, among others). I take a similar stand on this issue and support it by showing the plausibility of this view with respect to tense, aspect, and agreement in the verbal domain in the next subsection.

The first assumption is that verbs which denote past tense (perfective verbs) move to T, while verbs which denote a non-past tense (imperfective verbs) do not move to T. Aoun et al. give three arguments to support the assumption that past tense verbs move to T but non-past tense verbs do not. First, subject agreement appears as a suffix on past tense verbs but as a prefix on present tense verbs. In (28)a, the verb moves to T, so agreement shows up as a suffix. In (28)b, if we assume that the present tense verb does not move to T, we can explain how the agreement appears as a prefix on the verb:

(28) a.

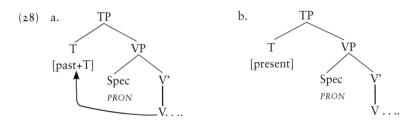

The second argument comes from idiomatic expressions. In these expressions, the past tense verb appears before the subject as in (29)a, but the present tense verb appears after the subject. Aoun et al. argue that the contrast can be explained if we assume that the past tense verb moves to T but the present tense verb stays in VP.

(29) a. ra-hm-u   llah   (MA)
          bless.3MSG.PFV-him   God
          'May God bless him.'

      b. llah   y-rə-hm-u   (MA)
          God   bless.3MSG.IPFV-him
          'May God bless him.'

The third argument comes from negation patterns in modern Arabic dialects such as Cairene Egyptian Arabic (CEA), where both the discontinuous negation pattern and the continuous pattern are possible in sentences with an imperfective verb as in (30), whereas only the discontinuous pattern is possible in sentences which have a perfective verb as in (31). Again, according to Aoun et al., the contrast can be explained if we assume that the past tense verb moves to T but the present tense verb does not. Recall that if the verb moves to T, there is no minimality violation since it incorporates with the negative morpheme, as is clear from the fact that the negative morphemes are clitics in (30) and (31).

(30) a. ana   ma-ba-hazzar-š   (CEA)
          I   NEG-ASP-joke.1SG.IPFV-NEG
          'I am not joking.'

      b. ana   muš   ba-hazzar   (CEA)
          I   NEG   ASP-joke.1SG.IPFV
          'I am not joking.'

(31) a. ana   ma-ruħt-iš   (CEA)
          I   NEG-go.1SG.PFV-NEG
          'I did not go.'

b. *ana muš ruħt   (CEA)
    I   NEG go.1SG.PFV

The fourth argument comes from the fact that there is no copula in sentences which have a non-verbal predicate when these sentences express the present tense, as in (32), while there is a copula when the sentence expresses the past tense, as in (33). The contrast can be explained if we assume that T^0 needs to be filled in sentences with a present tense interpretation. This in turn implies that the present tense verb in verbal sentences does not need to move to T^0.

(32) Ɂaħmad   zaʕlaan   (JA)
      Ahmad   sad
      'Ahmad is sad.'

(33) Ɂaħmad   kaan   zaʕlaan   (JA)
      Ahmad   be.3MSG.PFV sad
      'Ahmad was sad.'

This dichotomous analysis for verb movement is directly related to the distribution of bipartite negation in the Arabic dialects. Benmamoun's (2000) and Aoun et al.'s (2010) analyses of bipartite negation in Arabic dialects assume that past tense verbs move to T but non-past tense verbs do not. This assumption forms the basis of their account for why past tense verbs have to merge with negation but non-past verbs do not. They suggest that the past tense verb has to move to T to check its [+V] feature while a non-past verb does not move to T because its T head is not specified for [+V]. Under this assumption, movement of a past tense verb across negation (without incorporating with it) creates a minimality violation (i.e., violates the Head Movement Constraint). These are the relevant examples from EA:

(34) ana muš ba-hazzar   (EA)
      I   NEG ASP-joke.1SG.IPFV
      'I am not joking.'

(35) ana ma-ruħt-iš   (EA)
      I   NEG-go.1SG.PFV-NEG
      'I did not go.'

2.2.3 *Tense and aspect*

The perfective and imperfective distinction between verbs is one of many hotly debated issues among researchers in the syntax of tense and aspect in Arabic. There is a consensus in the literature that the morphological distinction displayed by perfective and imperfective verb forms in Arabic is not a reflection of the temporal past/non-past distinction (Shlonsky 1997; McCarthy 1979; Benmamoun 2000; Aoun et al. 2010; Soltan 2011; Hallman 2015). Instead, the affixes carried by these verb forms are a reflection of Person/Number/Gender (PNG) agreement features (phi-features φ), and tense is abstract (Aoun et al. 2010). Soltan (2011) proposes a connection between agreement and imperfective aspect. He proposes that imperfective verb forms get their agreement features under the aspectual projection (AspP), while their tense head has no phi-features. The imperfective verb form stays under AspP giving rise to the prefixal form of the imperfective verb.[8] The perfective verb forms, on the other hand, have a tense head that has phi-features requiring the verb to move to T and subsequently get their suffixal AGR.[9] The following representations are an illustration of the JA imperfective and perfective examples below.

(36) a. el-bint   b-t-ilʕab   (JA)
          DET-girl   ASP-3FSG-play.IPFV
          'The girl is playing.'

     b. el-bint   liʕba-t   (JA)
          DET-girl   play-3FSG.PFV
          'The girl played.'

(37) a. $[_{TP}$ T $_{[Nonpast]}$ $[_{AspP}$ Asp$_{\varphi}$ $[_{VP}$ V . . .]]]
     b. $[_{TP}$ T $_{[Past]\varphi}$ $[_{AspP}$ Asp $[_{VP}$ V . . .]]]

The analysis of tense and aspect in this chapter follows Soltan's proposal that imperfective verbs get their agreement under AspP. However, the analysis here differs in the following way. Soltan's analysis treats the marker *b-* in EA as a marker of imperfective aspect. Instead, I argue that in JA this marker is the head of a modal projection (ModP) dominating AspP. This ModP licenses the imperfective verb form and gives rise to either a progressive/habitual interpretation or an epistemic interpretation expressing certainty. This ModP is arguably the host for the future marker *raħ* in JA (cf. next section on simple tenses). I argue that the imperfective verb form is a defective tense that must be licensed by a head (the progressive/habitual particle *b-* in JA or an abstract aspectual head in GA and SA) because it fails to make reference to the utterance time. The perfective verb form, however, is not dependent and can make reference to the utterance time. This analysis of SA imperfective verbs assumes Hallman's (2015) analysis of SA imperfective verb forms, whereby the meaning of the progressive and habitual aspect is derived from covert operators rather than from the imperfective verb form.

The following sections put forward an analysis for tense and aspect in simple and complex tense constructions. I argue that *b-* is not a marker of imperfective aspect, nor is it a tense marker. I also argue that *raħ* is also not a tense marker. The markers *b-* and *raħ* are aspectual modals that express progressive/habitual aspect and future aspect, respectively. The next two subsections answer the following questions. Why is the imperfective verb form ungrammatical in the absence of *b-*? What is the nature of the inflectional category in sentences with *b-* and *raħ*? Finally, what is the structure of complex tense constructions?

2.2.3.1 Simple tenses

This section first develops an analysis of the JA tense and aspect system in order to instantiate the dependency between the imperfective verb form and the aspectual markers *b-* and *raħ*. This lays out the grounds for the claim that SA and GA have covert operators that correspond to the JA aspectual markers, concurring with Hallman's (2015) analysis of the SA imperfective verb. Hallman argues that the imperfective verb form in SA is the default lexical form and that the habitual/ progressive aspects associated with this form are derived from covert aspectual operators associated with the relevant aspectual interpretation. The JA data and its analysis in this section support Hallman's conclusion about SA. I show that the imperfective verb form is dependent on an aspectual operator in JA and the aspectual operator is lexicalized by the various aspectual markers such as *b-* and *raħ*.

The syntactic status of the markers *b-* and *raħ* can be determined based on their syntactic distribution and on their semantic contribution to the interpretation of the clause. The first significant observation regarding their syntactic distribution is that the imperfective verb form cannot occur by itself and *b-* must precede it, while the perfective form can occur by itself and *b-* cannot precede it.

(38)   a.   *(bi)-y-lʕab   (JA)
            ASP-3MSG-play.IPFV
            'He plays/is playing.' (Progressive/Habitual)

       b.   *(raħ)   y-lʕab   (JA)
            FUT   3MSG-play.IPFV
            'He will play.' (Future)

These facts suggest that the imperfective verb form is defective in some way, while the perfective form is not. What about the imperfective form makes it defective? Recall that this form occurs in

the context of Exceptional Case Marking (ECM) verbs and non-veridi-
cal contexts:

(39) a. *(ħabb-o)   y-lʕab   (JA)
          like.3MSG.PFV-him   3MSG-play.IPFV
          'He liked him to play.' (ECM)

      b. *(ʕašaan)   y-lʕab   (JA)
          in order to   3MSG-play.IPFV
          'In order to play.' (Purpose complementizer)

      c. *(laazim)   y-lʕab   (JA)
          necessary   3MSG-play.IPFV
          'He must play.' (Deontic: obligation)

      d. *(law)   y-lʕab   (JA)
          if   3MSG-play.IPFV
          'If he were to play.' (Irrealis conditional)

These contexts share a lack of direct temporal reference. With ECM constructions, the time of the embedded verb is determined by the time of
the matrix verb. There is no reference to the utterance time with subjunctive clauses, either. Therefore, I suggest that the imperfective verb form
is licensed by the subjunctive mood in these sentences. To explain the
nature of the dependency between the imperfective verb and the subjunctive, I follow the view that the verb has an event variable (e) that must be
bound by a temporal or modal/mood operator (Enc 1991; Pesetsky 1992;
Bošković 1996, 1997; Martin 1996, 2001; Giannakidou 2009, among
others). In the case of the subjunctive, an operator in a Mood projection
binds the event variable of the verb.

(40) [MoodP Subj $_{Op}$ [AspP e(-PFV) [vP. . .

How, then, does the imperfective verb get licensed in indicative sentences? Specifically, why is it that an imperfective verb in indicative sentences requires *b-* or *raħ* and cannot occur by itself? I propose that these
markers are required to license the imperfective verb form. Furthermore,
I argue that *b-* and *raħ* are aspectual modals rather than tense markers.

It is important to emphasize that *b-* is not a marker of imperfective
aspect. The imperfective verb form has an imperfective interpretation
without this marker:

(41) kaan   y-lʕab   (JA)
      be.3MSG.PFV   3MSG-play.IPFV
      'He was playing/used to play.'

This marker is also not a tense marker. It can co-occur with events that are simultaneous with, anterior to, or posterior to the utterance time:

(42) a. bi-y-lʕab   (JA)
          ASP-3MSG-play.IPFV
          'He plays/is playing.'

      b. kaan   bi-y-lʕab   (JA)
          be.3MSG.PFV   ASP-3MSG-play.IPFV
          'He was playing.'

      c. ba-šuf-ak   (JA)
          ASP-1SG.see-you
          'I will see you.'

This marker is, nonetheless, compatible with imperfective verbs and cannot precede perfective verbs. It is therefore reasonable to propose that *b-* is a modal that marks habitual/progressive aspect.

(43) a. *(bi)-y-lʕab   (JA)
          ASP-3MSG-play.IPFV
          'He plays/is playing.'

      b. (*bi)-liʕib   (JA)
          (*ASP)-play.3MSG.PFV
          'He played.'

The generative literature on the syntax of tense/aspect in Arabic supports the view that Arabic has distinct aspect and tense phrases (Benmamoun 2000; Fassi Fehri 2000/2004, 2012; Ouali and Fortin 2007; Aoun et al. 2010; Soltan 2011, among others). Following this view, I assume that there are distinct tense and aspect projections in JA. The resulting representation for sentences with simple tense is as follows:

(44) [TP (-Past) [ModP (PROG./Habit.) [AspP (-PFV) [vP. . .

The imperfective verb form has defective tense, hence the need for an element that can saturate it. The marker *b-* is a modal operator that has a progressive/habitual interpretation, and it is compatible with non-past tense, or a non-deictic tense. This modal operator licenses the event variable of the imperfective verb.

(45) [ModP *b-* $_{Op}$ [AspP e(-PFV) [vP. . .

This is consistent with the fact that imperfective aspect is ambiguous between progressive and habitual aspect. It is also consistent with the fact that *b-* has an epistemic modality interpretation, in addition to a future interpretation:

(46) a. bi-y-kuun   (bi)-y-lʕab[10]   (JA)
         ASP-3MSG-be.IPFV   (ASP)-3MSG-play.IPFV
         'He must be playing.'   (Epistemic: certainty)
         'He will be playing.'   (Future)

     b. bi-y-kuun   liʕib   (JA)
         ASP-3MSG-be.IPFV   play.3MSG.PFV
         'He must have played.'   (Epistemic: certainty)
         'He will have played.'   (Future)

Crucially, the interpretation of the marker *b-* preceding the auxiliary can have a posterior or an anterior interpretation. The event is posterior to the utterance time when the lexical verb is imperfective. With a perfective lexical verb, the marker *b-* preceding the auxiliary is ambiguous between an anterior and a posterior interpretation. The event is anterior to the utterance time under the epistemic reading, but posterior under the future reading. This suggests that this marker is not a tense marker.

   The future marker *raħ* is an aspectual modal that can give a posterior interpretation of an event. This interpretation is consistent with non-past tense, but it does not follow from non-past tense. This analysis is consistent with the fact that the presence of this marker does not give the interpretation that the event occurred after the utterance time (cf. Wurmbrand's (2014) analysis of English would).[11]

(47) min   šahr   qarrar   inn-o   kaan   (JA)
      since month   decide.3MSG.PFV   that-he be.3MSG.PFV
      raħ   ysaafir   nbaariħ
      FUT   3MSG.travel.IPFV   yesterday
      'A month ago, he decided that he would travel yesterday.'

Likewise, this marker can be used even when an event is simultaneous with the utterance time:

(48) raħ   y-isˤal   l-ʔaan   (JA)
      FUT   3MSG-arrive.IPFV   DET-now
      'He's arriving now.'

The idea that a clause can have a future interpretation without having a formal feature that can be interpreted as [FUT] 'future' is well supported in the literature. Wurmbrand (2014: 404) shows that English infinitives can have a future interpretation despite being tenseless. Wurmbrand proposes that these tenseless infinitives involve syntactic projection (ModP) with a future modal.[12]

(49) Leo decided to read a book.   (Future irrealis)

Therefore, *rah* is an aspectual modal with an operator that can bind the dependent variable of imperfective verbs. This analysis partly follows Giannakidou's (2009) proposal for the perfective non-past in Greek.

(50) [TP (-Past) [ModP (FUT. $_{Op}$) [AspP e(-PFV) [vP...

As for SA and GA, we do not find aspectual markers that co-occur with the imperfective verb to convey the habitual and progressive interpretations associated with an eventive verb like *ya-lʕabu* 'to play.' Instead, these meanings seem to be expressed by the imperfective verb form itself.

(51) a. ya-lʕabu   (SA)
          3MSG-play.IPFV
          'He plays/is playing.'

      b. ye-lʕab   (GA)
          3MSG-play.IPFV
          'He plays/is playing.'

If this analysis of the imperfective in JA is on the right track, it is reasonable to posit covert aspectual operators that can saturate the imperfective verb form and give rise to the habitual and progressive interpretations associated with it.

Indeed, Hallman (2015) argues convincingly that the imperfective verb form in SA is the default lexical form that does not have an imperfective meaning and therefore is similar to the English infinitive. The imperfective form in Hallman's analysis is a morphological form that does not contribute to the habitual/ progressive aspect interpretation. Hallman advances various arguments supporting the claim that the imperfective is not the source of the aspectual interpretation. Hallman cites examples showing that in the context of the model predicate *min l-muhtamali* (likely) the imperfective verb form fails to express the progressive or habitual reading available to eventive verbs like the above verb *ya-lʕabu* 'to play.' The model predicate *min l-muhtamali* is followed by the complementizer *ʔan* which selects a subjunctive imperfective verb:

(52) ʔa-ʕtaqid-u   ʔanna min l-muħtamal-i
      I-believe.IPFV-IND   that   of   the-likely-GEN
      ʔan   yakuun-a
      that be.IPFV-SBJV
      ðaalika ʕalaam-at-an ʕalaa stiʕdaad-i-himaa
      that   sign-F-ACC   of   readiness-GEN-their.dual
      li-t-taʕaawun-i   fii dʒadwal-i   ʔiʕmaal-in
      to-the-cooperation-GEN   in   agenda-GEN   actions-GEN
      siyaasiyy-in.
      political-GEN
      'I believe that this is likely to be a sign of their readiness to cooperate on
      a political agenda.'

At this point we have yet to account for the perfective verb form. Recall
that a perfective verb has deictic tense that refers to the utterance time by
anchoring the tense of the clause as anterior to the utterance time. This is
true of all the Arabic varieties:

(53) a. liʕib   (JA)
          play.3MSG.PFV
          'He played.'

      b. liʕab   (GA)
          play.3MSG.PFV
          'He played.'

      c. laʕiba   (SA)
          play.3MSG.PFV
          'He played.'

This explains its incompatibility with *b-* and *raħ* in JA and the
future marker *sa-* in SA (non-deictic aspectual modals associated with
non-past).

(54) a. (*bi-)liʕib   (JA)
          (*ASP-)play.3MSG.PFV
          'He played.'

      b. (*raħ)   liʕib   (JA)
          (*FUT)   play.3MSG.PFV
          'He played.'

      c. (*sa-)liʕib   (SA)
          (*FUT) play.3MSG.PFV
          'He played.'

    d. sa-yalʕabu   (SA)
        FUT-play.3MSG.IPFV
        'He will play.'

Therefore, it is reasonable to suggest that there is an AspP associated with perfective aspect (+PFV), and a tense phrase associated with past tense (+Past).

  (55) [TP (+Past) [AspP (+PFV) [vP...

There are rare cases in which the perfective can be used to denote an event simultaneous with the utterance time as in (56)a, or even posterior to the utterance time as in (56)b. Crucially, the aspectual marker *b-* is not allowed in such contexts:

  (56) a. ʔiða (*bi)-ruħt,   xabbir-ni   (JA)
          If   (*ASP)-go.2MSG.PFV, tell.3MSG.PFV-me
          'If you go, tell me.'

        b. lʔaan (*bi)-laaħaðˤt   l-farg   (JA)
          Now (*ASP)-notice.1SG.PFV DEF-difference
          'Now I see the difference.'

In such cases, the perfective verb form is associated with non-past tense. This gives further evidence that the AspP is distinct from the tense phrase in JA. This also supports the claim that the marker *b-* is not a marker of non-past tense. This is evident from the fact that *b-* is not allowed here despite the non-past interpretation of the sentence.

  As for the perfective verb form, recall that this form is independent. It can stand by itself, as in (53). But what does this lack of dependency mean? I would like to suggest that the perfective verb is independent because it is associated with a deictic tense head. Assuming the pronominal theory of tense (Partee 1973, 1984; Heim 1994; Abusch 1998, 2004; Giannakidou 2009, among others), I suggest that the T head associated with [Past] is a deictic head. Interestingly, it is highly plausible to suggest that it is phi-features that make it deictic. In other words, Soltan's (2011) proposal that Past T is specified for phi-features fits with the proposal that Past T is deictic. Therefore, the event variable of the perfective verb is identified by the deictic Past T head. The deictic nature of past tense is clear from the fact that perfective verbs with a past tense interpretation make a specific reference to the utterance time. Crucially, this is not the case with imperfective verb forms.

2.2.3.2 Complex tenses

Another issue in the syntax of complex tense constructions is whether the auxiliary and lexical verb are mono-clausal or bi-clausal.

(57) a. kaan   (bi)-y-lʕab   (JA)[13]
          be.3MSG.PFV   (ASP)-3MSG-play.IPFV
          'He was playing.'

      b. kaan   liʕib   (JA)
          be.3MSG.PFV   play.3MSG.PFV
          'He had played.'

(58) a. kaana   ya-lʕabu   (SA)
          be.3MSG.PFV   3MSG-play.IPFV
          'He was playing.'

      b. kaana   laʕiba   (SA)
          be.3MSG.PFV   play.3MSG.PFV
          'He had played.'

Specifically, the issue is whether they each have a tense head as in (59), or they each have their own VP, AspP and TP projection, as in (60).

(59) [T1 (±Past) [T2 (±Perf/Ant) [Asp (±Pfv/Term) [VP (±Telic)]]]]
      (Fassi Fehri 2000/2004)

(60) [TP [AspP [VP BE [TP [AspP [vP [VP main verb
      (Ouali and Fortin 2007)

Crucial to this monograph is where the locus of the auxilaiary *kwn* exists in the syntactic structure, and whether there are two tense phrases in complex tense constructions. I argue that the verbal copula *kwn* is lower than the tense head in a distinct projection (AuxP).

As for the two proposals analyzing complex tense constructions involving the auxiliary *kwn* and a lexical verb: the first is a bi-clausal analysis with two TPs, two AspPs, and two VPs (developed in Ouali and Fortin 2007 for Moroccan Arabic (MA); schematized in (61)), and the second is a mono-clausal two-TP analysis (developed in Fassi Fehri 2000/2004 for SA; schematized in (62)).

(61)

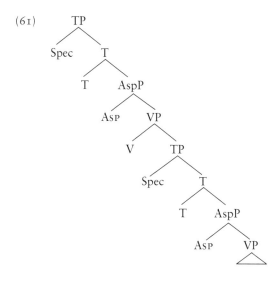

(62)

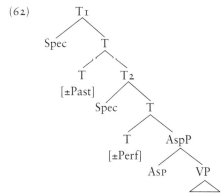

Which of these proposals do the JA facts support, and what modifications are required in light of the JA data and the analysis argued for in the previous section? The following facts support a bi-clausal analysis. The auxiliary and the lexical verb are not one syntactic tense head. The auxiliary and lexical verb each express agreement, aspect, and tense, and the negative marker can immediately precede either the auxiliary or the verb.

(63) a. bi-y-kuun   bi-y-lʕab   (JA)
          ASP-3MSG-be.IPFV   ASP-3MSG-play.IPFV
          'He will/must be playing.'

      b. bi-y-kuun   liʕib   (JA)
          ASP-3MSG-be.IPFV   play.3MSG.PFV
          'He will/must have played.'

(64) a. kaan   (bi)-y-lʕab   (JA)
         be.3MSG.PFV   (ASP)-3MSG-play.IPFV
         'He was playing.'

      b. kaan   liʕib   (JA)
         be.3MSG.PFV   play.3MSG.PFV
         'He had played.'

(65) (maa) bi-y-kuun   (maa) liʕib   (JA)
      (NEG)   ASP-3MSG-be.IPFV (NEG) play.3MSG.PFV
      'He will not have played.'

Moreover, the subject can immediately precede the lexical verb or the auxiliary verb:

(66) (l-walad)   kaan   (l-walad) bi-y-lʕab   (JA)
      (DEF-boy)   be.3MSG.PFV   (DEF-boy) ASP-3MSG-play.IPFV
      'The boy was playing.'

Adverbs display the same behavior:

(67) (bi-l-beit)   kaan   (bi-l-beit)   bi-y-lʕab   (JA)
      (in-DEF-house)   be.3MSG.PFV   (in-DEF-house) ASP-3MSG-play.IPFV
      'He was playing at home.'

And wh-words in situ can intervene between the auxiliary and lexical verb:

(68) kaan   (miin/ween)   bi-y-lʕab?   (JA)
      be.3MSG.PFV   (who/where)   ASP-3MSG-play.IPFV
      'Who was playing?/Where was he playing?'

While these facts from JA support the bi-clausal analysis Ouali and Fortin (2007) developed for Moroccan Arabic, I depart from their analysis by suggesting that the imperfective lexical verb following the auxiliary does not have a tense head, and that it merely has an aspectual modal head.

(69) [TP (-Past) [ModP b-/raħ [AspP (-PFV) [AuxP kwn
      [ModP b-/raħ   [AspP (-PFV) [vP. . .

(70) [TP (+past) [AspP (+PFV) [AuxP kwn
      [ModP ba-/raħ [AspP (-PFV) [vP. . .

What we have dominating the imperfective lexical verb is thus an aspectual modal rather than tense (cf. Fassi Fehri's 2004 imperfect tense).

A tense head with [+/- Perfect] is not justified morphologically or semantically. Morphologically, the aspectual markers *b-* and *raḥ* are not required in this context. Unlike imperfective verb forms in simple tenses such as (71)a, the imperfective verb in complex tenses such as (71)b does not have to include *b-*.

(71)   a.   *(bi)-y-lʕab   (SA)
           ASP-3MSG-play.IPFV
           'He plays/is playing.'

      b.   *(bi)-y-kuun   y-lʕab   (SA)
           ASP-3MSG-be.IPFV   3MSG-play.IPFV
           'He will/must be playing.'

Given that the imperfective form is licensed by the auxiliary, if there is a tense head dominating the lexical verb in (71)b then this tense head is the licensor of the imperfective verb form. If an abstract tense head can license the imperfective verb form, we incorrectly predict that it will do so in the sentence without an auxiliary as in (71)a.

This analysis consequently suggests that the auxiliary verb licenses the lexical verb. Recall that we argued that the imperfective verb form needs an operator to bind its event variable. In example (71)b, the marker *b-* preceding the auxiliary is obligatory. This suggests that the imperfective form of the auxiliary needs a licensor. Consequently, this suggests that the auxiliary has a VP projection with an event variable, supporting Ouali and Fortin's analysis of the auxiliary as a head that has an aspectual and a temporal projection. This auxiliary has a variable that needs to be bound by an operator, the aspectual marker *b-* in (71)b The structure of this example is shown in (72).

(72)   [TP (-Past) [ModP b- [AspP (-PFV) [AuxP kwn [AspP (-PFV) [vP...

As for perfective lexical verbs following the auxiliary, are they dominated by a tense head (one that is distinct from the tense head of the auxiliary) in addition to the aspectual head, or merely by the aspectual head alone? There are two possible analyses for such cases. The first is that there is no tense head dominating the AspP of the lexical verb, as in (73)a. The second is that there is a relative tense head (i.e., +Perfect) à la Fassi Fehri (2000/2004) dominating the AspP of the lexical verb, as in (73)b.

(73)   a.   [TP (±Past) [ModP b-/raḥ [AspP (±PFV) [AuxP kwn
            [AspP (+PFV) [vP...

      b.   [TP (±Past) [ModP b-/raḥ [AspP (±PFV) [AuxP kwn
            [TP (+Perfect) [AspP (+PFV) [vP...

Recall that the perfective lexical verb in simple sentences (without the auxiliary) has a deictic tense that anchors the event time prior to the utterance time. In the case of a lexical verb following an auxiliary, the perfective lexical verb can express an event whose time is anterior relative to a posterior event, as in (74), or anterior relative to the utterance time, as in (75):

> (74) lamma   b-tisʕal,   bi-y-kuun   liʕib   (JA)
>   when   ASP-arrive.2MSG.IPFV   ASP-3MSG-be.IPFV   play.3MSG.PFV
>   'When you arrive, he will have played.' (anterior relative to future)

> (75) bi-y-kuun   liʕib   nbaariħ   (JA)
>   ASP-3MSG-be.IPFV   play.3MSG.PFV   yesterday
>   'He must have played yesterday.' (anterior relative to utterance time)

Such cases suggest that the lexical verb does not make reference to the utterance time. It is possible to capture this lack of reference to the utterance time by allowing the lexical verb to project an AspP without a tense phrase, or by positing a relative tense head that specifies the time of the event as anterior to another event (à la Fassi Fehri's (2000/2004) [+Perfect] tense). This other event is the future event in (74) and the utterance time in (75).

A unified analysis for complex tenses, however, would favor an analysis which does not posit a relative tense head [+Perfect]. An analysis with relative tense head would complicate analyses of imperfective lexical verbs that follow the auxiliary. Recall that such cases arguably have a ModP projection, explaining the occurrence of the aspectual markers *b-* and *raħ* preceding the lexical verb. In these cases, adding another tense head for [-Perfect] would be superfluous. Moreover, recall that the imperfective verb following an auxiliary does not require the aspectual markers *b-* and *raħ*, which suggests a lack of ModP in such structures. Therefore, a unified analysis for imperfective and perfective verbs following the auxiliary is more plausible. This analysis has the following schematic structures for imperfective and perfective verbs in such context:

> (76) a. [Aux kwn...[(ModP b-/raħ) [AspP (-PFV) [vP...
>   b. [Aux kwn...[AspP (+PFV) [vP...

Having discussed the theoretical assumptions and key arguments for the syntax of subjects, verb movement, and tense, we have now laid out the grounds for an analysis of negation. The first issue that will be discussed is the morphological and syntactic status of negative markers in Arabic. After establishing their status, we can develop a multi-locus analysis of Arabic negation.

2.3 The morphological and syntactic status of negative markers in Arabic

Southern Levantine Arabic has five elements that appear in sentential negation. These are *maa, laa, -š, miš,* and *wala* in JA. SA has the markers *maa, laa, lam, lan,* and *laysa.* QA has *maa, laa,* and *mub.* The distribution of these elements is sensitive to the morphological, syntactic, and pragmatic context of the clauses in which they occur. The purpose of this section is to show the morphological and syntactic status of these various words. Morphological status here refers to whether the particular element is a free or bound morpheme. Syntactic status has to do with whether it is a head (X^0) or a phrase (XP).

Unlike the morphological status of the elements *ma* and *la,* the morphological status of the elements, *-š, miš,* and *wala* is transparent. The morpheme *-š* is a bound morpheme, and the morphemes *miš* and *wala* are free morphemes. The morpheme *-š* always appears as an enclitic on its host, the predicate, as in (77). The morpheme *miš* is free and usually immediately precedes the predicate or constituent it negates.[14] Consider the examples in (78). The morpheme *wala* is also a free morpheme. It occupies a sentence-final position, as can be seen in (79).

(77) b-aʕirf-iš   (JA)
      ASP-know.1SG.IPFV-NEG
      'I don't know.'

(78) a. ʔani   miš   zaʕlaan   (JA)
          I   NEG   sad
          'I am not sad.'

      b. miš   kull   tˤ- tˤullaab   hoon   (JA)
          NEG   all   DEF-students   here
          'Not all the students are here.'

(79) maa   saafar   wala   (JA)
      NEG   travel.3MSG.PFV   NEG
      'He did NOT travel.'[15]

Previous analyses of *ma* and *la* assume that they are bound morphemes (proclitics) in dialects which have bipartite negation such as JA, Moroccan Arabic, and EA. In these dialects, the morpheme *ma* is analyzed as a proclitic because it is phonologically weak and adjacent to the predicate it negates. Phonological weakness is manifested by the fact that *ma* is a weak syllable which consists of a consonant and a short vowel [ma]. Moreover, phonological weakness is manifested by the fact that *ma* is unstressed or at least does not carry sentential stress. In SA and the urban variety of JA, *ma* is a strong syllable which consists of a consonant and a long vowel [maa]. Consider the contrast between JA and SA in (80)–(81):

(80) a. ma-`b-aʕirf-iš   (JA)
          NEG-ASP-know.1SG.IMP-NEG
          'I don't know.'

     b. la-`truuḥ-iš   (JA)
          NEG-2.go.IMP-NEG
          'Don't go.'

(81) a. `maa   ʕarafa   (SA)
          NEG   ASP-know.3MSG.PFV
          'He didn't know'

     b. `la   taðhab   (SA)
          NEG   2.go.IMP
          'Don't go.'

As for adjacency, the negative marker *ma* must be adjacent to the predicate it negates when -*š* is present. For example NPs cannot intervene between *ma* and the predicate, as in (82)–(83):

(82) a. ʔaḥmad   ma   `b-aʕirf-iš   (JA)
          Ahmad   NEG   ASP-know.3MSG.IPFV-NEG
          'Ahmad doesn't know.'

     b. *ma   ʔaḥmad   `b-aʕirf-iš   (JA)
          NEG   Ahmad   ASP-know.3MSG.IPFV-NEG

(83) a. ʔaḥmad   la-`truuḥ-iš   (JA)
          Ahmad   NEG-2.go.IMP-NEG
          'Don't go.'

     b. *la   ʔaḥmad   `truuḥ-iš   (JA)
          NEG   Ahmad   2.go.IMP-NEG

While it is reasonable to assume that *ma* and *la* are proclitics in Levantine Arabic based on the fact that they are phonologically weak and adjacent to the predicate, I argue that they are free morphemes when they are used alone for sentential negation in Levantine Arabic, i.e., when -*š* is absent. First, when -*š* is absent, these morpheme carry sentential stress. Second, they are phonologically strong ([maa] and [laa]). This is also similar in QA:

(84) a. ˋmaa   b-aʕrif   (JA)
          NEG   ASP-know.1SG.IPFV
          'I don't know.'

      b. ˋlaa   truuħ   (JA)
          NEG   2.go.IMP
          'Don't go.'

      c. ˋmaa   ysaafir   (QA)
          NEG   travel.3MSG.IPFV
          'He does not travel.'

      d. ˋlaa   truuħ   (QA)
          NEG   2.go.IMP
          'Don't go.'

Interestingly, indefinite NPs can separate *maa* from the predicate it negates. Accordingly, I conclude that *ma* and *la* in JA can be either bound morphemes (proclitics) or free morphemes. The same claim can be extended to QA. The negative marker *ma* appears as a proclitic on the NPI *ħada* forming the compound *ma-ħħad* 'no one.' Even in SA, the negative marker appears with the NPI *ʔaħada* forming the compound *la-ʔaħada* 'no one.'

(85) a. ˋmaa   šaaf-ni   ħada   (JA)
          NEG   see.3MSG.PFV-me   one
          'No one saw me.'

      b. ˋmaa   ħada   šaaf-ni   (JA)
          NEG   one   see.3MSG.PFV-me
          'No one saw me.'

      c. ˋma-ħħad   šaaf-ni   (QA)
          no-one   see.3MSG.PFV-me
          'No one saw me.'

      d. ˋla-ʔaħada   raʔaa-ni   (SA)
          no-one   see.3MSG.PFV-me
          'No one saw me.'

We now turn to the syntactic status of the morphemes *ma*, *la*, *-š*, *miš*, and *wala*. The markers *ma* and *la* have been analyzed as heads of a NegP projection. The morpheme *-š* has been analyzed as a specifier in Spec/NegP (e.g., Ouhalla 1990) as well as a head which forms a discontinuous morpheme with *ma* (e.g., Benmamoun 2000). The morpheme *miš* has been assumed to be the result of a word formation process which takes place between the morphemes *ma* and *-š*. As Aoun et al. (2010) point out, the mechanism behind this word formation process is not clear under

Ouhalla's analysis. Under their analysis, *ma* and *-š* form a discontinuous morpheme (a circumfix). As for the morpheme *wala* in JA, it is clear that *wala* combines with an indefinite NP forming the compound *wala*-NP. This compound is a Negative Concord Item (NCI) which requires the use of a negative marker and does not contribute a negative meaning when it is postverbal, hence the concordant reading in the following example:

(86) ma-ʾb-aʕirf-iš   wala-iši   (JA)
      NEG-ASP-know.1SG.IPFV-NEG   NEG-thing
      'I don't know anything.'

However, *wala* is not a bound morpheme in JA because it can stand by itself without an NP in preverbal and postverbal positions:

(87) a. maa   saafar   wala   (JA)
          NEG   travel.3MSG.PFV   NEG
          'He did NOT travel.'

      b. wala   b-ħayaat-o   saafar   (JA)
          NEG   in-life-his travel.3MSG.PFV
          'He never traveled.'

Notice that *wala* in (87)a is used to reinforce the sentential negation carried out with *maa*. Hoyt (2010) gives a thorough description for its use in Negative Concord (NC) constructions in LA. However, to the best of my knowledge, the specific use of this morpheme as a reinforcer of sentential negation has not previously been reported in the literature. Hoyt reports its use as an NC word where it is used as a negative scalar focus particle *wala* 'not (even) (one), not a (single)' which combines with singular indefinite nouns in NC constructions. This marker is discussed further in Chapter 4.

I follow the standard analysis of *ma* and *la* as heads of a NegP projection (Ouhalla 1993; Bahloul 1996; Benmamoun 2000; Aoun et al. 2010, among others). I support this with various tests for the syntactic status of negative words. First, *ma* and *la* block V-to-T movement because of the Head Movement Constraint. This is based on the assumption that in Arabic, past tense verbs move to T (Benmamoun 2000; Aoun et al. 2010). If this assumption is right, and if *ma* is a head, then we can expect it to block V-to-T movement. This expectation is borne out in (88) where the past tense verb cannot cross over *ma* and precede it:[16]

(88) a. ma-saafartiš   (JA)
          NEG-travel.1SG.PFV
          'I did not travel.'

b. *saafart-iš   ma   (JA)
    travel.1SG.PFV-NEG   NEG

c. maa   saafart   (QA)
    NEG   travel.1SG.PFV
    'I did not travel.'

d. *saafart   maa   (QA)
    travel.1SG.PFV   NEG

e. maa   saafart-u   (SA)
    NEG   travel.1SG.PFV-IND
    'I did not travel.'

f. *saafart-u   maa   (SA)
    travel.1SG.PFV-IND NEG

The negative marker *laa* is used in negative imperative constructions in JA, QA, and SA. It can appear as a proclitic on an imperative verb suffixed by the negative marker *-š*, creating the bipartite marker *la. . .-š* used in JA negative imperatives. It can also be used to negate imperfective verbs in SA:

(89) a. laa   tsaafir   (JA)
         NEG   2.travel.IMP
         'Don't travel.'

     b. laa   tsaafir   (QA)
         NEG   2.travel.IMP
         'Don't travel.'

     c. laa   tu-saafir   (SA)
         NEG   2-travel.IMP
         'Don't travel.'

     d. laa   tsaafr-iš   (JA)
         NEG   2.travel.IMP-NEG
         'Don't travel.'

     e. laa   yusaafiru   daa?iman   (SA)
         NEG   travel.3MSG.IND always
         'He does not always travel.'

It is difficult to determine the syntactic status of this marker by looking at whether it can intercept the verb. *Laa* does not co-occur with perfective verbs that have a past tense interpretation, thus making this type of test impossible. Likewise, in SA, however, it co-occurs with imperfective verbs which arguably do not undergo V-to-T movement.

Nonetheless, one of the tests for determining the syntactic status of negative markers is the *Why Not* test (Zeijlstra 2004). The negative markers *ma* and *la* cannot be used in the *Why Not* construction. According to this test, negative markers which fail this test are syntactic heads, while those that PASS it are syntactic adverbs. Consider these examples which show that *maa* and *laa* (which are free morphemes rather than proclitics) fail this test:

(90)   a.   *leeš   laa/maa ?   (JA)[17]
            why   NEG
            'why not'

       b.   *leeš   laa/maa ?   (QA)
            why   NEG
            'why not'

       c.   lima   laa ?   (SA)
            why   NEG
            'why not'

Therefore, I conclude that these negative markers are syntactic heads, with the exception of *laa* in SA which is a syntactic adverb.

2.4 The multi-locus analysis: NegP below and above TP

There are two views in the literature on the syntax of negation regarding the position of negation in the clause structure. The first view is the parametric view in which within a given language NegP selects either a *v*P or a TP but not both (Benmamoun 1992, 2000; Ouhalla 1990, 1991; Mohammad 2000; Hoyt 2007; Soltan 2007; among others). This view restricts the locus of negation to one position in the syntactic structure, thus I will refer to it as the unilocus view. Under the second view, a certain language may opt for any position of negation, with the low position (selecting a vP) being the default and the higher position having special semantic/pragmatic and syntactic effects (cf. Ramchand 2001 for Bengali; Zanuttini 1998 for Romance languages; Alqassas 2015 for JA). This second view does not restrict the locus of negation to two positions. Therefore I will refer to this view as the multi-locus view.

In this section, I propose that the morphologically weak *ma/la* is the head of a NegP projection below TP, while morphologically strong *maa/laa* is the head of a NegP projection on top of TP. The morpheme *-š* is an agreement clitic which reinforces the weak proclitics *ma* and *la*. The difference between high and low negation is motivated by syntactic and semantic/pragmatic reasons. I argue that the variation in the position of NegP is not due to a syntactic parameter (whether NegP selects TP or VP), but is instead due to certain syntactic or semantic/pragmatic properties of negation (cf. Ramchand 2001 for Bengali; Zeijlstra 2004; Alqassas 2015 for Jordanian). According to this view, the semantic properties of negation differ in terms of whether the negative marker binds an event variable (vP) or a time variable (TP) (Zeijlstra 2004). Furthermore, the unmarked way to express sentential negation is by binding an event variable so that NegP is on top of vP (cf. Acquaviva 1997; Giannakidou 1999; Zeijlstra 2004; Alqassas 2015).

Ramchand (2001) uses Bengali as a case for illustration to explain why only the negative marker *ni* can license the NPI adverb *kokhono* 'ever,' while the negative marker *na* cannot do so as seen in the contrast below:

(91) a. Ami kokhono an   khai ni   (Bengali)
          I   ever   mangoes   ate   NEG
          'I never ate mangoes.'

     b. *Ami kokhono an   khai na   (Bengali)
          I   ever   mangoes   ate   NEG
          'I never ate mangoes.'

The negative marker *ni* happens to be the marked one. The NPI adverb is presumably in a position above TP since it is a time adverb. The negative marker *ni* can thus license this NPI because it is in a NegP on top of TP. That is to say, the negative marker binds a time variable in addition to binding the event variable. On the other hand, failure of the negative marker *na* to license the NPI adverb suggests that *na* is in a NegP on top of vP. In other words, *na* binds an event variable rather than a time variable. The details of the binding relationship and its consequences in Arabic are discussed in Chapter 3 in which Arabic data is used to analyze the relationship between negation and adverbs of time. As will be seen, this proposal suffices to account for word order restrictions and semantic ambiguities in Arabic. The focus in the present section, however, is to motivate the multi-locus analysis by investigating the interaction between adverbs and subjects on the one hand and negation on the other hand, as well as the interaction between negative markers and complementizers.

To begin with, it is important to explain why sentential (nuclear) stress falls on the preverbal negative marker *maa* when -*š* is absent, but on the negated predicate when -*š* is used. First, single negation involves a preverbal negative marker that is a separate word morphologically. It is a strong morpheme that receives primary stress. This differs from bipartite negation, in which primary stress falls on the

appropriate syllable in the morphological complex NEG-verb-NEG following the JA rules of word stress.[18] The verb happens to be the appropriate one in example a below. If *maa* and the verb in (92)b below were
one word, we would expect stress to fall on the second syllable (the
verb) on a PAR with the two syllable word *baa`zaar* 'market' in (92)a.
Yet, stress falls on *maa* when single negation is used to negate a verb that
has a heavy monosyllabic structure such as *zaar* 'visited' (cf. Alqassas
2015):

(92) a. baa `zaar l-batra   (JA)
          bazar   DEF-Petra
          'Petra's bazar.'

      b. `maa zaar   l-batra   (JA)
          NEG   visit.3MSG.PFV DEF-Petra
          'He did not visit Petra.'

In the case of the negative marker in bipartite negation, there is a
straightforward answer if the verb merges with the negative marker
via the syntactic process of incorporation. No such incorporation
takes place with single negation. This is based on the assumption that
sentential negation falls on the leftmost word in the sentence. This
word is *maa* or *laa* when there is no incorporation with the predicate,
but when the predicate merges with negation the leftmost word is the
negated predicate. This can help predict where sentential stress falls.
Why, then, does the predicate only sometimes merge with the negative
marker but sometimes does not? I propose that this is caused by the
availability of two positions for NegP. The first position is on top of TP
(the high NegP) and the second one is below TP, on top of *v*P (the low
NegP). In this case, the strong negative markers *maa* and *laa* occupy
the head position of the high NegP, while the weak ones *ma* and *la*
occupy the head position of the low NegP. The following is a schematic
representation:

(93) a.

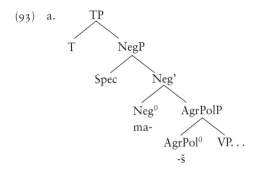

b.

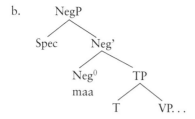

2.4.1 *Adverbs and subjects*

A crucial point for bipartite negation is that the enclitic -*š* is not dependent on the proclitic negative marker *ma-* in certain contexts. The preverbal marker is optional. In these very contexts, *ma-*, when used, must be adjacent to the verb.

(94) a. (ma)-basaamiḥ-k-iš   (JA)
          NEG-forgive.1SG.IPFV-you-NEG
          'I will not forgive you.'

      b. *ma b-yoom   basaamiḥ-k-iš   (JA)
          NEG in-day   forgive.1SG.IPFV-you-NEG
          'I will not forgive you in any day.' (Alqassas 2015: 114)

Since the preverbal marker is optional in these contexts, adjacency is not a requirement imposed by the enclitic. It is a syntactic requirement that follows from the bipartite markers (*ma* and enclitic -*š*) being below tense, adjacent to the verb or predicate. On the other hand, single negation (*maa* by itself) allows for syntactic constituents to intervene between negation and the verb. These constituents can be adverbs or subjects (cf. (1)b and (4) in section 2.1), or the verbal copula *kunt*, suggesting that *maa* is higher than the TP. In generative syntactic terms, bipartite negation is lower than TP, while single negation is higher than TP.

(95) a. maa (*Zeid) (*fiʕlan) bi-saafir
          NEG   (*Zeid) (*really) ASP-travel.3MSG.IPFV
          (Zeid) (fiʕlan) kul yoom   (JA)
          (Zeid) (really) every day
          'Zeid doesn't really travel every day.'

      b. maa ḥada   fiʕlan bi-saafir   kul yoom   (JA)
          NEG anyone really ASP-travel.3MSG.IPFV every day
          'No one really travels every day.'

Moreover, there are contexts where certain adverbs and definite subjects can intervene between *maa* and the verb such as *b-yoom*:

(96) wallah   maa   b-yoom   Zeid   bisaamħ-ak   (JA)
      by-God   NEG   in-day   Zeid   forgive.3MSG.IPFV-you
      'Zeid will not forgive you in any day.' = 'Zeid will never forgive you.'
      (adapted from Alqassas 2015: 114)

(97) a. kunt   miš   zaʕlaan   (JA)
          be.1SG.PFV   NEG   upset
          'I was not upset.'

      b. maa   kunt   zaʕlaan   (JA)
          NEG   be.1SG.PFV   upset
          'I was not upset.'

Thus, I claim negation can occupy a position below or above TP. This analysis will also be extended to complex tense constructions in Arabic.

(98) a. [$_{TP}$ [$_{NegP}$ [$_{AspP}$ [$_{VP}$ ···
      b. [$_{NegP}$ [$_{TP}$ [$_{AspP}$ [$_{VP}$ ···

So far we can find contrast between the higher and the lower negatives in JA because JA has both bipartite and single negation. Gulf Arabic (GA) displays the same contrasts regarding the ability of subjects and adverbs to intervene between the negative marker and the verb. However, GA does not have bipartite negation. Nonetheless we can see the contrasts between higher negation and lower negation by contrasting the behavior of the negative marker in unmarked and marked contexts. Recall that unmarked contexts arguably involve use of the negative marker that projects below TP in the canonical position. Therefore, we can predict that these contexts do not allow the subject to intervene between the negative marker and the verb. This prediction is born out:

(99) a. maa   xallaw   šay   maa   xað-uu   (Kuwaiti)
          NEG   leave.3MPL.PFV   thing NEG   take.3MPL.PFV-it
          'They didn't leave anything they didn't take.' (Brustad 2000: 285)

      b. ʔal-awlaad   maa   xallaw   šay   maa
          DEF-boys   NEG   leave.3MPL.PFV   thing NEG
          xað-uu   (QA)
          take.3MPL.PFV-it
          'The boys didn't leave anything they didn't take.'

      c. *maa   ʔal-awlaad   xallaw   šay   maa
          NEG   DEF-boys   leave.3MPL.PFV   thing NEG
          xað-uu   (QA)
          take.3MPL.PFV-it

In pragmatically marked sentences, the negative marker *maa* precedes the subject. Negation here presupposes that 'his mother and sister did not call.'

(100)   a.   leeš   maa   ʔumm-a   w   leeš maa   ʔuxt-a
             why   NEG   mother-his   and   why NEG   sister-his
             daggat-li   (Kuwaiti)
             call.3FSG.PFV-to.me
             'Why didn't his mother and why didn't his sister call me?'
             (Brustad 2000: 293)

        b.   leeš   maa   ʔumm-a   tasˤlat-li!   (QA)
             why   NEG   mother-his   call.3FSG.PFV-me
             'Why didn't his mother call me!'

        c.   leeš   maa   tasˤlat-li   ʔumm-a?   (QA)
             why   NEG   call.3FSG.PFV-me   mother-his
             'Why didn't his mother call me?'

(101)   a.   ʔintu   ma-antu   hali   (Kuwaiti)
             you.PL   NEG-you.PL   family.my
             'You are not my family.' (Brustad 2000: 297)

        b.   ma-anta   (b-)rifidʒ-i   min   alyoom   w-raayeh   (QA)
             NEG-you.SG   ASP-friend.my   from   today   and-going
             'You are not my friend from now on!' (expressing anger)

The negative marker *maa* can also precede the adverb *gad* 'never' in Qatari:

(102)   maa   gad   kallamt-a   (QA)
        NEG   ever   talk.1SG.PFV-him
        'I've never talked to him.'

Similarly, in pragmatically marked contexts the negative marker in QA and JA can precede the subject of the non-verbal predicate in verbless sentences:

(103)   a.   ma-ani   (b-)maakil   l-yoom   kaamil   (QA)
             NEG-I   ASP-having eaten   DEF-day   entire
             'I will not be eating the whole day!' (expressing anger)

        b.   ma-ani   maakil   tˤuul   l-yoom   (JA)
             NEG-I   having eaten   throughout   DEF-day
             'I will not be eating the whole day!' (expressing anger)

But the negative marker is adjacent to the non-verbal predicate in unmarked contexts:

(104) a. ʔana mub maakil   l-yoom kaamil   (QA)
           I   NEG having eaten DEF-day entire
           'I haven't eaten the whole day.'

       b. ani miš maakil   tˤuul   l-yoom   (JA)
           I   NEG having eaten throughout DEF-day
           'I will not be eating the whole day.'

The same contrasts can be found in QA and JA when comparing interrogative and rhetorical questions:

(105) a. ʔinta mub ʕaarif   al-dʒawaab?   (QA)
           you   NEG knowing   DEF-answer
           'You don't know the answer?'

       b. mub int ʕaarif   al-dʒawaab!   (QA)
           NEG you knowing   DEF-answer
           'Don't you know the answer!'
           (speaker presupposes that addressee knows the answer)

SA, on the other hand, resembles JA in that it has two different negative markers that are associated with the two different positions in the syntactic structure. The negative marker *maa* is adjacent to the verb while the negative marker *laa* is not, suggesting that *maa* is above TP while *laa* is below TP. The negative marker *maa* can precede subjects of verbless sentences, while *laa* cannot:

(106) a. maa Muħammad-un   kaatib-un   (SA)
           NEG Mohammad-NOM   writer-NOM
           'Mohammad is not a writer.' (Aoun et al. 2010: 116–17)

       b. *laa Muħammad-un   kaatib-un   (SA)
            NEG Mohammad-NOM   writer-NOM

The negative marker *maa* can also precede the subjects of verbal sentences, while *laa* cannot:

(107) a. maa ʔana qul-tu   haaða   (SA)
           NEG I   say.ISG.PFV   this
           'I did not say this.' (Fassi Fehri 1993: 165)

       b. maa/*laa ʔana ʔaquulu   haaða   (SA)
           NEG/*NEG I   say.ISG.IPFV this
           'I do not say this.'

The indefinite subject *ʔaḥad-un* can intervene between *maa* and the verb suggesting that this subject is in Spec-TP, while this is not possible with *laa*. The negative *laa* and *ʔaḥad* can form the lexical compound *laa-ʔaḥada* that can occur preverbally. Since *ʔaḥad* does not carry the nominative case, *laa-ʔaḥada* must be a lexical compound rather than the combination of a negative head *laa* and a subject pronoun subject *ʔaḥad*.

(108) a. maa   ʔaḥad-un   yašukku   fii   qawli-ka   (SA)
           NEG   one-NOM   doubt.3MSG.IPFV in   saying-you.ms
           'No one is questioning what you said.' (Fassi Fehri 1993: 165)
           [$_{NegP}$ maa [$_{TP}$ ʔaḥad-un [$_{VP}$ yašukku   fii   qawli-ka

       b. maa   yašukku   ʔaḥad-un fii   qawli-ka   (SA)
           NEG   doubt.3MSG.IPFV   one-NOM   in   saying-you.ms
           'No one is questioning what you said.'
           [$_{NegP}$ maa [$_{TP}$ [$_{VP}$ yašukku   ʔaḥad-un fii   qawli-ka

(109) a. laa-ʔaḥada yašukku   fii   qawli-ka   (SA)
           no one   doubt.3MSG.IPFV in   saying-you.ms
           'No one is questioning what you said.'
           [$_{TP}$ laa-ʔaḥada [$_{VP}$ yašukku   fii   qawli-ka

       b. laa   yašukku   ʔaḥad-un fii   qawli-ka   (SA)
           NEG   doubt.3MSG.IPFV   one-NOM in   saying-you.ms
           'No one is questioning what you said.'
           [$_{TP}$ [$_{NegP}$ laa [$_{VP}$ yašukku   ʔaḥad-un fii   qawli-ka

2.4.2 *Complementizer deletion*

In this section, I show that single negation can be used as a complementizer in contexts that require a complementizer, while bipartite negation cannot. I argue that bipartite negation is ungrammatical because it occupies a position lower than TP. I discuss these sentences where only single negation is allowed under the term 'negative complementizers' because the negative marker *maa* functions as a negative complementizer. While I do not suggest that the negative marker in these sentences is in a CP projection, sentences which allow complementizer deletion select the high NegP. This in turn explains the ungrammaticality of bipartite negation as a complementizer.

I assume Rizzi's hierarchical order for the different CP layers based on cross-linguistic evidence. The Fin IP is for complementizers like *for* and *to* that select nonfinite verbs. The focus and topic projections correspond to FocP and TopP respectively. The Force projection is for complementizers which indicate the illocutionary force of the clause, such as *whether* for interrogative clauses and *that* for indicative clauses.

(110)   Force ... (Topic) ... (Focus) ... Fin IP
        Rizzi (1997: 288)

Recall that preverbal definite NPs are topics in Spec-CP. Within the
context of this discussion, the position of the preverbal definite NP is
specifically Spec-TopP. In this section, I show that *maa* functions both
as a negative marker and a complementizer. In some cases, the negative
marker *maa* can optionally appear before the definite NP, i.e., the topic. I
take this as evidence for movement of the negative marker *maa* from the
head of high NegP to the head of ForceP.

In SA, *maa* functions either as a complementizer or as a negative
marker. Notice that *maa* and *baʕda* form one compound word, the
complementizer *baʕda-maa*. It corresponds to the English word 'after' in
terms of its function and there is no negative force for *maa*, unlike its use
as a marker of sentential negation.

(111)   a.   baʕda-maa   qadima   (SA)
             after-COMP   come.3MSG.PFV
             'After he came.'

        b.   maa   qadima   baʕdu   (SA)
             NEG   come.3MSG.PFV   yet
             'He hasn't come yet.'

In JA, *maa* functions either as a complementizer, a negative operator, or
both. Similar to SA, *maa* is used as part of the complementizer *baʕd*. In
the first example, as in SA, *maa* in JA is used when *baʕd* connects two
clauses. But in the second example where *baʕd* connects NPs, *maa* cannot
be used and only *baʕd* is used. In the last example, *maa* is used as a complementizer without being part of any other word. This complementizer
connects two clauses. The first clause is represented by one word *ʕadʒzaan*
'unable,' and the second clause is *yištari siyyara* 'buy a car.' This is possible because Arabic allows dropping the subject (Arabic is pro-drop) and
present tense copular sentences have a null copula.

(112)   a.   baʕd-maa   raaħ   (JA)
             after-COMP   go.3MSG.PFV
             'After he went.'

        b.   gaabalt   ʔaħmad   baʕd   ʕali   (JA)
             meet.1SG.PFV   Ahmad   after   Ali
             'I met Ahmad after Ali.'

        c.   ʕadʒzaan   maa   yištari   siyyara!   (JA)
             unable   COMP   buy.3MSG.IPFV   car
             'Is he unable to buy a car! = He is able to buy a car.'

In the example below, *maa* functions as a negative marker. However, it also functions as a complementizer connecting two clauses. The first clause has the adjective *maliiħ* 'it is good/fortunately' which is a predicate of a copular sentence. The subject of this sentence is silent since Arabic is pro-drop, and the copula is null because the present tense copula is usually covert.

(113) maliiħ maa rasabt-(*iš)   (JA)
       good NEG fail.2MSG.PFV-(*NEG)
       'It is good that you didn't fail.'

To test whether negation is part of the second clause, we can look at the affirmative counterpart of this sentence. If negation is part of the second clause, in the TP of the lower clause, and the structure has a null complementizer, we expect the affirmative counterpart to not need an overt complementizer. On the other hand, if the affirmative counterpart requires a complementizer, then it is reasonable to assume that the negative marker *maa* functions as a complementizer. The following example shows that a complementizer is required in the affirmative sentence:

(114) a. maliiħ *(inn-ak)   rasabt   (JA)
         good *(COMP-you) fail.2MSG.PFV
         'It is good that you failed.'

      b. maliiħ maa l-walad rasab-(*iš)   (JA)
         good NEG DEF-boy fail.3MSG.PFV-(*NEG)
         'It is good that the boy didn't fail.'

      c. maliiħ maa l-walad rasab-(*iš)   (JA)
         good NEG DEF-boy fail.3MSG.PFV-(*NEG)
         'It is good that the boy didn't fail.'

Further evidence that the negative marker is higher than TP comes from the fact that the subject intervenes between the negative marker and the verb. The following example gives evidence for the use of *laa* as a negative complementizer in JA:

(115) a. ʔilbas   dʒakeet laa yidʒmad-(*iš)   (JA)
         2.wear.IMP jacket NEG freeze.3MSG.SBJV-(*NEG)
         dʒism-ak
         body-your
         'Wear a jacket so that your body doesn't freeze.'

      b. ?? ʔilbas dʒakeet laa dʒism-ak yidʒmad-(*iš)   (JA)
         wear   jacket NEG body-your freeze.3MSG.SBJV-(*NEG)
         'Wear a jacket so that your body doesn't freeze.'

In the first example, as is clear from the English translation, *laa* functions as a complementizer to express purpose. The following example shows that *laa* can be replaced by the regular complementizer *mišan* 'so as to' and bipartite negation using *ma* and *-š*.

(116) ʔilbas   dʒakeet   <u>mišan</u>   ma-tidʒmad-iš   (JA)
       wear   jacket   COMP   NEG-freeze.2MSG.SBJV-NEG
       'Wear a jacket so as not to freeze.'

Notice also that the affirmative counterpart below requires the use of the complementizer *mišan* 'so as to.' This suggests that *laa* here functions as a negative marker and a complementizer at the same time.

(117) ʔilbas   dʒakeet   *mišan*   tidfa   (JA)
       wear   jacket   COMP   warm.2MSG.SBJV
       'Wear a jacket so as to get warm.'

Further evidence for the use of *maa* as a complementizer in JA comes from the interaction between the superlative adjective *ʔaħsan* and the negative marker *maa*. This adjective can be used along with *maa* to form a negative complementizer *ʔaħsan maa* which corresponds to the English 'so as not to.' Note that without the use of the negative word *maa*, *ʔaħsan* cannot be used alone as a complementizer to express the meaning of 'so as to.'

(118) ʔilbas   dʒakeet   ʔaħsan maa   tidʒmad   (JA)
       wear   jacket   COMP   NEG   freeze.2MSG.SBJV
       'Wear a jacket so as not to freeze.'

(119) *ʔilbas   dʒakeet   ʔaħsan   tidfa   (JA)
       wear   jacket   COMP   warm.2MSG.SBJV
       'Wear a jacket so as to get warm.'

Therefore, it is *maa* that makes the superlative adjective a complementizer. Consider the following contrasts showing that bipartite negation is ungrammatical with the negative complementizer *ʔaħsan maa* while it is grammatical with the affirmative complementizer *mišan*. This can be instantiated by adopting the proposal I argue for in this chapter. The use of bipartite negation is grammatical because bipartite negation is located below TP in a NegP projection which can select a functional projection (which I later call AgrPolP, a negative agreement projection) headed by the agreement clitic *-š*. We know that low negation is acceptable because the complementizer (*mišan*) functions as a connector and thus there is no need for the high NegP.

(120) *ʔilbas   dʒakeet   ʔaħsan maa   tidʒmad-iš   (JA)
      wear   jacket   COMP   NEG   freeze.2MSG.SBJV-NEG
      'Wear a jacket so as not to freeze.'

(121) ʔilbas   dʒakeet   mišan   ma-tidʒmad-iš   (JA)
      wear   jacket   COMP   NEG-freeze.2MSG.SBJV-NEG
      'Wear a jacket so as not to freeze.'

Accordingly, the absence of a complementizer like *mišan* in a sentence that requires one forces the negative marker to function as a complementizer. It could be that Force^0 has to be filled in these sentences, suggesting that the negative marker *maa* moves from Neg^0 to Force^0. But it could also be that Force^0 can be null only in sentences which have a high Neg^0. Example (122)b shows that an intervening subject between the negative marker and the verb is not acceptable. This suggests that the negative marker *maa* is not moving from Neg^0 to Force^0.

SA provides further evidence with respect to the two negatives *maa* and *laa*. Consider the following distributional contrasts with respect to negating nonfinite verbs (occurring after *ʔan*):

(122) a.   ʔuriid-u   ʔan   laa   tadxul-a   (SA)
           I-want-IND   that NEG   enter.2MSG-SBJV
           'I want you not to enter.' (Fassi Fehri 1993: 172)
      b. * ʔuriid-u   ʔan   maa   tadxul-a   (SA)
           want.1SG.IPFV.IND   that NEG   enter.2MSG.SBJV

Notice that the embedded verb *tadxul-a* cannot carry tense:

(123) a.   ʔaradt-u   ʔan   laa   tadxul-a   (SA)
           I-wanted-IND   that NEG   enter.2MSG.SBJV
           'I wanted you not to enter.'
      b. *ʔaradt-u   ʔan   laa   daxalta   (SA)
           want.1SG.IPFV.IND   that NEG   entered.2MSG

and its subject can be case marked by the matrix verb

(124) a.   ʔuriid-u   ʔan   yadxulu   (SA)
           I-want-IND   that enter.3MPL.SBJV
           'I want them to enter.'

      b.   ʔuriid-u-hum   ʔan   yadxulu   (SA)
           I-want-IND-them   that enter.3MPL.SBJV
           'I want them to enter.'

If the embedded verb does not have a TP (following Ouali and Fortin's (2007) proposal for *want* verbs in Moroccan Arabic), the contrasts in (90) follow from the fact that *maa* selects TP while *laa* does not (that is to say, *laa* does not dominate TP).

(125)   [TP [AspP [vP [VP WANT [AspP [vP [VP (Ouali and Fortin 2007: 182)

(126)   a.   [TP [AspP [vP [VP WANT [NegP laa [AspP [vP [VP
        b.   [TP [AspP [vP [VP WANT [*NegP maa [AspP [vP [VP

With evidence from SA negation, I argue that *maa* differs from *laa* and its variants (*lam, lan*) in its location in the clause structure. Specifically *lam* occupies the head position of a NegP below TP, while *maa* is the head of a NegP above TP. Negative *maa* also occupies a position in the CP layer in cases where it has a contrastive focus interpretation.

(127)

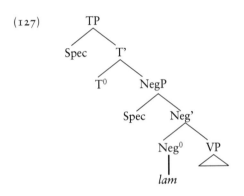

(128)

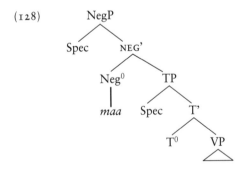

2.4.3 *Expectative modal* qad *and future modal* sawfa

Further evidence for the two negatives *maa* and *laa* can be found in differences in compatibility with the future modal *sawfa*. There are distributional contrasts in modality between *maa* on the one hand and *laa* and *lam* on the other hand. Consider the following contrasts with respect to the future modal *sawfa*:

(129) a. sawfa   laa   yaħsˤulu   haaða   (SA)
           FUT.   NEG   happen.3MSG.IPFV   this
           'This will not happen.' (Fassi Fehri 1993: 173)

       b.* sawfa   maa   yaħsˤulu   haaða   (SA)
           FUT.   NEG   happen.3MSG.IPFV   this (Fassi Fehri 1993: 173)

Consider also the following contrasts with respect to the expectative modal *qad*:

(130) a. qad   lam   yaʔti   (SA)
           may   NEG.past   come.3MSG.IPFV.JUSS
           'He may not have come.' (Fassi Fehri 1993: 172)

       b. qad   laa   yaʔti   (SA)
           may   NEG   come.3MSG.IPFV
           'He may not come.' (Fassi Fehri 1993: 172)

       c.* qad   maa   yaʔti   (SA)
           may   NEG.past   come.3MSG.IPFV (Fassi Fehri 1993: 172)

If Arabic modals are heads that project a Mod(al) projection that selects IP/TP (as in Fassi Fehri 1993: 159–60), these contrasts again follow from the fact that *maa* selects a TP while *laa* and its tensed variants do not. In other words *maa* is incompatible with modals because both compete to select TP, whereas *laa* and *lam* do not compete with Mod:

(131) [ModP [*NegP maa [TP [NegP laa [VP

The sentential negative marker *maa* is above TP (selects TP) and displays syntactic restrictions such as incompatibility with the modals *sawfa* and *qad* which compete with it to select TP. Being below TP (i.e., not selecting TP), the sentential negative marker *laa* and its variants do not display syntactic restrictions on co-occurring with the modals *sawfa* and *qad* since they do not compete with it in selecting TP.

The next chapter provides more evidence from semantics to show how the two types of NegP (the low NegP and the high NegP) create subtle semantic and pragmatic differences.

Notes

1. Some of the ideas in this chapter were presented at meetings of the Annual Symposium on Arabic Linguistics held in the University of Wisconsin-Milwakee in 2015 and Stony Brook-New York in 2016. I thank the audience for their helpful feedback and comments. I especially thank Youssef Haddad, Peter Hallman, Hamid Ouali, Usama Soltan, Mohammad Mohammad, among others. Needless to say, all errors are mine.
2. This is based on the Mirror Principle (Baker 1985), which holds that the order of affixes on the verb mirrors the order in which they are picked up by verb movement.
3. Cited in Benmamoun et al. (2013).
4. Zanuttini adopts Cinque's (1999) framework for analyzing adverbs and functional heads.
5. Note that this approach does not argue that all parameters can be reduced to semantic or pragmatic variability. However, it can be argued that this approach is preferred to the parametric one from a minimalist perspective. This is because under the parameter approach if an element in a certain language can have two (or more) different positions this translates as optionality, and optionality is not preferred (or even allowed) under the strong minimalist thesis. However, under the non-parametric approach, there is no optionality. The mere availability of the two positions in the same language is conditioned by some semantic or pragmatic factor like scope even though the two available positions can be interchangeable in some contexts.
6. Speas (1991) uses the order of the bound morphemes within the verbal complex to determine the position of NegP.
7. Another approach is to use the distribution of and interaction between tense and negation (Mitchell 2004). Using morphological data, Mitchell shows that in the Finno-Ugric family, NegP is generated below TP in some of the languages, and above TP in others. She argues that this cross-linguistic variation is due to language-specific feature specifications of Neg^0 within the lexicon. She specifically argues that in this family, languages in which tense is expressed by the negative marker (Mordva, Mari, Komi, Udmurt, and Livonian) have NegP on top of vP, while NegP is on top of TP in languages in which the main verb expresses tense in both positive and negative sentences (Finnish, Karelian, Ingrian, Veps, Votian, Estonian, and Saami).
8. Imperfective verb forms have both prefixes and suffixes in certain cases such as third person masculine and feminine plurals.
9. This analysis is an alternative to the analysis that relies on categorical features to distinguish the present tense from the past tense (Benmamoun 2000). Under Benmamoun's analysis, the T head of the present tense is not specified for a [+V] feature that requires the lexical verb or auxiliary to move to T; while the T head of the past tense is.

10. The details of the derivation for these complex tenses are developed in the next subsection.

11. Details of these complex tense constructions are laid out in the next section.

12. Ritter and Wiltschko (2004, 2005) show that it is possible to have a future interpretation without having the syntactic category tense.

13. GA is similar to JA, but without the use of *b-*.

14. I say 'usually' because *miš* can express metalinguistic negation where it appears preverbally, although it can be construed as a predicate or a postverbal constituent (cf. Alqassas 2012 for details).

15. Note that this element makes sentential negation emphatic, which is why 'NOT' is capitalized in the translation.

16. The underlying assumption here is that the past tense verb moves to NegP and incorporates with *ma* (i.e., this is a head-to-head movement) on its way up to the TP head (cf. Aoun et al. 2010 for this analysis). In this book, I show that this is plausible when analyzing bipartite negation, but I depart from this analysis by arguing that the negative marker *maa*, when used by itself (i.e., single negation), occupies the head position of a negative projection above the TP. Thus negation does not intercept the past tense verb movement from V-to-T.

17. It should be pointed out that the negative adverb which can pass the *why not* test is *laʔ(a)* rather than *la*. While *laa* and *laʔ(a)* are related historically, it is still reasonable to argue that they now have different statuses syntactically: a head and an adverb respectively. This adverb is only used as a negative interjection when answering a yes/no question, as in (i) below:

    (i) badd-ak   tsaafir ?   laʔ(a),   ma-badd-iš   (JA)
         want-you   travel.2MSG.IPFV   no,   NEG-want.1SG.IPFV-NEG
         'Do you want to travel?'   'No, I don't want to.'

18. For rules of stress in JA, see de Jong and Zawaydeh (1999).

3

Semantic and pragmatic effects of negative markers

The previous chapter argued for a multi-locus analysis for negation in Arabic. The primary focus in that chapter was to display the key distributional contracts between the NegP projection below TP and the one above TP in relation to the position of adverbs and subjects in the syntactic structure, the availability of complementizer deletion, and the availabity of certain negative markers in the context of modals. This chapter focuses on the semantic and pragmatic effects associated with the various positions of negation. Particularly, presuppositional readings for negative statements can arguably be explained by a difference in the position of negation (higher in the TP) as opposed to the non-presuppositional interpretations associated with the lower NegP below TP. Some of the JA data and analysis in this chapter are taken in part from my 2012 Ph.D. dissertation. Extra data from JA and analogous data from GA (Qatari in particular) is included in this chapter.[1] The examples in (1)a–c show pragmatic contexts in which only higher negation (*maa* by itself) is grammatical (Alqassas 2012: §4 126–46):

(1)　a.　maliiħ　maa　rasabt-(*iš)　　　　　　　　　　　(JA)
　　　　　good　NEG　fail.2MSG.PFV-(*NEG)
　　　　　'It is good that you didn't fail.' (presupposition)

　　　b.　ʔilbas　　dʒakeet　laa　yidʒmad-(*iš)
　　　　　wear.imp　jacket　NEG　freeze.3MSG.IPFV-(*NEG)　　(JA)
　　　　　dʒism-ak
　　　　　body-your
　　　　　'Wear a jacket so that your body doesn't freeze.' (imperative mood: cautioning)

　　　c.　laa　t-igaʕ-(*iš)　　　　　　　　　　　　　　(JA)
　　　　　NEG　2-fall.imp-(*NEG)
　　　　　'Don't fall/Be careful not to fall.' (imperative mood: cautioning)

This chapter also analyzes contrasts between SA *maa* on the one hand and *laa* and its variants on the other hand. These contrasts are related to scope readings, presupposition, mood and speech acts.

I argue that presuppositional negation is a product of the interplay between syntax and pragmatics. Specifically, I propose that presuppositional negative markers are higher in the syntactic structure. They occupy a position above the tense phrase in the clausal structure, namely NegP above TP.

This proposal bears on the cross-linguistic debate over whether the locus of negation is parametric (either above TP or below TP in a given language, as in Ouhalla 1993) or non-parametric (a particular language may opt for any position of negation for syntactic and pragmatic reasons, as in Zanuttini 1997a, 1997b; Ramchand 2001, 2002; Zeijlstra 2004; Alqassas 2012, 2015). This book advocates the second view. However, research on negation in Arabic has largely followed the parametric view with some proposals placing NegP below TP (e.g., Benmamoun 1992, 1997, 2000; Ouhalla 1990, 1991) and others placing it above TP (Fassi Fehri 1993; Mohammad 2000; Hoyt 2007; Soltan 2007). This book advocates the view that a particular language may opt for any position of negation for syntactic and pragmatic reasons, building on proposals in Alqassas (2012, 2015) for JA, Zanuttini (1997a, 1997b) for Romance languages, and Ramchand (2001, 2002) for Bengali.

This chapter shows that in Arabic the pragmatically marked negation is above TP while pragmatically neutral negation is below TP. Zanuttini (1997a, 1997b) shows the same effects in various Romance languages and dialects.

In this chapter, pragmatically marked negation includes presuppositional negation, categorical negation, and what I will refer to here as cleft negation. The former two are in a NegP above TP, while the latter is in CP.

3.1 Scope of negation and the locus of negative markers

This section shows the semantic contrasts exhibited by single negation on the one hand and bipartite negation along with *laa* and its variants on the other hand. I argue that these contrasts follow from the different positions negation has as well as their mapping from syntax to semantics.

3.1.1 *Wide and narrow scope*

In the previous chapter, I argued that bipartite negation is lower than TP while single negation is higher than TP in JA. I also argued that in SA *laa* and its variants (*lam* and *lan*) are lower than TP while *maa* is higher. Furthermore, the negative marker *maa* in QA can occupy a position

higher than TP or lower than TP. In this section, I argue that lower negation (NegP below TP) binds the event variable of the verb while higher
negation (NegP above TP) binds the time variable of tense. This proposal
is argued for in Alqassas (2015) using JA data. This section extends the
analysis to QA and SA. The contrasts between lower and higher negation yield different scope readings (narrow and wide) for negation in the
context of time adverbials. With higher negation (*maa* by itself), only a
wide scope reading is possible, while both a narrow and a wide scope
reading is possible with lower negation (bipartite negation) (cf. (2)a, b
from Alqassas (2015: 116–17).

(2) a. maa štayalt   la-muddit ʔusbuuʕ (# bas štayalt   (JA)
         NEG work.1SG.PFV   for-period week   (# but work.1SG.PFV
         θalaθt-iyyam)
         three days)
         'I did not work for a week.'
         i.   'I did not work at any point during the week.'
         ii. #'I did not work for seven days, but I worked for three days.'

     b. ma-štayalt-iš   la-muddit ʔusbuuʕ   (JA)
         NEG-work.1SG.PFV-NEG for-period week
         (bas štayalt   θalaθt-iyyam)
         (but work.1SG.PFV   three days)
         'I did not work for a week.' (but I worked for three days)
         i.   'I did not work at any point during the week.'
         ii. 'I did not work for seven days, but I worked for three days.'

What, then, makes negation above TP a pragmatically marked option?
First, the locus of an element in the syntactic structure affects its scope.
Consider the following examples on the scope of the adverb *frequently* in
English (Engels 2012):

(3) John could frequently lift 200 pounds.
     i.   'John was frequently able to lift 200 pounds.'
     ii. 'John was able to lift 200 pounds several times (in a row).'

(4) John frequently could lift 200 pounds.
     i.   'John was frequently able to lift 200 pounds.'
     ii. #'John was able to lift 200 pounds several times (in a row).'

The position of the adverb lower than the copula yields an ambiguous
reading with the adverb 'frequently' having wide scope reading, i.e.,
scoping over the modal verb 'could,' or having narrow scope reading, i.e.,
scopeing over the verb 'lift.' By contrast, the position of the adverb higher
than the modal verb 'could' only allows for a wide scope reading.

The different scope readings are the result of the two different positions of the adverb in relation to tense. In this chapter, I put forward an analysis for Arabic negation in which I capitalize on similar scope effects that the different positions of negation display.

Building on proposals in Ramchand (2001, 2002) and Alqassas (2015), I propose that negation introduces an existential quantifier that binds the variables introduced by the predicate and its arguments. The following is a simple illustration:

(5) $[Op\neg \exists e, x [\ldots(e)\ldots(x)\ldots]]$

When negation is below TP, this quantifier binds the event variable of the predicate. Assuming a neo-Davidsonian framework of semantic representation (Davidson 1967; Parsons 1990), we get the following formal illustration:

(6) $\exists t:[t< t^*] No\ e:[t_f \in _T (e) = t]\ [(e)\ \&\ \Theta_1 (e)\ \&\ \Theta_2 (e)]$

Negation specifies that the event did not happen at a specific moment in the past, but does not rule out the possibility that the event took place at some other time in the past. In other words, there is a time during which the event did not take place. Note: here the time variable is linked to the event via context and not grammar.

When negation is above TP, this quantifier binds both the time variable of tense and the event variable of the predicate.[2]

(7) $No\ t:[t< t^*] \exists e:[t_f \in _T (e) = t]\ [(e)\ \&\ \Theta_1 (e)\ \&\ \Theta_2 (e)]$

Negation specifies the entire time period of the past as the interval during which the event did not take place. In other words, there is no time during which the event took place.

Formally, this means:

maa $\Rightarrow$ *ma-*. . . *š*; but *ma-*. . . *š* $\nRightarrow$ *maa* (*maa* implies *ma-*. . . *š*; but *ma-*. . . *š* does not imply *maa*).

And in SA the implication is as follows:

maa $\Rightarrow$ *lam*; but *lam* $\nRightarrow$ *maa* (*maa* implies *lam*; but *lam* does not imply *maa*)

It is worth pointing out that the wide scope effect attributed to *maa* under the multi-locus analysis finds support from the fact that *maa* can combine with question words to form the following compounds where the question word has a wide scope interpretation equivalent to the function of *ever* in compounds like 'whatever, whenever, whoever . . . etc' in both colloquial and standard Arabic:

(8) a. miin maa,   ween maa,   mata maa, ma-h-maa,   (JA)
         who ever,   where ever,   when ever, what-epenthetic-ever,
         šuu   maa
         what ever

     b. ʔayna-maa,   ma-h-maa,   kayfa-maa,   mata-maa   (SA)
         where-ever,   what-epenthetic-ever   how-ever,   when-ever

Negation above TP thus scopes over the whole proposition (including the time variable of tense). This gives rise to the perceived sense of a stronger negation, hence the suitability of higher negation for denying a presupposition and for expressing emphatic negation.

Assuming a neo-Davidsonian framework of semantic representation (Davidson 1967; Parsons 1990), we get (9)a, b (representations for (2)a, b, respectively). In (a) there is no time during which the event happened. In (b) the structure specifies that there is a time during which the event took place, but it leaves open the possibility that the event could have taken place during some other time, hence the possibility of either a wide or a narrow scope reading.

(9) a. maa štaɣalt   la-muddit ʔusbuuʕ   (JA)
         NEG work.1SG.PFV for-period   week
         (# bas štaɣalt   θalaθt-iyyam)
         (# but work.1SG.PFV three days)
         'I did not work for a week.'
         iii. 'I did not work at any point during the week.'
         iv. #'I did not work for seven days, but I worked for three days.'
         No t:[t< t* and t *in* I] $\exists$e:[$t_f \in {}_T(e) = t$] [working(e) & Θ_1 (e, 'I') & 'for a week'(I)]

     b. ma-štaɣalt-iš   la-muddit ʔusbuuʕ   (JA)
         NEG-work.1SG.PFV-NEG for-period   week
         (bas štaɣalt   θalaθt-iyyam)
         (but work.1SG.PFV three days)
         'I did not work for a week.' (but I worked for three days)
         iii. 'I did not work at any point during the week.'
         iv. 'I did not work for seven days, but I worked for three days.'
         $\exists$t:[t< t* and t *in* I]No e:[$t_f \in {}_T(e) = t$] [working(e) & Θ_1 (e, 'I') & 'for a week'(I)]

Semantic notions and pragmatic notions are included here in the same chapter because they are related to each other. The semantic notions are specifically related to the operator-variable binding relationship between negation on the one hand and tense and the verb/event on the other hand. Pragmatics comes into play when we consider notions such as presupposition and rhetorical questions. These semantic and pragmatic concepts are related in that the negative markers that have a wider semantic scope are the ones that are also pragmatically marked. Interpretation of these markers thus involves a presupposition or a rhetorical interpretation. I argue that pragmatically marked negation is above TP while pragmatically neutral negation is below TP. Pragmatically marked negation includes presuppositional negation and categorical negation in a NegP above TP, as well as cleft negation in CP.

Typological studies of negation in colloquial Arabic (Harrell 1962; Cowell 1964; Johnstone 1967; Woidich 1968; Holes 1990; Brustad 2000, among others) have identified various negation strategies in the dialects, including verbal negation, predicate negation, and categorical negation (Brustad 2000). These studies also report a presuppositional function of these negation strategies. The categorical negation is an emphatic negation that is expressed with a negative marker that I analyze above TP in this chapter. Consider the following examples where the negative marker *maa* expresses categorical negation. There is evidence that *maa* here is higher than tense. The negative marker precedes the subject in both the Kuwaiti and Qatari examples:

(10) a. ʔintu   ma-antu   hali   (Kuwaiti)
          you-PL NEG-YOU.PL   family.my
          'You are not my family.' (Brustad 2000: 297)

      b. ma-anta   (b-)rifiʤ-i   min   alyoom   w-raayeh   (QA)
          NEG-you.SG   ASP-friend.my from   today   and-going
          'You are not my friend from now on!' (expressing anger)

Another context where *maa* expresses categorical negation is in the context of the Negative Sensitive Item (NSI) *qad* 'never.' The negative marker *maa* can also precede the negative sensitive item *gad* 'never' in Qatari:

(11) maa   gad   kallamt-a   (QA)
      NEG   ever   talk.1SG.PFV-him
      'I've never talked to him.'

Another form of categorical negation reported in Brustad (2000) is the use of the negative marker *wala* in Kuwaiti, which is also used in QA and JA:

(12) a. wala   ʕumr-i   tħatšet   (Kuwaiti)
          NEG   life-my   talk.1SG.PFV
          'Never did I say a word.' (Brustad 2000: 309)

      b. wala   ʕumr-i   kallamt-a   (QA)
          NEG   life-my   talk.1SG.PFV-him
          'I've never talked to him.'

      c. wala   ʕumr-i   zurt-o   (JA)
          NEG   life-my   visit.1SG.PFV-him
          'I've never visited him.'

Following the analysis of negation presented in the previous chapter, unmarked negation projects a NegP below TP such that the preverbal subject cannot intervene between the negative marker and the verb. The fact that the preverbal subject precedes negation in unmarked contexts in GA is to be expected if negation is below TP and the preverbal subject is above TP. Consider the following examples:

(13) a. maa   xallaw   šay   maa   xað-uu   (Kuwaiti)
          NEG   leave.3MPL.PFV thing NEG   take.3MPL.PFV-it
          'They didn't leave anything they didn't take.' (Brustad 2000: 285)

      b. ʔal-awlaad   maa   xallaw   šay   (QA)
          DEF-boys   NEG   leave.3MPL.PFV thing
          maa   xað-uu
          NEG   take.3MPL.PFV-it
          'The boys didn't leave anything they didn't take.'

      c. *maa   ʔal-awlaad   xallaw   šay   (QA)
          NEG   DEF-boys   leave.3MPL.PFV thing
          maa   xað-uu
          NEG   take.3MPL.PFV-it

(14)

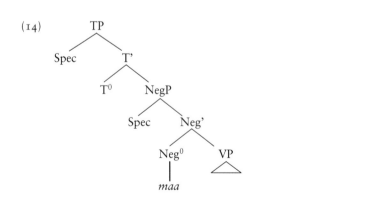

The negative marker can precede the subject pronoun of verbless sentences in marked contexts when negation expresses a strong denial (categorical negation). In contrast, the unmarked counterpart of these instances of negation cannot precede the subject. The unmarked negative marker in verbless sentences, *mu* in Kuwaiti Arabic and *mub* in QA, must follow the subject pronoun.

(15) a. ʔinta   mub   rifidʒ-i   (QA)
          you.SG   NEG   friend.my
          'You are not my friend.'

      b. ma-anta   (b-)rifidʒ-i   (min alyom   w-raayeh)   (QA)
          NEG-you.psg   ASP-friend.my   (from today   and-going)
          'You are not my friend from now on!'

(16) a. ʔana   mub   maakil   l-yoom   kaamil   (QA)
          I   NEG   having eaten   DEF-day   entire
          'I haven't eaten the whole day.'

      b. ʔana   mu   maakil   šay   tˤuul   iðˤ-ðˤuhr   (Kuwaiti)
          I   NEG   having eaten thing   throughout   DEF-afternoon
          'I hadn't eaten anything all afternoon.' (Brustad 2000: 301)

      c. ma-ani   (b-)maakil   l-yoom   kaamil   (QA)
          NEG-I   having eaten   DEF-day   entire
          'I will not be eating the whole day!' (expressing anger)

With adverbs that express categorical negation such as *gad* 'never,' we also find that the adverb intervenes between the negative marker and the verb.

(17) a. maa   gad   fi-sˤsˤˤaf   kallamt-a   (QA)
          NEG   ever   in class   talk.1SG.PFV-him
          'I've never talked to him in class.'

      b. *maa   fi-sˤsˤˤaf   kallamt-a   (QA)
          NEG   in class   talk.1SG.PFV-him

      c. mub   fi-sˤsˤˤaf   kallamt-a   (QA)
          NEG   in class   talk.1SG.PFV-him
          'I did not talk to him in class.'

Similarly, in cases of categorical negation in Kuwaiti (Brustad 2000: 309), an element, namely the negative polarity adverb *ʔumr-i* 'my life,' can intervene between the negative marker and the verb. This is consistent with the view that negation is above the tense phrase.

(18)   wala   ʕumr-i   tħatšet   (Kuwaiti)
       NEG   life-my   talk.1SG.PFV
       'Never did I say a word.' (Brustad 2000: 309)

SA displays the same semantic effect with respect to negation. The negative markers associated with a marked interpretation are higher in the syntactic structure (above TP), whereas those that are not marked are lower (below TP). I give semantic evidence for the different positions of these negatives below. The negative marker *maa* in (19)a, as opposed to *lam* in (19)b, has a special pragmatic effect in SA. In the Quranic verse in (19), the use of *maa* denies the truth value of a presupposed proposition that God has taken a son (al-Zamakhshari 1859). The negative marker *lam* denies a proposition that is not presupposed, and the sentence is simply informative and does not negate any presupposition (al-Zamakhshari 1859).

I propose that this special pragmatic effect results from having the negative marker *maa* above TP. This marker can then bind the time variable of tense (and the event variable of the verb) resulting in the semantic interpretation of absolute/emphatic negation, as in (20)a. On the other hand, the negative marker *lam* is below TP and binds the event variable of the verb but not the tense variable, as in (20)b.

(19) a.   maa   ʔittaxaða   Allaahu   min   waladin   (SA)
            NEG   take.3MSG.PFV   Allaahu   any   child
            'Allah has not taken any son.' (al-Mu'minun, ch. 23: verse 91)

      b.   wa   lam   yattaxið-ø   waladan   (SA)
           and   NEG.past   take.3MSG.IPFV.-JUSS   child
           'And who did not take a son.' (al-Furqan, ch. 25: verse 2)

(20) a.   No t:[t< t* and t *in* Allah] $\exists$e:[$t_f \in {}_T(e) = t$] [taking(e) & Θ_1(e, 'Allah')]
           [$_{NegP}$ maa [$_{TP}$ [$_{vP}$ ʔittaxa . . .

      b. $\exists$t:[t< t* and t *in* Allah]No e:[$t_f \in {}_T(e) = t$] [taking(e) & Θ_1(e, 'Allah')]
           [$_{TP}$ [$_{NegP}$ lam   [$_{vP}$ yattaxið . . .

Other cases of absolute/emphatic negation can be found where *maa* negates the imperfect in examples like (21). Such examples are very frequent in SA. These cases involve a presupposed proposition with *maa* used to convey an emphatic negation.

(21)   yuxaadiʕ-uuna   Allaaha   wa-allaðiina   (SA)
       deceive.3MPL.IPFV   Allah   and-those
       ʔaamanuu   wa-maa
       believe.3MPL.PFV   and-NEG

yaxdaʕ-uuna   ʔilla   ʔanfusahum   wa-maa   yašʕur-uun
deceive.3MPL.IPFV   except   themselves   and-neg   feel.3MSPL.IPFV
'They [think to] deceive Allah and those who believe, but they deceive not except themselves and perceive [it] not.' (al-Baqarah, ch. 1: verse 9)

(22) [$_{NegP}$ *maa* [$_{TP}$ [$_{vP}$ *yaxdaʕ-uuna   ʔilla   ʔanfusahum*
No t:[t< t* and t *in* They] ∃e:[t$_f$ ∈ $_T$(e) = t] [deceiving(e) & Θ$_1$ (e, 'They') & Θ$_2$ (e, 'Themselves')]

Placing *maa* in a position scoping over tense and the verb may explain the emotional load it has.

(23) a. lam   ya-ktub   (SA)
          NEG.past   3MSG-write.IPFV
          'He did not write.'
          [$_{TP}$ [$_{NegP}$ lam   [$_{vP}$ ya-ktub
          ∃t:[t< t* and t *in* He]No e:[t$_f$ ∈ $_T$(e) = t] [writing(e) & Θ$_1$ (e, 'He')]

      b. maa   kataba   (SA)
          NEG   write.3MSG.PFV
          'He has NOT written.' 'Emphatic negation'
          [$_{NegP}$ *maa* [$_{TP}$ [$_{vP}$ *kataba*
          No t:[t< t* and t *in* He] ∃e:[t$_f$ ∈ $_T$(e) = t] [writing(e) & Θ$_1$ (e, 'He')]

Furthermore, another interesting aspect of *maa* is that it tends to negate events related to the present (Wehr 1953 in Van Mol 2003: 259–260; Kouloughli 1988). These previous authors explain that negating with *lam* yields a simple past, while negating with *maa* yields a present perfect. Notice that in these examples negation denies a presupposition using *maa*. The pragmatic difference between *maa* and *lam* thus cannot be reduced to contrastive focus. Reporting on Wehr (1953), van Mol (2003: 260–263) explains that the use of *maa* is associated with 'subjective' and 'heavily emotional' content. The negative marker *maa* here is used for denying a proposition and showing emotional tension (emphasis). This can explain the sharp contrast in the distribution of *maa* in classical Arabic compared to modern SA. Consider the following results on the distribution of these negative marker in SA. The data is extracted from the Quran and MARC-2000 corpus by Mark Van Mol at KU-Leuven.[3]

The negative marker *maa* occurs only 6.6 percent of the time in the Modern Standard Arabic corpus (LBA corpus, which is Literary Fiction from Lebanon), while *maa* occurs 23.40 percent of the time in the classical Arabic corpus (Quranic corpus). Given that modern literary Arabic is restricted to the academic domain which tends to be objective and is

Table 3.1 Distribution of *maa* in classical and modern corpus

Particles	LBA Fiction		Quran	
maa	132	6.60%	732	23.40%
lam	509	25.60%	346	11%
Total NEG words	1986		3125	
Total corpus words	86032		85933	

less likely to reflect the emotional state of the writer, we expect *maa* to be limited in its use compared to its use in classical Arabic. The drop in using *maa* in the modern corpus is correlated with the higher use of *lam* in the modern corpus. The particle *lam* is used 25.60 percent of the time in the modern LBA Fiction corpus compared to only 11 percent in the Quranic corpus.

I argue that *maa* and *lam* in SA differ from each other in their location in the clause structure. Specifically, *lam* occupies the head position of a NegP below TP, while *maa* is the head of a NegP above TP. Negative *maa* also occupies a position in the CP layer in cases where it has a contrastive focus interpretation.

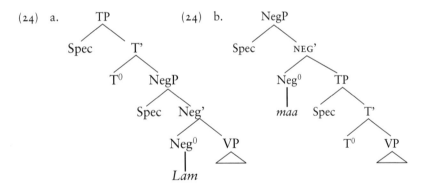

Improbable conditional sentences provide interesting contrasts where *lam* occurs in the protasis, whereas *maa* in the apodosis.

(25) law lam   tadrus,   la-maa   nadʒaħat
      If   NEG.past study.3FSG.IPFV   PAR-NEG   succeed.3FSG.PFV
      'Had she not studied, she would not have succeeded.'

lam specifies that the event did not take place in the hypothetical scenario, while *maa* specifies that there is no time during which the event could have taken place.

Under this analysis, semantic contrasts follow from *lam* scoping over the event, yielding the reading 'there is a time during which the event did not take place,' while *maa* scopes over tense and thus yields the wide scope interpretation 'there is no time during which the event took place.' It is reasonable to assume that the wide scope interpretation also gives rise to the 'present perfect' aspectual interpretation.

Moreover, since negation above TP scopes over the whole proposition (including the time variable of tense) use of *maa* gives rise to the perceived sense of a stronger negation, making it suitable for denying a presupposition. The negative markers *laa*, *lam*, and *lan* are heads of a NegP below TP. They only bind the event variable yielding neutral (pragmatically unmarked) negation.

3.1.2 *Cleft negation*

Another type of negation that displays a pragmatically marked interpretation is cleft negation, for example 'Isn't it the case that . . .':

(26) a. ʔinta mub ʕaarif   al-dʒawaab?   (QA)
         you   NEG knowing   DEF-answer
         'You don't know the answer?'

     b. mub int ʕaarif   al-dʒawaab!   (QA)
        NEG you knowing   DEF-answer
        'Don't you know the answer!'/'Isn't it the case that you know the answer!'
        (speaker presupposes that addressee knows the answer)

There is evidence that *mub* here is above TP but not in a NegP projection. This negative marker cannot license NPIs as seen in the following example:

(27) a. ʔinta mub ʕaarif   ʔayya   ħal   (QA)
         you   NEG knowing   NPI-any   solution
         'You don't not know any solution.'

     b. *mub int ʕarif   ʔayya   ħal!   (QA)
        NEG   you knowing   NPI.any   solution

     c. mub int mub ʕaarif   al-dʒawaab!   (QA)
        NEG you NEG knowing   DEF-answer
        'Isn't it the case that you don't know the answer!'
        (speaker presupposes that addressee doesn't know the answer)

Assuming that NPIs are syntactically licensed by a negative marker that scopes over them (Benmamoun 1997; Alqassas 2015), and given that *mub* fails to license the NPI *ʔayya*, it follows that *mub* is not a form of sentential negation where the negative marker scopes over the whole sentence or proposition. This is consistent with the analysis that *mub* is not in a NegP projection co-commanding the NPI (cf. Chapter 4 for details on NPI licensing).

Where, then, is it located in the syntactic structure? Presumably, it is buried in the CP domain (in a Focus projection) where it does not c-command the NPI. The negative marker here forms a constituent with the pronoun *inta* (constituent negation).

(28)   *[CP mub inta C [TP T [AP ʕarif   ʔayya   ħal

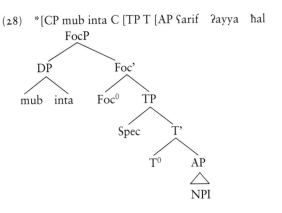

Notably, this chapter provides a unified analysis for the presuppositional negatives which in previous analyses have been classified under different negation strategies. These presuppositional negatives can all be classified as pragmatically marked negation. This includes presuppositional negation, categorical negation, and cleft negation. The former two are in a NegP above TP, while the latter is in CP.

(29)   [CP CLEFT NEGATION [NegP PRESUPPOSITIONAL & CATEGORICAL NEGATION [TP [NegP NEUTRAL NEGATION [VP/AP. . .

3.1.3 *Contrastive focus* maa

Contrastive focus *maa* is a form of meta-linguistic negation in which *maa* is in a Focus projection FocP at the left periphery in a layered CP. Previous analyses place *laa* and its variants (*lam, lan, laysa*) as the head of a NegP below TP, and *maa* as the spell-out of a negative feature in the CP (FocusP) (Ouhalla 1993; also adopted in Aoun et al. 2010).

Consistent with the parametric view on the locus of negation, Ouhalla (1993) maintains that NegP in SA is below TP, but that *maa* is not in that NegP projection. Instead, *maa* is the spell-out of the functional category

NegP. It is merely the spell out of a negative feature [+neg] under the functional category FP (Focus projection).

There are a number of challenges to Ouhalla's analysis. First, *maa* does not have a contrastive focus reading in the examples below. Notice that negation, in these examples, denies a presupposition using *maa*. Thus the pragmatic difference between *maa* and *lam* cannot be reduced to contrastive focus. Recall that the use of *maa* here is associated with 'subjective' and 'heavily emotional' content:

(30) a. lam   ya-ktub   (SA)
          NEG.past   3msg-write.IPFV
          'He did not write.'

      b. maa   kataba   (SA)
          NEG   write.3MSG.PFV
          'He has NOT written.' (emphatic negation)

Crucially, however, no contrastive focus is associated with *maa* here.

Second, Focus itself is a poorly understood phenomenon. Focus can be expressed using tonic accent, using a morpheme like *bi-*, *li*, or by preposing to the left periphery.

A third challenge is that Focus/topic cannot intervene between *maa* and the verb (cf. contrast below). If *maa* is in C, adverbs should be able to intervene between *maa* and the verb. However this is not borne out:

(31) maa   y-uḥibbu   Zaydun   al-qira'ata   (SA)
      NEG   like.3MSG.IPFV   Zaydun   DEF-reading-ACC
      'Zayd does not like reading.' (Ouhalla 1993: 276)

(32) a. maa   qaabaltu   ʔaḥad-an   (SA)
          NEG   meet.3MSG.PFV   one-ACC
          'I have not met anyone.'

      b. maa   l-baariḥata   qaabaltu   Zaydan   (SA)
          NEG   DEF-yesterday   meet.1SG.PFV   Zayd
          'I did not meet Zayd yesterday.'

      c. *maa   l-baariḥata   qaabaltu   ʔaḥadan   (SA)
          NEG   DEF-yesterday   meet.1SG.PFV   one-ACC

Fourth, placing *maa* as the head of a Focus projection in examples where it scopes over the whole proposition as well as where it scopes over a postposed constituent cannot account for the different scope each example has. Capitalization is applied to focused elements.

(33) a. maa ?allafat   Zaynabu   RIWAAYAT-AN   (SA)
          NEG write.3FSG.PFV   Zaynab   novel-ACC
          (bal qasiidat-an)
          (but poem-ACC)
          'It is not a novel that Zaynab has written (but a poem).'
          (Ouhalla 1993: 287)

      b. maa ?allafat   Zaynabu   riwaayat-an   (SA)
          NEG write.3FSG.PFV   Zaynab   novel-ACC
          'Zaynab did NOT write a novel.'

When it does not have a contrastive focus interpretation, I treat *maa* as a
sentential negative marker that can license NPIs. When it has a contrastive focus interpretation, however, *maa* cannot license NPIs and is thus
referred to separately as contrastive focus *maa*. Similar contrasts are in
Moutaouakil (1991: 274–275):

(34) a. maa   qaabaltu   ?ahad-an   (SA)
          NEG   meet.1SG.PFV   one-ACC
          'I have not met anyone.'

      b. *maa l-baarihata   qaabaltu   ?ahadan   (SA)
          NEG   DEF-yesterday   meet.1SG.PFV   one-ACC
          bal   al-yawma
          but   DEF-today

      c. *maa qaabaltu   ?ahadan   l-baarihata   (SA)
          NEG   meet.1SG.PFV   one-ACC   DEF-yesterday
          bal   al-yawma
          but   DEF-today

Moreover, a clitic left dislocated NP cannot follow sentential negation *maa*.
The following examples include an NPI to ensure that negation is sentential:

(35) a. maa   qaabala   ?ahad-un   Zaydan   (SA)
          NEG   meet.3MSG.PFV one-NOM   Zayd-ACC
          'No one has met Zayd.'
          [NegP *maa* [TP [vP qaabala ?ah ad-un Zaydan

      b. *maa Zayd-un   qaabala-hu   ?ahad-un   (SA)
          NEG   Zayd-NOM   meet.3MSG.PFV-him   one-NOM

This ungrammaticality is expected if *maa* is the head of a NegP on top
of TP. The clitic left dislocated NP *Zaydan* cannot occupy a position
between NegP and TP, hence it cannot intervene between *maa* and the
verb. However, if *maa* is in the CP layer, there is nothing to prevent

Zaydan from intervening between *maa* and the verb. Indeed, a clitic left dislocated NP can precede and follow contrastive focus *maa*. Consider the following examples from SA (Moutaouakil 1991: 276–277):

(36) a. al-kitaab-u   maa   allaftu-hu   (SA)
          DEF-book-NOM   NEG   write.1SG.PFV-it
          bal   sˤaħħahtu-hu
          but   correct.1SG.PFV-it
          'I haven't written this book; I have only corrected it.'
          [_FP al-kitaab-u [_FocusP maa [_VP allaftu-hu   bal   sˤaħħahtu-hu

     b. maa   al-kitaab-u   allaftu-hu   (SA)
          NEG   DEF-book-NOM   write.1SG.PFV-it
          bal   sˤaħħahtu-hu
          but   correct.1SG.PFV-it
          'I haven't written this book; I have only corrected it.'
          [_FocusP maa [_FP al-kitaab-u [_VP allaftu-hu   bal   sˤaħħahtu-hu

Finally, sentential negation *maa* can occur in embedded clauses preceding the verb (Fassi Fehri 1993: 167) suggesting that there is no requirement for it to be in root clauses and that it can intervene between the complementizer and the verb. This is consistent with its analysis as a head of a NegP between CP and TP. Crucially in example (36)b, we are not coordinating two CPs but rather two TPs. Thus negation in this case must be part of the lower conjoined TP.

(37) a. zaʕama   ʔan   maa   ħadaθa   šayʔ-un (SA)
          pretend.3MSG.PFV that   NEG   happen.3MSG.PFV thing
          'He pretended that nothing has happened.'
          [_TP [_VP zaʕama [_CP ʔan [_NegP maa [_TP [_VP ħadaθa   šayʔ-un

     b. zaʕama   ʔanna-hu   qaʕada
          pretend.3MSG.PFV that-him   sit.3MSG.PFV
          wa   maa   btasama   (SA)
          and   neg   smile.3MSG.PFV
          'He pretended that he sat and has not smiled.'
          [_TP [_VP zaʕama [_CP ʔanna-hu [_TP [_VP qaʕada wa
          [_NegP maa [_TP [_VP btasama

I restrict Ouhalla's (1993) analysis of *maa* as focused negation in FocP to the special use of *maa* with a contrastive reading as when *maa* negates preposed NPs and PPs (Ouhalla 1993; also Moutaouakil 1993). I treat this use of *maa* as a form of meta-linguistic negation. Use of *maa* in SA and dialectal Arabic differs in this context in that some dialects have developed a different negative marker for meta-linguistic negation, such as *miš* in Egyptian and Jordanian (Mughazy 2003; Alqassas 2012).

(38) maa   riwaayat-an   ʔallafat   Zaynabu   (bal qasiidat-an) (SA)
      NEG   novel-acc   write.3FSG.PFV   Zaynab   (but poem-ACC)
      'It is not a novel that Zaynab has written (but a poem).' (Ouhalla
      1993: 227)

(39)

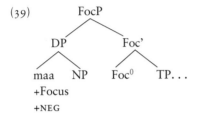

The negative constituent (the whole DP *maa riwaayat-an*) moves from a *v*P internal position to Spec-FocP (Ouhalla 1993). But in cases where the focused constituent is postverbal, *maa* is the spell-out of the focus head specified for +Focus and +NEG.

(40) maa   ʔallafat   Zaynabu   (SA)
      NEG   write.3FSG.PFV   Zaynab
      RIWAAYAT-AN   (bal qasiidat-an)
      novel-ACC   (but poem-ACC)
      'It is not a novel that Zaynab has written (but a poem).' (Ouhalla
      1993: 287)

(41)

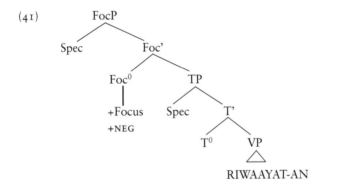

It is not clear, however, why this should be the case. One can propose that the negative *maa* in both cases is in Spec-FocP. The focused constituent can then enter into a dependency relation with Spec-FocP regardless of whether this happens in situ or via movement to Spec-FocP.

(42)

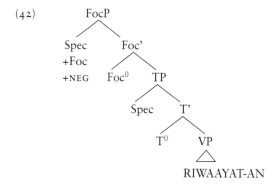

Finally, consider the following example in which contrastive focus *maa* cannot license NPIs, whereas *maa* with no contrastive focus can:

(43) a. maa   ʔaʕtˤat   Zaynabu   ʔayya
          NEG   give.3MSG.PFV   Zaynab   any
          ʔaħadin   riwaayatan   (SA)
          one   novel
          'Zaynab has not given anyone a novel.'

      b. *maa   ʔaʕtˤat   Zaynabu   ʔayya   ʔaħadin   (SA)
          NEG   give.3MSG.PFV   Zaynab   any   one
          RIWAAYAT-AN   (bal qasiidat-an)
          novel   (but poem-ACC)

Similar contrasts are in Moutaouakil (1991: 274–275):

(44) a. maa   qaabaltu   ʔaħad-an   (SA)
          NEG   meet.1SG.PFV   one-ACC
          'I have not met anyone.'

      b. *maa   l-baariħata   qaabaltu   ʔaħadan   (SA)
          NEG   DEF-yesterday   meet.1SG.PFV   one-ACC
          bal   al-yawma
          but   DEF-today

      c. *maa   qaabaltu   ʔaħadan   l-baariħata   (SA)
          NEG   meet.1SG.PFV   one-ACC   DEF-yesterday
          bal   al-yawma
          but   DEF-today

This is expected under the analysis that contrastive negation is a form of constituent negation, and thus contrastive focus *maa* cannot license NPIs.

To sum up this section, we can conclude that the sentential negative marker *maa* is the head of NegP above TP. It binds the tense
variable and has a wider scope (including over the time variable of
tense) which gives rise to the perceived sense of a stronger negation.
Thus, it has a pragmatically marked distribution and is suitable for
denying presuppositions and for emphasis. On the other hand, the
negative markers *laa*, *lam*, and *lan* are heads of a NegP below TP. They
bind the event variable to yield neutral (pragmatically unmarked)
negation, hence their wider distribution. The following table shows
the distribution of the negative markers in the Lebanese Arabic literay
corpus (LBA fiction) and the Quranic corpus. The data is extracted
from the Quran and MARC-2000 corpus by Mark Van Mol at
KU-Leuven.

The negative marker *maa* occurs only 6.6 percent of the time in the
LBA corpus and only 23.4 percent of the time in the Quranic corpus. This
limited distribution contrasts sharply with the distribution of *laa* and its
variants *lam* and *lan* which, when combined, occur 84.9 percent of the
time in the LBA corpus, and 73.5 percent of the time in the Quranic
corpus.

Contrastive focus *maa* is a form of meta-linguistic negation/constituent
negation where *maa* is in a Focus projection FocP in a layered CP. This
negative cannot license Negative Priority Items (NPIs), and can be followed by a (clitic) left dislocated NP or a preposed PP. The following
structural representation summarizes the locus of the negative markers in
the syntactic structure:

(45) [FocusP CONTRASTIVE FOCUS MAA/CLEFT NEGATION [NegP PRESUPPSOTIONAL/
EMPHATIC MAA [TP [NegP UNMARKED NEGATION LAA/LAM/LAN [*v*P . . .

Table 3.2 Distribution of *maa*, *laa*, *lam*, *lan*, and *laysa* in classical and
modern corpus

Particles	LBA fiction		Quran	
laa	1115	56%	1853	59.20%
maa	132	6.60%	732	23.40%
lam	509	25.60%	346	11%
lan	67	3.30%	106	3.30%
laysa	163	8.30%	88	2.80%
Total NEG words	1986		3125	
Total corpus words	86032		85933	

3.2 Presuppositional negation in Jordanian, Gulf, and Standard Arabic

It is well known that negation interacts with the truth conditions of an utterance in various ways that go beyond expressing denial. In other words, negation can be used to object to elements external to the truth conditions of an utterance. This is precisely the case with meta-linguistic negation. Negation can be used to object to the style, register, pronunciation, or essentially any aspect of an utterance other than its truth conditional content. Horn (1989: 121) considers this non-canonical use of the negative operator as 'a device for objecting to a previous utterance on any grounds whatever—including its conventional or conversational implicata, its morphology, its style or register, or its phonetic realization.' This contrasts with the canonical use of negation, which is to deny the truth of the proposition. This kind of negation is usually referred to as propositional negation, truth functional descriptive negation, or categorical negation (cf. descriptive negation in Horn 1985:132). Consider the following examples:

(46) a. A: Mary dislikes chocolate.
          B: Mary doesn't dislike chocolate. John does.

      b. A: Mary dislikes chocolate.
          B: Mary doesn't dislike chocolate. She hates chocolate.

In example (46)a, the speaker is denying the proposition or assertion that Mary dislikes chocolate. However, in example (46)b the speaker is not denying the proposition that Mary dislikes chocolate, but rather is objecting to the use of the verb 'dislike' and thinks that 'hate' is more suitable to describe that event. Similarly, consider the following examples from Alqassas (2012):

(47) ani   miš   šuf-t   Chomisky-, ani   (JA)
      I   NEG   see.PFV-1SG   Chomisky,   I
      šuf-t   Chomsky
      see.PFV-1SG   Chomsky
      'I didn't see Chomisky – I saw Chomsky.'

In example (47), the use of the negative morpheme *miš* is grammatical only when a meta-linguistic negation interpretation is intended. The use of the rectification clause clarifies what the addressee objects to. Moreover, there is contrastive intonation, achieved by making the objection (the mispronunciation of Chomsky as Chomisky) the focus.

Accordingly, negation can be used to deny the truth conditional content of an utterance or to object to non-truth conditional content such as the style or pronunciation of the utterance. Even when denying the truth conditional content, however, negation can not only be used to deny the proposition of the utterance, but it can also be used create presuppositional negation (cf. Zanuttini 1997a, 1997b for presuppositional negation in Romance languages). Consider the following examples in which negative rhetorical questions are used to express an objection based on a presupposition in Arabic:

(48) a. leeš   inbaariħ   maa   dʒaab-hin-(*iš)!   (JA)
          why   yesterday   NEG   bring.3MSG.PFV-them-(*NEG)
          laazim   dʒaab-hin
          should   bring.3MSG.PFV-them.F
          'Why didn't he bring them yesterday!' = 'He should have
          brought them' (presupposition: rhetorical)

      b. miin   maa   dʒaab-hin-(*iš)!   (JA)
          who   NEG   bring.3MSG.PFV-them.F-*(NEG)
          'Who could bring them!' = 'No one could bring them'
          (presupposition: rhetorical)

      c. bigdaru   ma-yruħu-š?   (JA)
          can.3PL.IPFV   NEG-go.3PL.IPFV-NEG
          'Can they not go?' = 'They have to go'
          (presupposition: rhetorical)

These examples express objections that are based on presuppositions. The first example presupposes that the items should have been brought. The second presupposes that no one can bring the items. The third one presupposes that no one can go.

The following examples also show that bipartite negation is unacceptable in rhetorical questions that involve a presupposition about the truth conditions of an utterance:

(49) miin   ma-dʒaab-hin-*(iš)?   (JA)
      who   NEG-bring.3MSG.PFV-them.F-*(NEG)
      'Who didn't bring them?'

(50) miin   maa   dʒaab-hin-(*iš)!   (JA)
      who   NEG   bring.3MSG.PFV-them. F-*(NEG)
      'Who could bring them!' (rhetorical: no one could bring them)

In the examples below, notice that the complementizer (*in*) can fill the CP head position in a yes/no question, although it is not required in either a negative statement, as in (51)a, or in its affirmative counterpart, as in (51)b.

(51) a. bigdaru   (in-hum)   maa   yruuħu?   (JA)
         can.3PL.IPFV   comp-they   NEG   go.3PL.IPFV
         'Can they not go?'

      b. bigdaru   (in-hum)   yruuħu?   (JA)
         can.3PL.IPFV   COMP-they   go.3PL.IPFV
         'Can they go?'

Optional use of the complementizer *inn* in such sentences explains the optional use of high negation, since high negation is used in sentences where the negative marker functions as a complementizer, as argued earlier in Chapter 2.

Another contrast found in rhetorical questions is shown in (52)a and (52)b. While it is grammatical to have a relative pronoun with question words such as 'who' *miin*, as in (52)a, this is not possible in questions that express an indirect speech act, as in (52)b:

(52) a. miin   ʔilli   ma-dʒaab-hin-iš?   (JA)
         who   that   NEG-bring.3MSG.PFV-them.F-NEG
         'Who didn't bring them?'

      b. *miin   ʔilli   maa   dʒaab-hin!   (JA)
          who   that   NEG   bring.3MSG.PFV-them.F   (rhetorical question)

I suggest that the question word *miin* above functions as a quantifier phrase (QP) and that this QP selects a NegP on top of TP. The QP and the negative marker form a negative quantifier. In other words, the question word *miin* and the negative marker *maa* are interpreted as 'no one' as seen in the translation in (50). Therefore, while in (52)a the relative pronoun is in C^0, there is no such position available in (50), hence the ungrammaticality of the use of *ʔilli* in (52)b. The representation in (53) is for (50):

(53)

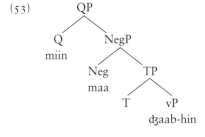

The following is another example of the use of high negation in sentences which make an indirect suggestion that something should be done. In (54) a the speaker is denying the proposition or presupposition that he has been in touch with his family, while in (54)b he is criticizing himself for the fact that he has not talked to his family for a long time, something he suggests is important or necessary to do. Consider the JA examples below:

(54) a. min   zamaan   ma-b-aħtš-is   (JA)
          from   long time   NEG-ASP-speak.1SG.IPFV-NEG
          maʕ   ʔihl-i
          with   family-my
          'I haven't been talking with my family for a long time.'

      b. zamaan   maa   ħatšeet-(*iš)   maʕ   ʔihl-i   (JA)
          long time NEG   speak.1SG.PFV-(*NEG)   with   family-my
          (laazim   ʔaħtši   maʕ-hum)
          (should   speak.1SG.IPFV with-them)
          'It has been a long time that I did not talk to my family.'

Assuming that the use of high negation marks special pragmatic functions, the ungrammaticality of (54)b should be due to a syntactic reason. I argue that *maa* in (54)b functions as a complementizer. First, the interpretation of the sentence shows that *zamaan* is a predicate that is part of an elided clause. The subject of that clause in the English translation is an expletive pronoun, which is null in Arabic. Since the copula of a present tense sentence is also usually null in Arabic, *zamaan* is the only overt element in the clause. This makes the rest of the sentence (*ma-ħatšeet-(*iš) maʕ ʔihl-i*) 'I did not talk to my family' in (54)b an embedded clause. (54)b should thus have the following representation shown in (55):

(55)
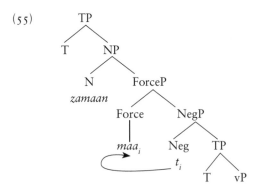

On the other hand, the prepositional phrase *min zamaan* in JA in example (54)a is simply an adjunct and the sentence is one clause.

The contrast between (56)a and (56)b below further supports this analysis. In (56)a the PP adjunct *min zamaan* can be in sentence-final position, but the predicate *zamaan* in (56)b cannot.

(56) a. ma-b-aḥtš-iš   maʕ   ʔihl-i   (JA)
          NEG-ASP-speak.1SG.IPFV-NEG   with   family-my
          min   zaman
          from   long time
          'I haven't been talking with my family for a long time.'

      b. *maa   ḥatšeet   maʕ   ʔihl-i   zamaan   (JA)
          NEG   speak.1SG.PFV   with   family-my   long time
          (laazim   ʔaḥatši   maʕ-hum)
          (should   speak.1SG.IPFV   with-them)

The position of the preverbal definite NP gives evidence that *maa* moves from its position in the high NegP to Force^0. Under the assumption that preverbal definite NPs are topics in Spec-TopP, we can predict that topics will always precede *maa* even when it is in NegP on top of TP. This prediction is borne out. When *maa* precedes the topic, however, it is reasonable to argue that *maa* has moved out of Neg^0 to Force^0. Consider example (57)b where *maa* can precede the topic in sentences which have the word *zamaan*. Example (57)c is an illustration from JA:

(57) a. zamaan   li-wlaad   maa   ḥatšu-(*š)   maʕ-na (JA)
          long time   DEF-boys   NEG   speak.3MPL.PFV-(*NEG)   with-us
          'It has been a long time that the boys did not talk to us.'

      b. zamaan   maa   li-wlaad   ḥatšu-(*š)   maʕ-na (JA)
          long time   NEG   DEF-boys   speak.3MPL.PFV-(*NEG)   with-us
          'It has been a long time that the boys did not talk to us.'

      c.
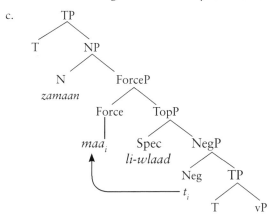

In GA, we find the same presuppositional negation. In pragmatically marked sentences, the negative marker precedes the subject. This suggests that negation is above the tense phrase. This type of negation gives us the presuppositional meaning that 'his mother and sister did not call.'

(58) a. leeš   maa   ?umm-a   w   leeš maa   ?uxt-a   (Kuwaiti)
why   NEG   mother-his and   why NEG   sister-his
daggat-li
call.3FSG.PFV-to.me
'Why didn't his mother and why didn't his sister call me?'
(Brustad 2000: 293)

b. lees   maa   ?umm-a   tasˤlat-li!   (QA)
why   NEG   mother-his call.3FSG.PFV-me
'Why didn't his mother call me!'

c. lees   maa   tasˤlat-li   ?umm-a?   (QA)
why   NEG   call.3FSG.PFV-me   mother-his
'Why didn't his mother call me?'

Notice here that the subject does not precede the question word, suggesting that it is not a topic in the CP domain but a grammatical subject in Spec-TP. Note that this is not possible in SA in which the NP must precede the question word, suggesting that the NP is a topic in CP (Bakir 1980; Fassi Fehri 1993; Plunkett 1993; Ouhalla 1994b).

(59) (al muʕalliumu) limaaða (*al-muʕalliumu) ħadˤara   (SA)
DEF-teacher   why   DEF-teacher   come.3MSG.PFV
muta?axiran?
late
'Why did the teacher come late?'

Moreover, *maa* in GA is not as high as *maa* in SA. SA *maa* can precede focus-fronted constituents as seen in example (60) below:

(60) maa   riwaayat-an ?allafat   Zaynabu (bal qasiidat-an) (SA)
NEG   novel-ACC   write.3FSG.PFV   Zaynab   (but poem-ACC)
'It is not a novel that Zaynab has written (but a poem).' (Ouhalla
1993: 227)

Recall that such occurrences are explained by analyzing *maa* in SA as the spell-out of a negative feature in a Focus projection in the CP domain (Ouhalla 1993). However, such structures are ungrammatical in GA.

These facts are expected under a structure in which negation is above TP:

(61)

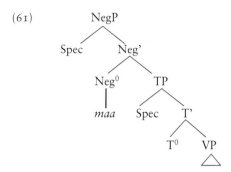

Other pragmatically marked sentences in GA include cases where the question is rhetorical. It is obvious that negation is above TP because it precedes the subject:

(62) a. ʔinta   mub   ʕaarif   al-ʤawaab?   (QA)
          you   NEG   knowing   DEF-answer
          'You don't know the answer?'

      b. mub   int   ʕaarif   al-ʤawaab!   (QA)
          NEG   you   knowing   DEF-answer
          'Don't you know the answer!'
          (speaker presupposes that addressee knows the answer)

SA also displays a similar interaction between negation and presupposition. The negative marker *lam* can only negate imperfective verbs, carries a past tense interpretation, and does not negate a presupposition. It is simply informative and does not negate any presupposition (al-Zamakhshari 1859). Recall that the negative marker *maa* contrasts with *lam* in that it has a special pragmatic effect in SA. In the Quranic verse in (63)a, the use of *maa* denies the truth value of a presupposed proposition that God has taken a son (al-Zamakhshari 1859). In contrast, the negative marker *lam* in (63)b denies a proposition without a presupposition and is thus simply informative.

(63) a. maa   ʔittaxaða   Allaahu   min   waladin   (SA)
          NEG   take.3MSG.PFV   Allahu   any   child
          'Allah has not taken any son.' (al-Mu'minun, ch. 23: verse 91)

      b. wa   lam   yattaxið-ø   waladan   (SA)
          and   NEG.past   take.3MSG.IPFV-juss   child
          'And who did not take a son.' (al-Furqan, ch. 25: verse 2)

Recall that there are other cases in which *maa* also negates the imperfective verb. Such examples are very frequent in SA and involve negation of a presupposed proposition, hence the need for emphatic negation using *maa*.

(64)   yuxaadiʕ-uuna   Allaaha   wa-allaðiina   ʔaamanuu   (SA)
        deceive.3MPL.IPFV   Allah   and-those   believe.3MPL.PFV
        wa-maa   yaxdaʕ-uuna   ʔilla   ʔanfusahum
        and-NEG   deceive.3MPL.IPFV except   themselves
        wa-maa   yaʃʕur-uun
        and-NEG   feel.3MPL.IPFV
        'They [think to] deceive Allah and those who believe, but they deceive not except themselves and perceive [it] not.' (al-Baqarah, ch. 1: verse 9)

3.3 Negation and mood/modality

This section focuses on the interaction between negation and modality. This interaction is interesting because it can explain the division of labor between the various negative markers and their syntactic positions in producing an intricate system for negating modality. The various types of modalities that will be discussed are related to Speech Act theory, but the aspects of modality particularly relevant to this analysis are grammaticalized via the use of certain negative markers in various syntactic positions. Therefore, I will briefly introduce the basic notion of Speech Act theory before proceeeding into a discussion of the interaction between modality and negation.

Speech Act theory was developed by the philosophers John Austin and John Searle. Austin (1962) argued that truth conditions are not central to language understanding. He argued that utterances do not only say things; they also do things. Austin explains that any utterance in real speech is composed of three components: a locutionary act, which refers to the utterance itself (the words and their literal meanings), an illocutionary act, which refers to the function of the utterance, such as declaring, asking, answering, threatening, promising, and so on, and a perlocutionary act, which refers to the effect of the utterance on the hearer's feelings and thoughts. Because they denote the speaker's intention in delivering an utterance, illocutionary speech acts are of particular importance to the present analysis.

The speech acts relevant to the discussion in this chapter are the performatives. For Austin, performatives classify the way a speaker performs an action by uttering specific words. They can be grouped into three main types: declarations, directives, and commissives. Declarations are exemplified by sentences used in marriage, such as 'I now pronounce you husband and wife.' In directives, the speaker directs a command or a request to the listener. As such, imperatives and questions usually fall under this category. In commissives, the speaker commits him- or herself to a future course of action. This could be a promise or a threat, such as 'I promise to tell you the truth,' or 'I will fire you if you don't show up on time tomorrow.' For more details including an exhaustive list of all possible speech acts, the reader is referred to Searle (1975).

3.3.1 *Commissive modality*

In this section, I discuss other kinds of pragmatic functions of negation in which high negation is used. I show that -š is ungrammatical in sentences that have commissives. The grammatical form of negation in these sentences is formed not only by deleting -š but also by using the strong version of *ma* as a free morpheme, *maa*.

One interesting aspect of -š is that it is in complementary distribution with oath words such as *wallah* and *inšaallah* and NPIs such as *ʔumr*. These facts have been reported for rural Palestinian Arabic, Egyptian Arabic (Lucas 2007, 2009), and Moroccan Arabic (Ouhalla 1993). Lucas has reported oath words like *wallah* in (65) and *inšaallah* (66) as ungrammatical when occurring with -š in Palestinian Arabic:

(65) wallah   ma-ba-ʕrif-(*iš)   (PA)
      by God   NEG-ASP-know.1SG.IPFV-(*NEG)
      'By God, I don't know.'

(66) inšaallah   ma-ba-rsub-(*iš)   (PA)
      god willing   NEG-ASP-fail.1SG.IPFV-(*NEG)
      'God willing, I will not fail.'

Lucas (2007) proposes that these are relics of an earlier stage of Arabic. He specifically proposes that -š is an NPI and words like *wallah*, *inšaallah*, and *ʔumr* are in complementary distribution with -š because it is ungrammatical to have more than one NPI in a sentence with only one negative operator, namely *ma*. Another proposal made by Lucas (2009) is the 'Emphasis' analysis. Lucas explains the restriction on the use of -š to negate sentences similar to the above two examples in terms of the emphatic value that use of *ma. . .-š* (a form of negation that is a recent development in the language) would have in unmarked contexts when competing with the use of *ma* by itself, an earlier form of negation in the language. This analysis claims that stage II negation was emphatic at the early stage of its development. For this reason, it is redundant to use stage II negation in sentences emphasized by words like oath words. Subsequently, when stage II negation became unmarked (non-emphatic) as it is now, the ungrammaticality of stage II negation in (57) and (58) remains as a relic.

However, both analyses suffer from at least three problems. The first problem is that multiple NPIs are allowed in a negative sentence with only one negative marker in Arabic (Ouhalla 2002). The second problem is that there are cases in JA in which -*š* co-occurs with NPIs, for example *ma-ʔumr-iš* 'I never.' The third problem is that these analyses cannot explain the fact that the use of -*š* in sentences with oath words can be less offensive or acceptable for some native speakers under certain pragmatic conditions. The fourth problem is that Lucas's account does not extend to cases where -*š* is unacceptable for the other pragmatic reasons discussed in the previous sections of this chapter.

Let us now explore these issues in greater detail. First, it has been shown that more than one NPI can co-occur with *ma* (cf. Ouhalla 2002 for Moroccan Arabic below). In (67)a, the negative marker *ma* co-occurs with the two NPIs *hətta haʒa* 'anything' and *hətta waħəd* 'anyone.' In (67) b, there are three NPIs *hətta haʒa* 'anything,' *hətta waħəd* 'anyone,' and *hətta blasa* 'any place.'

(67) a. ma-ʕtat   Nadia hətta haʒa   (Moroccan)
          NEG-give.3FSG.PFV Nadia any   thing
          l-hətta waħəd
          to-any body
          'Nadia did not give anything to anybody.'

      b. hətta waħəd ma-šaf   hətta   (Moroccan)
          any   body   NEG-see.3MSG.PFV   any
          haʒa   (f-hətta blasa)
          thing (in-any place)
          'Nobody saw anything (anywhere).'

The second problem is caused by JA sentences which allow -*š* to co-occur with NPIs. Before discussing these sentences in JA, I will present Ouhalla's (2002) analysis of the complementary distribution between -*š* and NPIs. Ouhalla (2002: 314) reports that -*š* is in complementary distribution with NPIs in the Arabic dialects. He also reports that more than one NPI can be used with *ma*, and concludes that the absence of -*š* cannot be because -*š* and the NPI are competing for the same Spec/NegP position. He argues that -*š/ši* is a dummy variable that is required because *ma* is a negative operator which needs a variable to bind. When an NPI is present in a negative sentence, the negative operator binds the argument variable of the NPI. The insertion of -*š* is thus unnecessary. For Ouhalla, -*š* is regulated by the same last-resort measure that regulates insertion of other 'semantically vacuous' elements such as expletive subjects and

Do-support. However, the following example from JA shows that -*š* can occur even when the NPI *ʕumr* is used.

(68)   a.   ma-ʕumr-i-š   ruḥt   (JA)
            NEG-ever-my-NEG   go.1SG.PFV
            'I have never gone.'

       b.   ʕumr-i   ma-ruḥt-(*iš)   (JA)
            NPI-ever-my   NEG-go.1SG.PFV-(*NEG)
            'I have never gone.'

Third, none of Lucas's analyses can explain the fact that the use of -*š* in sentences that have oath words can be ameliorated under certain pragmatic conditions. To understand how speech acts can explain the deletion of -*š* with oath words and predict the amelioration, consider the following contrast in (69)–(70):

(69)   ??wallah   ma-ba-ʕrif-iš   (JA)
       by God   NEG-ASP-know.1SG.IPFV-NEG
       'By God, I don't know.'

(70)   t'ayyib   bι-tšuf,   wallah   (JA)
       ok   ASP-see.2MSG.IPFV   by God
       ma-b-asaaʕd-ak-(*-iš)
       NEG-ASP-help.1SG.IPFV-you-(*-NEG)
       'Ok, you'll see, by God I won't help you.'

The sentence in (69) expresses an assertive speech act, while in (70) it expresses a commissive speech act (specifically, a threat). The use of -*š* in example (69) is less offensive (and even fully acceptable for many native speakers) when compared with the use of -*š* in example (70). The two examples thus differ primarily in that the first is an assertion (its function is only to convey information), while (70) is a commissive speech act in which the speaker is threatening the hearer. Additionally, he is committing himself to a course of action in the future, namely not to help the hearer. It thus seems that -*š* cannot appear in sentences which perform a commissive speech act such as threatening.

More evidence that the contrast between (69) and (70) is due to a difference in the speech acts employed in each sentence comes from the contrast in the use of the NPI *ʕumr* with negation between (71) and (72) below:

(71)   ma-ʕumr-i-š   ruḥt   hnaak   (JA)
       NEG-ever-my-NEG   go.1SG.PFV   there
       'I have never gone there.'

(72) a. tˤayyib   bi-tšuuf,   ʕumr-i   (JA)
          ok   ASP-see.2MSG.IPFV   NPI-ever-my
          ma-b-asaaʕd-ak-(*-iš)
          NEG-ASP-help.1SGIPFV-you-(*-NEG)
          'Ok, you'll see, I will never help you.'

      b. *tˤayyib   bi-tšuuf,   ma-ʕumr-i-š   (JA)
          ok   ASP-see. 2MSG.IPFV   NEG-ever-my-NEG
          b-asaaʕd-ak
          ASP-help.1SG IPFV-you
          'Ok, you'll see, I will never help you.'

In (71), the speech act is an assertion. The speaker is only stating that he 'never went there.' In context, this utterance would be answering a question about whether or not he went somewhere. In (72), the speaker is threatening never to help the hearer. He is committing himself to a course of action in the future and thus this is a commissive speech act. Accordingly, the use of -š in (72)a and (72)b is ungrammatical (i.e., the use of low negation is unacceptable). On the other hand, it is grammatical in (71) because the speech act is an assertive one.

The use of *inšaallah* in certain sentences to express the pragmatic function 'promise' adds more empirical support to the claim that high negation is used in commissive speech acts, since promises, like threats, are classified as commissives. Consider the following example:

(73) inšaallah   ma-b-ansaa-k-(*iš)   (JA)
      god willing   NEG-ASP-forget.1SG.IPFV-YOU-(*NEG)
      'God willing, I will not forget you.'

Accordingly, it is not because *wallah* and *inšaallah* are oath words and oath words are used for emphasis that they are in complementary distribution with -š. Rather it is because utterances with a commissive speech act (a threat or a promise) are marked by the use of the negative marker that is located above TP, i.e., *maa* by itself.

3.3.2 Directive modality

In this section I highlight how different degrees of directive speech acts exhibit a contrast with respect to the position of negation. The relationship between directive modality and negation is exemplified by clauses in which the negative imperative does not allow the use of -š and only *la* can be used. When the function of the imperative is cautioning rather than prohibition, only high negation is possible, as seen below where the use of -š is ungrammatical:

(74) a.   laa   t-ruuħ-iš   (JA)
           NEG   2-go.IMP-(*NEG)
           'Don't go.'

      b.   laa   t-igaʕ-(*iš)   (JA)
           NEG   2-fall.IMP-(*NEG)
           'Don't fall/Careful not to fall.'

The difference in the pragmatic function expressed by the negative imperative is marked by a difference in intonation. Specifically, the intonation of a cautioning phrase has a high boundary tone at the end of the utterance, but a low boundary tone when the pragmatic function is prohibition. Consider the grammaticality of *miš* below:

(75) miš   t-ruuħ   (JA)
      NEG   2-go.IMP
      'Don't go.'

The function of (75) is similar to that of (74). The pragmatic function 'cautioning' is marked by the absence of -š. The use of the high negative marker which is morphologically strong (it is a free morpheme which carries sentential stress) in (74) contrasts with the use of *miš* in (75). Additionally, the use of *la* alone in (74) is to be expected, since negative imperatives can be negated by *laa* or *la* and -š. However, the use of *miš* in (75) is unexpected and needs an explanation since *miš* is not otherwise used in negative imperatives which function as prohibitions. Consider the fact that the double negation in example (76) is grammatical. This suggests that *miš* is in a higher clause. In (77), we see that the negative marker *la* cannot replace *ma* in this type of structure.

(76) miš   ma   t-ruuħ-(iš)   (JA)
      NEG   NEG   2-go.IMP-(NEG)
      'Lit. You shouldn't not go.' = 'You should go'

(77) *miš   la   t-ruuħ-(iš)   (JA)
      NEG   NEG   2-go.IMP-(NEG)

When negation has the function of cautioning rather than prohibition, the negative marker *laa* is used and -š is ungrammatical, as in (78). The speaker here sees that the addressee is about to fall and so warns them not to fall. Example (79) is not possible if the function is cautioning.

(78) laa   t-igaʕ-(*iš)   (JA)
      NEG   2-fall.IMP-(*NEG)
      'Don't fall/Careful not to fall.'

(79)   *miš   t-igaʕ   (JA)
        NEG   2-fall.IMP

In example (80), the negative marker *laa* has a special pragmatic function, namely cautioning rather than prohibition. I suggest that this negative marker is in a NegP projection on top of TP (high NegP or high negation). Recall that high negative markers are free morphemes which carry sentential stress.

(80)   laa   t-ruuħ-(*iš)   (JA)
        NEG   2-go.IMP-(*NEG)
        'Don't go.' (cautioning, no prohibition)

The previous example can be reinterpreted as having a main clause. This main clause has undergone ellipsis and so can be reconstructed as follows:

(81)   bansˤaħa-k   laa   t-ruuħ   (JA)
        advise.1SG.IPFV-YOU   NEG   2-go.IMP
        'I advise you not to go.'

In JA, I suggest that cautioning is grammaticalized in the sense that the negative marker *laa* moves to ForceP to show the difference between prohibition and cautioning. Assuming a layered CP structure à la Rizzi (1997), we can find motivation for the movement through the Force projection. The complementizer occupying this Force projection determines the illocutionary force of the sentence. The common types of force observed cross-linguistically are indicative, interrogative, and imperative. Other types such as cautioning are usually assumed to be determined by pragmatics only. That is, cautioning is implied by the context rather than a result of the structure. Accordingly, I give the following representation to the cautioning examples in (82) below:

(82)

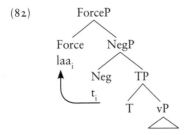

In languages which do not have true negative imperatives, Zeijlstra argues that this can be taken as evidence that the negative marker

is in Neg^0 (Zeijlstra 2004: 182). He assumes that imperative verbs move to check a mood feature, which is either in T^0 or in C^0, depending on the language. So, if a language does not have true negative imperatives, this is because the imperative verb cannot cross over negation.

In order to capture the ungrammaticality of -*š* in cases where negation has a cautioning rather than prohibitive interpretation, I propose that the imperative verb in JA moves to check the mood feature in T^0. When negation is low (for example with *la*. . . .*š*), the imperative moves to I^0 after incorporating with neg heads. With high negation *laa*, the fact that the negative marker is a free morpheme suggests that the verb does not move or incorporate with it. So, one might argue that sentences which have a cautioning reading in JA are not true negative imperatives, since the verb does not move to T^0 to check an IMP feature.

We now turn to another example of negative imperatives where the pragmatic function of a negative marker other than *la* is also cautioning. This word is *miš*:

(83) mič   t-ruuħ   (JA)
      NEG   2-go.IMP
      'It is not for you to go.'

It is unclear here why the use of *miš* is grammatical. This question is puzzling for a number of reasons. First, the morphemes *ma* and -*š* are ungrammatical in negative imperatives. Second, if we were to assume that negative imperatives with the function of cautioning allow the use of *ma* and -*š* and that the predicate does not move to -*š*, we cannot explain how movement is possible in the following example:

(84) miš   ma-t-ruuħ-iš   (JA)
      NEG   NEG-2-go.IMP-NEG
      'It is not for you not to go.' = 'You should go'

In this example, the surface form shows double negation as is clear from the translation 'You should go.' However, Arabic does not allow double negation. Therefore, *miš* in example (83) must be in a higher clause which has its own NegP.[4] Aoun et al. (2010: 102) give a different syntactic context in which *miš* is used in a clause that has the discontinuous morpheme *ma*. . .-*š*. The following is their example:

(85) maši   ma-kunti-š   f   d-daar?   (Moroccan)
      NEG   NEG-be.2FSG.PFV-NEG   in   DEF-house
      'Isn't it the case that you were not in the house?'

In (85), Aoun et al. show that the interpretation of *maši* in Moroccan Arabic is 'isn't it the case,' and that this is made possible by the fact that expletive subjects and the present tense are null in Arabic. Moreover, there is no verbal copula in the present tense, so the negative marker is the only overt element in the sentence 'isn't it the case.' Based on this and the fact that Arabic does not allow double negation (except in meta-linguistic negation as was explained earlier), they argue that the independent negator *maši* is in the NegP projection of a higher clause as shown below.

(86)

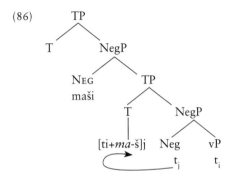

Therefore, it should not be surprising that the independent morpheme *miš* is the only word pronounced in the higher clause. The subject of the clause is an expletive and the copula is in the present tense. Also, the deontic modality interpred as 'should' in the translation of such cases is grammaticalized via the marked use of *miš* to express cautioning.

In conclusion, high negation occurs in sentences implying cautioning, in commissive speech acts, and in rhetorical questions, all of which are marked constructions. Cautioning is marked relative to the common use of negative imperatives as prohibitions. Commissive speech acts are marked relative to assertions, and rhetorical questions are marked relative to the more common use of questions as interrogatives.

3.3.3 Volitive modality

Volitive modality expresses the speaker's wish or fear toward the proposition of the utterance (cf. Pei and Gaynor 1954; Palmer 1986). This type of modality employs single negation to express the negative counterpart of the affirmative utterance. The negative marker that is used here is *laa*.

(87) a. Allaah (laa)   yi-wafga-k   (JA)
          God   NEG.IMPR   3MSG-help.IPFV-you.MSG
          'May God not help you!'

b. laa   waffaqa-ka   Allaah   (SA)
   NEG.IMPR help.3MSG.PFV-you.MSG God
   'May God not help you!'

This specific type of mood is known as imprecative mood, whereby the speaker wishes something bad befalls someone. The single negative marker *maa* can also be used to express this modality. In such cases, *maa* follows the modal verb *reit* 'may,' as in:

(88)   reet-ak   maa   tindʒaħ   (JA)
       may-you   NEG   succeed.2MSG.IPFV
       'May you not succeed!'

The negative marker *maa* is also used in negating volitive modality expressed by the expression *inšallah* 'God willing':

(89)   inšallah   maa   b-tindʒaħ   (JA)
       God willing   NEG   asp-succeed.2MSG.IPFV
       'May you not succeed!'

3.3.4 (Ir)realis modality

SA employs the distinction between *maa* and *laa* in the domain of realis/irrealis modality. The two negatives *maa* and *laa* display contrasts in compatibility with embedded verbs. There are distributional contrasts with respect to negating nonfinite verbs that occur after the complementizer *ʔan*:

(90)   a.   ʔuriid-u   ʔan   laa   tadxul-a   (SA)
             want.1SG.IPFV-IND   that   NEG   enter.2MSG-SBJV
             'I want you not to enter.' (Fassi Fehri 1993: 172)

       b.   *ʔuriid-u   ʔan   maa   tadxul-a   (SA)
             want.1SG.IPFV-IND   that   NEG   enter.2MSG-SBJV

Notice that the embedded verb *tadxul-a* cannot carry tense:

(91)   a.   ʔaradt-u   ʔan   laa   tadxul-a   (SA)
             want.1SG.PFV-IND   that   NEG   enter.2MSG-SBJV
             'I wanted you not to enter.'

       b.   * ʔaradt-u   ʔan   laa   daxalta   (SA)
             want.1SG.PFV-IND   that   NEG   enter.2MSG.PFV

The subject of the embedded verb can be case marked by the matrix verb:

(92) a. ?uriid-u   ?an   yadxulu   (SA)
          want.1SG.IPFV-ND   that   enter.3MPL.SBJV
          'I want them to enter.'

      b. ?uriid-u-hum   ?an   yadxulu   (SA)
          want.1SG.IPFV-IND-them   that   enter.3MPL.SBJV
          'I want them to enter.'

Recall that if the embedded verb does not have a TP, the contrasts in (90) can be explained by allowing *maa* to select TP, an option not available to *laa* since it does not dominate TP (cf. Ouali and Fortin's analysis for Moroccan Arabic below).

(93)   [TP [AspP [*v*P [VP WANT [AspP [*v*P [VP (Ouali and Fortin 2007: 182)

The following is a representation for this structural dichotomy between *maa* and *laa*:

(94) a. [TP [AspP [*v*P [VP WANT [NegP laa [AspP [*v*P [VP
      b. [TP [AspP [*v*P [VP WANT [*NegP maa [AspP [*v*P [VP

Furthermore, there are distributional contrasts in modality between *maa* on the one hand and *laa* and *lam* on the other hand. Consider the following contrasts with respect to the future modal *sawfa*:

(95) a. sawfa   laa   yaħsˤulu   haaða   (SA)
          FUT   NEG   happen.3MSG.IPFV   this
          'This will not happen.' (Fassi Fehri 1993: 173)

      b. *sawfa   maa   yaħsˤulu   haaða   (SA)
          FUT   NEG   happen.3MSG.IPFV   this (Fassi Fehri 1993: 173)

Additionaly, there are contrasts with respect to the expectative modal *qad*:

(96) a. qad   lam   ya?ti   (SA)
          may   NEG.past   come.3MSG.JUSS
          'He may not have come.' (Fassi Fehri 1993: 172)

      b. qad   laa   ya?ti   (SA)
          may   NEG   come.3MSG.IPFV
          'He may not come.' (Fassi Fehri 1993: 172)

      c. *qad   maa   ya?ti   (SA)
          may   NEG.past   come.3MSG.IPFV (Fassi Fehri 1993: 172)

If Arabic modals are heads that project a Mod(al) projection that selects IP/TP (as in Fassi Fehri 1993: 159–160), these contrasts follow from *maa* being a negative that selects a TP while *laa* and its tensed variants do not. In other words, *maa* is incompatible with modals because both compete for selecting TP, whereas *laa* and *lam* do not compete with Mod:

(97)   [ModP [*NegP maa [TP [NegP laa [VP

Notes

1. Some of the ideas in this chapter and in Chapter 4 were presented at the Annual Symposium on Arabic Linguistics held at the University of Florida-Gainsville, and at the 5th Conference on Linguistics in the Gulf-5 at Qatar University. I thank the audience of both conferences for their helpful questions and comments. I especially thank Abbas Benmamoun, Youssef Haddad, Usama Soltan, Fassi Fehri, Ali Idrissi, among others, for their helpful feedback and comments.

2. Negation (whether below or above TP) also binds the variables of the internal and external arguments.

3. Negative sentences were extracted from two corpora: (1) MARC-2000 (Modern Arabic Representative Corpus – 2000), and (2) the Quran. The negative sentences cover the SA negative markers in a range of well-defined grammatical contexts. These contexts include the distribution of the negative markers in the context of verbal and non-verbal predicates, question words, conditional particles, among the other contexts. The corpora included two subcorpora: (1) Literary Fiction from Lebanon (86,000) words, in Mark Van Mol's corpus MARK-2000 compiled at KU-Leuven, and (2) The Quran, which is also 86,000 words.

4. Interestingly, Rowlett gives a similar French construction which allows for double negation, although double negation is also generally ungrammatical in French. He gives the following example where the gloss interprets the infinitive as imperative:

(i) Ne jamais ne pas avoir d'argent sur soi,   mais très peu, 40 francs max

    NEG never NEG not have of-money on oneself but very little 40 francs max(imum)

    'Never have no money on one's person, but very little, 40 francs max.'

Rowlett (2007) proposes two IPs, one on top of the other, each with its own NegP, to account for the double negation reading. However, he notes that the question of what *ne* attaches to in the higher clause, and why there is no apparent verbal material in that higher IP, must still be solved. Note that in the JA example, the fact that Arabic is pro-drop and has a null present tense copula explains why it is possible to have the higher TP filled with only *miš*. For French, see also Hirschbühler and Lahelle (1992/3).

4

Licensing Negative Sensitive Items

The term 'Negative Sensitive Items' (NSIs) describes a category of words and expressions that interact with negation in various ways. This interaction takes place in at least three different ways. First, negation is (usually) required in simple declarative sentences containing an NSI. Second, certain NSIs have a negative interpretation when used as fragment answers (the Fragment Answer Test), despite the absence of overt negation. Third, certain negative markers are in complementary distribution with certain NSIs. This chapter introduces the key contrasts between two major NSI categories and shows the explanatory adequacy of a multi-locus analysis of negation to account for the mutual exclusivity between certain NSIs on the one hand and bipartite negation in JA and the negative marker *maa* in SA on the other hand. The chapter starts by defining the major NSI types along with their lexical categories. It then lays out the theoretical background of NSI licensing as this is necessary to develop an analysis for NSIs based on the multi-locus analysis of negation. This chapter extends this analysis to the Qatari and SA data giving further evidence that the different positions of negation have different effects on the licensing of Negative Polarity Items (NPIs). This chapter also discusses the interaction between higher negation and determiner NCIs (*wala*-NP) as well as the interaction between *maa* and NPIs in SA.

4.1 Types of NSIs and their lexical categories

At least two different categories of words fall under the term NSI. They differ from each other with respect to their sensitivity to negation.[1] NPIs form the first category. These words always require negation in simple declarative sentences and may be in complementary distribution with certain negative markers, but cannot stand alone as fragment answers without negation.

The NPIs *ʔaħadun* 'one' and *ʔayyu ʔaħadin* 'anyone' in Standard Arabic (SA), *hada* 'one' and *ʔayy hada* in Jordanian Arabic (JA), and *ʕumr* 'ever' in JA all require a negative marker (see (1)a, (2)a, and (3)a) and cannot

PASS the Fragment Answer Test (see (1)b, (2)b, and (3)b). The NPI *ʕumr* is in complementary distribution with the enclitic negative marker *-š* in JA (Alqassas 2015), in Moroccan Arabic (Ouhalla 2002; Benmamoun 2006), and in Egyptian Arabic (Soltan 2012; Brustad 2000).

(1) a. *(lam)   yaʔti   ʔaħadun/ ʔayyu ʔaħadin   (SA)
       NEG.past come.3MSG.PFV one/   any   one
       'No one came.'

    b. Question: Answer:
       man   dʒaaʔa?   *(laa)   ʔaħad   (SA)
       who   come.3MSG.PFV   NEG   one
       'Who came?'   'No one.'

(2) a. *(ma)-ʔadʒaa-š   ħada/ ʔayy ħada   (JA)
       NEG-come.3MSG.PFV-NEG one/   any one
       'No one came.'

    b. Question: Answer:
       miin   ʔadʒa?   *(ma) ħada   (JA)
       who   come.3MSG.PFV   NEG   one
       'Who came?'   'No one.'

(3) a. ʕumr-o   *(ma)   zaar(*-iš)   el-batra   (JA)
       NPI-ever-his NEG   visit.3MSG.PFV-NEG DEF-Petra
       'He has never visited Petra.'

    b. Question: Answer: (JA)
       ʕumr-o   zaar   el-batra?   *ʕumr-o
       NPI-ever-his visit.3MSG.PFV DEF-Petra   NPI-ever-his
       'Has he ever visited Petra?'

The second category of NSIs are called Negative Concord Items (NCIs) and need not always co-occur with negation. Words in this category may be in complementary distribution with certain negative markers and receive a negative interpretation when used as fragment answers despite the absence of negation. The NCI *wala-ħada* 'no one' in JA, in (4)a, and the Moroccan Arabic *ħətta wəld* 'no one', in (5)a, both require a negative marker when they occur postverbally. Interestingly, the preverbal NCI in JA cannot co-occur with the negative marker, while the NCI in Moroccan Arabic must co-occur with the negative marker (cf. (4)b and (5)b). The fundamental distinction between NPIs and NCIs in JA and MA is that only the latter PASS the fragment answer test (cf. (4)c and (5)c). We observe, as well, that the enclitic negative marker *-š* cannot co-occur with the MA NCI in (5)d.

(4) a. *(ma)-ʔadʒaa-š   wala-ħada   (JA)
       NEG-come.3MSG.PFV-NEG   NCI-one
       'No one came.'

   b. wala-ħada   (*ma)-ʔadʒa-(*š)   (JA)
       NCI-one   NEG-come.3MSG.PFV-NEG
       'No one came.'

   c. Question: Answer:
       miin   ʔadʒa?   wala-ħada   (JA)
       who   come.3MSG.PFV   NCI-one
       'Who came?'   'No one'

(5) a. *(ma)-dʒa   ħətta wəld   (MA)
       NEG-come.3MSG.PFV   NCI boy
       *'Any boy didn't come.' (Benmamoun 1996: 49)

   b. ħətta waħəd   *(ma)-dʒa   (MA)
       even one   NEG-come.3MSG.PFV
       'Anyone didn't come.' (Benmamoun 1997: 273)

   c. Question: Answer:
       škuun šəf-ti?   ħətta   waħəd   (MA)
       who see.PFV-2S   not-even   one
       'Who did you see?'   'Nobody.' (Ouali and Soltan 2014: 162)

   d. *ma-dʒa-š   ħətta wəld   (MA)
       NEG-come.3MSG.PFV-NEG even boy (Benmamoun 1996: 49)

Closely related to NSIs is the category of Negative Quantifiers (NQs). This category includes inherently negative words that express universal quantification, such as the Standard English *no*-indefinite noun compounds, including *no one*, *nothing*, etc. NQs carry a negative interpretation in the absence of an negative marker. When a negative marker does co-occur with an NQ, the result is double negation.

(6) ma-ħadaa-š   rasab   bi-li-mtiħaan   (JA)
    NEG-one-NEG   fail.3MSG.PFV   in-DEF-exam
    'No one failed the exam.'

(7) ma-ħadaa-š   ma-rasab-iš   bi-li-mtiħaan   (JA)
    NEG-one-NEG   NEG-fail.3MSG.PFV-NEG   in-DEF-exam
    'No one didn't fail the exam.'

Both NPIs and NCIs can belong to a range of different lexical categories. Under the category of NPIs, for example, we find determiner

NPIs, nominal NPIs, adverbial NPIs, and idiomatic NPIs. Examples of determiner NPIs include the SA/JA *ʔayy*, which always combines with an indefinite, such as *ʔaḥad/ḥada* in examples (1) and (2) or *šayʔ/ʔiši* in example (8) below.

(8)   a.   *(lam)   yaštari   šayʔ/   ʔayya   šayʔ   (SA)
              NEG.past   buy.3MSG.PFV   thing/   any   thing
              'He didn't buy anything.'

       b.   *(ma)-štaraa-š   ʔiši /   ʔayy ʔiši   (JA)
              NEG-buy.3MSG.PFV-NEG   thing/   any thing
              'He didn't buy anything.'

The indefinite nouns *ʔaḥad/ḥada* and *šayʔ/ʔiši* are nominal NPIs that occupy the subject and object positions in examples (1), (2), and (8), respectively. The temporal adverbial NPI *ʕumr* in JA and EA and the MA equivalent *ʕəmmər* tend to occur sentence-initially. The NPI *baʕd* 'yet' in SA, however, is a sentence-final adverb:

(9)   *(lam)   yaʔti   baʕd   (SA)
         NEG.past   come.3MSG.PFV   yet
         'He hasn't come yet.'

Finally, idiomatic NPIs include expressions like *girš* 'piaster [small unit of currency],' and *fils ʔiḥmar* 'red cent.'

(10)   ma-maʕ-huu-š   girš/   fils ʔiḥmar   (JA)
          NEG-with-he-NEG   penny/cent red
          'He doesn't have a penny/red cent.'

NCIs can be classified into determiner NCIs and adverbial NCIs. Determiner NCIs include JA *wala* in (4), and MA *ḥatta* in (5). Adverbial NCIs include *never*-type words *ʔabadan/bilmarrah* 'not at all' (Hoyt 2010), and *still*-type words *baʕd/lissa* 'yet' in Levantine Arabic (Hoyt 2010) and Egyptian Arabic (EA) (Soltan 2012), and *baqi* 'yet' in MA (Benmamoun 2006).

(11)   ma-biḥibb-iš   l-tˤayyarah   ʔabadan/bilmarrah   (JA)
          NEG-like.3MSG.IPFV-NEG   DEF-plane   ever/at all
          'He doesn't like planes at all.'

(12)   ma-saafar-iš   baʕdo   (JA)
          NEG-travel.3MSG.PFV-NEG   yet-him
          'He hasn't traveled yet.'

(13)   mona   maa-saafir-it-š   lissah   (EA)
        Mona   NEG-travel.3FSG.PFV-NEG   yet
        'Mona has not traveled yet.' (Soltan 2012)

(14)   nadya   baq-a   ma-ʒat   (MA)
        Nadia   yet-FS   NEG-come.3FSG.PFV
        'Nadia hasn't come yet.' (Benmamoun 2006)

4.2 NSI licensing in the syntactic structure

Although early analyses distinguished between NPIs and NQs, NCIs were typically treated as a subset of either NPIs or NQs in the earlier studies. I briefly lay out the difference between NPIs and NQs below. In later sections, I briefly review the previous analyses of NPIs and NCIs, respectively.

The NPI *anyone* and the NQ *no one* are classic Standard English NSIs. In negative polarity environments, use of the NPI anyone requires the presence of the English negative marker *not/n't* or an NQ like *no one*, as in (15):

(15)   a.   I haven't seen anyone.
        b.   No one has seen anyone.

The NQ *no one*, by contrast, does not require negation. In fact, when negation co-occurs with an NQ in Standard English, the result is double negation:

(16)   a.   I haven't seen no one (= I have seen someone).
        b.   No one has seen nothing (= Everyone has seen something).

NPIs can occur in a number of environments, including clause-mate negation, superordinate negation, yes/no questions, conditionals, and adversative (semantically negative) predicates like *forget* and *doubt*. The English NPs *anyone*, *anything*, and so on are typical examples of NPIs.[2]

4.2.1 *NPI licensing*

Discussion of NPIs in the literature has centered on identifying ways to capture the dependency between NPIs and negation, taking into account the fact that some NPIs follow negation and others precede it. Syntactic accounts capture this dependency through specific structural configurations, such as c-command and the Spec-Head relation, although different accounts take different views regarding the level of representation at which licensing takes place – i.e., in an overt syntactic structure or covertly in the logical form (LF). For instance, when an NPI follows negation, the configuration is interpreted as a dependency between the NPI and the negation marker, mediated through a c-command relation-ship (Jackendoff 1969, 1972; Lasnik 1975; Linebarger 1981, 1987; Benmamoun 1997, 2006; Giannakidou 1998, 2006, 2011). C-command is defined here as in Reinhart (1976: 32):

(17)   Node A c-commands node B if neither A nor B dominates the other and the first branching node dominating A dominates B.

(18)   *(lam)   ya?ti   ?aħadun/ ?ayyu ?aħadin   (SA)
       NEG.past   come.3MSG.PFV one/   any   one
       'No one came.'

(19)

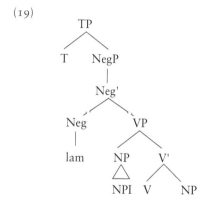

In (19), the representation for (18), the negative marker *lam* is the head of NegP and thus c-commands the NPI subject in Spec-VP. Neither the NEG head node nor the NP node dominates the other, and the first node dominating NEG, namely NEG', also dominates the NP.

Early analyses of NPIs claim that they are licensed overtly, that is to say at surface structure (Jackendoff 1969, 1972; Lasnik 1975). Lasnik proposes that NPIs need to be under the scope of negation at surface structure in order to be specified [+NEG] and [-referential], under the so-called 'Not-Scope Rule.' The scope of negation here is understood to encompass any element to the right of, and c-commanded by, negation. This assumption is based on the following contrasts:

(20)   a.   *Anybody didn't see me.
       b.   I didn't see anybody.

In (20)a, the NPI composed of the quantifier *any* and the indefinite noun *body* fails to receive a non-referential reading because it is not under the scope of negation at surface structure. The ability of negation to give a [-referential] marking to quantifiers can be seen in examples where the quantified NP is under the scope of negation and cannot be referential:

(21) a. Many students (namely, James, Robert, and Sarah) attended the class.
      b. *Not many students (namely, James, Robert, and Sarah) attended the class.

Evidence from passivization and topicalization suggest that the requirement for negation to precede and c-command the NPI is a surface-level constraint, rather than a deep-structure constraint (Linebarger 1980):

(22) a. I never saw anyone.
      b. *Anyone was never seen by me.
      c. *Anyone I never saw.

Recent analyses of NPIs in Hindi (Benmamoun and Kumar 2006) have maintained the surface structure approach, arguing that these NPIs are licensed overtly before scrambling. Evidence for this claim comes from reconstruction effects that argue against covert licensing.

(23) a. Raajiiv-ne   kah-aa ki [vo   ek bhii   pikcar jo (Hindi)
          Rajive-ERG   said   that that one EMPH   pictures which
          Sariitaa$_i$-ne   lii]$_j$ usko$_i$ pasand nahiiN hai   t$_j$
          Sarit-ERG   took   she   likes   NEG   PRS
          'Rajiv said that she does not like any picture that Sarita took.'

      b. *Raajiiv-ne   kah-aa ki   usko$_i$ pasand nahiiN hai (Hindi)
          Rajive-ERG   said   that she   likes   NEG   PRS
          [vo   ek bhii   pikcar   jo   Sariitaai-ne lii]
          that one EMPH   pictures which Sarit-ERG   took

Assuming the copy theory of movement, Benmamoun and Kumar (2006) show that LF reconstruction of the constituent *vo ek bhii pikcar jo Sariitaai-ne lii* to a position c-commanded by negation results in a violation of Binding Principle C. Accordingly, licensing of the NPI via LF reconstruction is rejected. Instead, the authors argue that NPI licensing in this case must have occurred prior to scrambling of the NPI object from its VP-internal position to pre-subject position.

Nonetheless, positing that the NPI is preceded and c-commanded by negation is insufficient to explain the behavior of NPIs in other languages. Consider, for instance, data from Greek (Giannakidou 1998), where NPIs precede negation at surface structure. Giannakidou shows that the Greek

NPI preceding negation must be c-commanded by negation at LF. In other words, the NPI is covertly licensed. Consider the contrast shown below (Giannakidou 1998: 235–236):

(24) a. *Dhen lipame   pligosa kanenan   (Greek)
        not regret.1SG that hurt anyone
        'I do not regret that I hurt anyone.'

    b. Fimes oti sinelavan   kanenan dhen kikloforisan (Greek)
        rumors that arrested.3PL anybody not   were.circulated.3PL
        'Rumors that they arrested anybody were not circulated.'

For Giannakidou, the contrast in grammaticality between (24)a, where the NPI *kanenan* 'anyone' is (unsuccessfully) c-commanded by negation, and (24)b, where the same NPI is not c-commanded by negation, is evidence that licensing takes place at LF. In (24)a, the NPI undergoes LF movement to a position above negation adjoined to IP. This movement, schematized in (25)a, is motivated by the presuppositional force of the complementizer *pu*. After this LF movement, the NPI is no longer c-commanded by negation, which leads to ungrammaticality. In (24)b, by contrast, the NPI is part of the topicalized complex NP *Fimes oti sinelavan kanenan*. At LF, this NP reconstructs to a position c-commanded by negation, as in (25)b, yielding the grammatical structure below:

(25) a. [IP [CP[pu pligossa kanenan]1 [IP dhen lipame [VP [CP t1]]]]
    b. [IP [NP fime oti sinelavan kanenan]1 [IP dhen kikloforisan [VP [NP fimes oti sinelavan kanenan]1]]]

In Arabic, adverbial NPIs can precede the negative marker, as can be seen in example (3) above, repeated here below.

(26) Sumr-o   *(ma) zaar(*-iš)   el-batra   (JA)
     NPI-ever-his NEG   visit.3MSG.PFV-NEG   DEF-Petra
     'He has never visited Petra.'

The question of whether these NPIs are also licensed under c-command by negation is complicated by the head-like properties that they exhibit. Moreover, recent analyses have proposed other licensing configurations for these NPIs.

4.2.2 NPI analyses in Arabic

The dependency between negation, functional categories, and post-verbal determiner and nominal NPIs in Arabic is also instantiated as a licensing requirement that the NPI be c-commanded by negation (Benmamoun 1996).

(27) a. *(lam)   ya?ti   ?aħadun/ ?ayyu ?aħadin   (SA)
          NEG.past come.3MSG.PFV one/   any   one
          'No one came.'

      b. *(ma)-?adʒaa-š   ħada/ ?ayy ħada   (JA)
          NEG-come.3MSG.PFV-NEG one/   any one
          'No one came.'

(28)

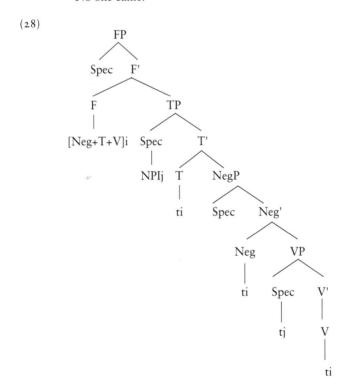

The NPIs in these examples function as subjects. Assuming a VP-internal subject position (Mohammad 1989; Fassi Fehri 1993), the subject NPIs are merged in Spec-VP, where they are within the c-command domain of the negative markers that occupy the head of NegP. Moreover, we assume that the verbal complex, including negation, moves to a functional projection above TP (Ouhalla 1994) where it continues to c-command the NPI even after it moves to Spec-TP to receive overt case assignment (Benammoun 1995a). Accordingly, the postverbal NPI in Spec-TP is c-commanded by the negative marker in FP. This means that the NPI can be licensed under c-command by negation.

   Assuming that NPIs can be licensed by being in a Spec-Head relationship with negation,[3] Benmamoun raises the question of why determiner and nominal NPIs in Arabic cannot precede negation. He suggests that this ungrammaticality can be reduced to a well-known general principle that bans nonspecific indefinite NPs from occurring preverbally (Ayyoub 1981; Mohammad 1989; Fassi Fehri 1993).

(29) a. ʤa   ši   wəld   (MA)
         come.3MSG.PFV   some boy
         'Some boy came.'

      b. ši   wəld   ʤa   (MA)
         some boy   come.3MSG.PFV
         'Some boy came.' (Benmamoun 1996: 62)

Determiner and nominal NPIs are inherently indefinite, nonspecific NPs. The derivation in (28) assumes that verb-initial sentences have a topicalized verb (in Focus projection here). One direct consequence for this analysis is that preverbal NPs must be analyzed as left dislocated elements. That is, given that the verb is in the CP layer already, whatever precedes it must be in a higher CP. This left dislocated position cannot be occupied by nonspecific indefinite NPs (including determiner and nominal NPIs), which drives the ungrammaticality of these elements in preverbal position.

   Recall, however, that nominal NPIs in SA can precede the verb (and negation) in subordinate clauses (cf. (31)a–c). It is possible to extend Benmamoun's analysis here. If the past tense negative marker is in T, then when the NPI subject moves to Spec-TP for case assignment it is in a position to be licensed by negation.

(30) ʔaðˤunnu [CP C ʔanna [TP ʔaħadan T lam [VP V yaʔti]]]

In Levantine Arabic, too, nominal NPIs can precede the verb/negation in subordinate clauses (Hoyt 2010: 250–251):

(31) a. leeš   ħada   ma-ʤaawab   ɣeer-i?   (LA)
         why   one   not-answer.3MSG.PFV other-my
         'Why didn't anyone answer other than me?'

      b. zaʕlaana   liyinnu   ħada ma-radd   (LA)
         angry.1fs.IPFV because   one   not-answer.3MSG.PFV
         ʕala   mawduuʕ-ik.
         upon   subject-your.2FSG
         'I am angry because anyone didn't respond to your thread.'

c. wa-batmanna   innu ħada ma-yizʕal   (LA)
and-desire.1FSG.IPFV that one   not-anger.3MSG.IPFV
min-ni
from-me
'. . .and I hope that anyone doesn't get angry at me.'

Hoyt's (2010) analysis distinguishes preverbal nominal NPIs in root clauses from those in subordinate clauses. In root clauses, these NPIs are interpreted as topical elements. Since topical elements must occupy a position in the CP layer, preverbal nominal NPIs in root clauses do not enter into a Spec-Head relation with negation and hence are ungrammatical. By contrast, preverbal nominal NPIs in subordinate clauses or following a question word have an existential rather than a topical interpretation and are therefore in an appropriate licensing configuration with negation.

So far the discussion has centered on the licensing of determiner and nominal NPIs. The research suggests that both c-command and Spec-Head configuration are available for licensing these NPIs. However, we do not yet have a clear answer concerning the possibility of satisfying the licensing requirement covertly at LF. To answer this question, we need to look at the licensing of idiomatic NPIs which can precede or follow the verb/negation:

(32) a. ʔaħmad   ma-waffar   girš/fils ʔiħmar   (JA)
Ahmad   NEG-save.3MSG.PFV penny/red cent
'Ahmad did not save a penny/red cent.'

b. girš/fils ʔiħmar   ʔaħmad   ma-waffar   (JA)
penny/red cent   Ahmad   NEG-save.3MSG.PFV
'Ahmad did not save a penny/red cent.'

It is obvious that the preverbal NPI here is not in a Spec-Head relation with negation, since the subject can intervene between the NPI and the negative marker. As such, the NPI must be interpreted as a left dislocated element occupying an XP position in the CP layer. Moreover, the preverbal NPI is not c-commanded by negation. How, then, is it licensed? Since overt licensing via c-command or the Spec-Head configuration is not possible, c-command at LF is the only possibility:

(33) [CP *girš/fils ʔiħmar* [TP ʔaħmad   T ma-waffar]]   (JA)

Another argument for covert licensing comes from the grammaticality of nominal NPIs embedded in focus-fronted CPs (Alsarayreh 2012: 133).

(34) ʔənnu Maryam ðarbat   ħada   *(ma)-basʕaddig.   (JA)
that   Mary   hit.3FSG.PFV one   NEG-believe.1SG.IPFV
'I do not believe that Mary hit anyone.'

The NPI here is not overtly c-commanded by negation, since it is embedded in the focus-fronted clause. The grammaticality of this construction can only be explained if c-command as a licensing condition obtains at LF. At LF, the focus-fronted clause reconstructs to its base-generated position as the complement of the verb:

(35) [CP [CP C ?ənnu Maryam ðarbat ħada]i [NegP NEG ma-basˤaddig [CPi]]

The last issue surrounding NPI licensing has to do with the NPI *ʕumr* 'ever.' This NPI tends to occur preverbally:

(36) ʕumr-o   *(ma) zaar   el-batra   (JA)
      NPI-ever-his NEG   visit.3MSG.PFV DEF-Petra
      'He has never visited Petra.'

The simplest analysis for this NPI is to assume that it is licensed in the Spec-Had relation with negation. However, this analysis is challenged by at least two empirical facts from MA (Benmamoun 2006) and JA, as shown below. First, the subject can intervene between the NPI and negation.

(37) ʕumr   ?aħmad *(ma) zaar   el-batra   (JA)
      NPI-ever Ahmad   NEG   visit.3MSG.PFV DEF-Petra
      'He has never visited Petra.'

Second, the NPI exhibits head-like properties. It can host clitics below and can assign genitive or accusative case to the clitic pronoun (cf. examples a–b below).

(38) a. ʕumr-i   *(ma) zurt   el-batra   (JA)
          NPI-ever-my NEG   visit.1SG.PFV DEF-Petra
          'I have never visited Petra.'

      b. ʕumr-ni   *(ma) zurt   el-batra   (JA)
          NPI-ever-me NEG   visit.1SG.PFV DEF-Petra
          'I have never visited Petra.'

Benmamoun convincingly argues against the possibility that this NPI may be licensed by covert movement of the negative marker. The proposal that the negative marker can covertly raise to a position c-commanding the NPI incorrectly predicts that the negative head can license the NPI *ʕumr* even when the auxiliary *kaan* 'be' separates the NPI from negation. Consider the MA contrasts illustrated in (39):

(39) a. Ɛəmmər-u   ma-kan   taybɣi   nadya   (MA)
        never-him   NEG-be.PFV   love.3MSG.PFV Nadia
        'He never loved Nadia.'

     b. *Ɛəmmər-u   kan   ma-taybɣi   nadya   (MA)
        never-him   be.PFV   NEG-love.3MSG.PFV Nadia

Benmamoun (2006) analyzes this NPI as the head of a clausal projection, XP, in Moroccan Arabic.

(40)

XP
X   NegP
Ɛəmmər

Building on the idea that the head-complement relation between T and VP is a checking configuration in English (Bobaljik and Thráinsson 1998), as well as the observation that the head-complement configuration satisfies categorical selection (e.g., V may select DP or PP), Benmamoun proposes that the head-complement relation between the NPI and negation in (40) is a licensing configuration in MA.

4.2.3 *Adverbial and determiner NPIs in Jordanian and Qatari*

One intriguing property of bipartite negation is the absence of the enclitic negative marker -š in the context of NSIs. This property is reported in the literature as a phenomenon of complementary distribution between the relevant NSIs and the enclitic marker. Consider the following examples where the enclitic negative marker -š cannot co-occur with the MA NSI from Benmamoun (2006) and EA NSIs from Soltan (2012):

(41) a. nadya   Ɛəmmər-ha   ma-ʒat(*-š)   (MA)
        Nadia   never-her   NEG-come.3FSG.PFV(*-NEG)
        'Nadia never came.'

     b. ma-dʒa(*-š)   ħətta waħəd   (MA)
        NEG-come.3MSG.PFV(*-NEG)   even one
        'No one came.'

(42) a. Ɛumr-i   maa-saafirt(*-iš)   Masr   (EA)
        NPI-ever-me   NEG-travel.1SG.PFV-NEG   Egypt
        'I have never traveled to Egypt.'

b. maa-saafirt-iš   Masr   ʕumr-ii   (EA)
   NEG-travel.1SG.PFV-NEG   Egypt   ever-me
   'I have never traveled to Egypt.'

c. ma-zaar-iš   ʕumr-o   el-batra   (JA)
   NEG-visit.3MSG.PFV-NEG   NPI-ever-his   DEF-Petra
   'He has never visited Petra.'

It is important to question whether these NSIs are in complementary distribution with enclitic negation, that is to say, whether the enclitic negative marker disappears in this context. The multi-locus analysis offers an interesting explanation to this phenomenon. It is now possible to explain the lack of the enclitic negative marker when the NPI is preverbal by recasting this as an epiphenomenon of the availability of two negatives (cf. Alqassas 2015). Arabic exhibits two different negatives: a single negation marker and a bipartite negation marker. These negative markers differ in their syntactic position. Single negation occurs above TP and bipartite negation occurs below TP. To see how this works, let us take the NPI ʕumr in preverbal position in JA as an example. This NPI cannot co-occur with enclitic negation. It also tends to occur at the left periphery of the sentence, preceding the verb and the preverbal subject:

(43) ʕumr   ʔaħmad   ma   saafar   bi-l-qitˤaar   (JA)
    NPI-ever   Ahmad   NEG   travel.3MSG.PFV   by-DEF-train
    'Ahmad never traveled by train.'

If this NPI can only be licensed in Spec/NegP or under c-command, and if bipartite negation is below TP, it follows that bipartite negation cannot license this NPI. Being above TP, single negation, however, can license the NPI. Evidence in favor of locating single negation in this context above TP can be seen in the example below, where an adverb intervenes between single negation and the verb:

(44) ʕumr   ʔaħmad   maa   b-yoom   saafar   bi-l-qitˤaar   (JA)
    NPI-ever   Ahmad   NEG   in-day   travel.3MSG.PFV   by-DEF-train
    'Ahmad never traveled by train on any day.'

I argue that the higher negative can license the adverbial NPIs that are merged above TP while the lower negative cannot do so because it is too low in the structure (below TP) for the NPI to be licensed in the specifier of NegP (cf. Alqassas 2015 for JA).

(45) a. ʕumr-o   maa zaar   el-batra   (JA)
          NPI-ever-his   NEG visit.3MSG.PFV   DEF-Petra
          'He has never visited Petra.'

      b. *ʕumr-o   ma-zaar-iš   el-batra   (JA)
          NPI-ever-his   NEG-visit.3MSG.PFV-NEG   DEF-Petra
          'He has never visited Petra.'

      c. maa gad   fi-sˤsˤaf   ʔaħmad kallam-a   (QA)
          NEG ever in class   Ahmad   talk.3MSG.PFV-him
          'Ahmad has never talked to him in class.'

      d. *gad   fi-sˤsˤaf   ʔaħmad maa kallam-a   (QA)
          ever   in class   Ahmad   NEG talk.3MSG.PFV-him

The validity of this type of analysis is supported by the fact that the
NPI ʕumr in posterbal position can in fact co-occur with bipartite negation in both EA in (42)b and JA in (42)c. Given that this NPI can occur
in postverbal position, and given that bipartite negation c-commands
this postverbal NPI, it follows that bipartite negation can co-occur with
this NPI.

The ability of the higher negative to license NPIs is also attested
with adverbs that express categorical negation such as *gad* 'never.' Here
we also find that the adverb can intervene between negation and the
verb.

(46) a. maa gad   fi-sˤsˤaf   kallamt-a   (QA)
          NEG ever in class   talk.1SG.PFV-him
          'I've never talked to him in class.'

      b. *maa fi-sˤsˤaf   kallamt-a   (QA)
          NEG   in class   talk.1SG.PFV-him

      c. mub   fi-sˤsˤaf   kallamt-a   (QA)
          NEG   in class   talk.1SG.PFV-him
          'I did not talk to him in class.'

Recall that there are arguments for analyzing the status of temporal NPIs
such as *ʕumr/ʕammər* 'ever' and *baʕd/bagi* 'yet' as heads, but it remains
unclear whether they are clausal heads or phrasal heads. Consider the
following example from JA, where the NPI *ʕumr* can be followed by a
dislocated object in (47)a or by a relative clause in (47)b:

(47) a. ʕumr   l-walad   maa ħabbat-o   bint   (JA)
          NPI-ever DEF-boy   NEG love.3FSG.PFV-him girl
          'A girl never loved the boy.'

b. ʕumr   ʔilli   budrus   maa   bursub   (JA)
    NPI-never who   study.3MSG.IPFV   NEG   fail.3MSG.IPFV
    'He who studies never fails.'

If the NPI is a clausal head in a projection above NegP, and if this NPI must be followed by NegP for licensing under the head-complement configuration (Benmamoun 2006), it follows that the NPI cannot be licensed, since the object *l-walad* and the relative clause *ʔilli budrus* already serve as complements for the NPI. Thus, the NPI projection cannot select NegP as a complement. See the illustration below:

(48) a. [XP X ʕumr [DP *l-walad*   [NegP *ma* . . .]]]
      b. [XP X ʕumr [CP *ʔilli budrus* [NegP *ma* . . .]]]

A solution to this problem is to assume that the NPI is a phrasal head that is licensed in Spec/NegP and selects either the object or the relative clause as a complement. Refer to the illustration below:

(49) a. [NegP [XP [X ʕumr] [DP *l-walad*] [NEG *ma* . . .]]]
      b. [NegP [XP [X ʕumr] [CP *ʔilli   budrus*] [NEG *ma* . . .]]]

This analysis is developed and argued for in Alqassas (2016). Future research on this NPI in other Arabic dialects can lead us to a better understanding of the syntax of such items.

(50)

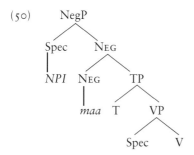

Recall that there is another type of negation in which the negative marker can precede the subject, referred to in this book as 'cleft negation' exemplified by the phrase 'Isn't it the case that . . . .'

(51) a. ʔinta   miš/mub   ʕaarif   al-dʒawaab?   (JA/QA)
          you   NEG   knowing   DEF-answer
          'You don't know the answer?'

b. miš/mub int   ʕaarif   al-dʒawaab!   (JA/QA)
    NEG   you   knowing   DEF-answer
    'Don't you know the answer!'/'Isn't it the case that you know the
    answer!'
    (speaker presupposes that addressee knows the answer)

There is evidence that the negative marker here is above TP but not in a
NegP on top of TP. This negative cannot license NPIs:

(52) a. ʔinta miš/mub ʕaarif   ʔayya   ħal   (JA/QA)
          you   NEG   knowing   NPI-any   solution
          'You don't not know any solution.'

      b. * miš/mub int   ʕarif   ʔayya   ħal!   (JA/QA)
          NEG   you   knowing   NPI-any   solution

      c. miš/mub int   mub   ʕaarif   al-dʒawaab!   (JA/QA)
          NEG   you   NEG   knowing   DEF-answer
          'Isn't it the case that you don't know the answer!'
          (speaker presupposes that addressee doesn't know the answer)

This is consistent with the analysis that *mub* is not in a NegP projection
co-commanding the NPI.

Where, then, is it located in the syntactic structure?

Presumably, it is buried in the CP domain (in a Focus projection) where
it does not c-command the NPI. The negative marker here would form a
constituent with the pronoun *inta* (constituent negation).

(53)   *[CP miš/mub inta C [TP T [AP ʕarif   ʔayya   ħal

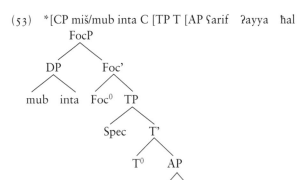

4.2.4 *Standard Arabic* maa *and NPI licensing*

The negative marker *maa* in SA can license the NPI *ʔaħad-an* in (54)a
where negation scopes over the whole proposition, but it cannot do so

in (54)b where negation precedes the fronted adverb and scopes over the focused adverb *l-baariħata*:

(54) a. maa   qaabaltu   ʔaħad-an   (SA)
          NEG   meet.1SG.PFV   one-ACC
          'I have not met anyone.'

      b. *maa   l-baariħata   qaabaltu   ʔaħadan   bal al-yawma (SA)
          NEG   DEF-yesterday meet.1SG.PFV   one-ACC   but DEF-today
          '*It was not yesterday that I met anyone, but today.'

Moreover, a clitic left dislocated NP cannot follow sentential negation *maa* (examples include an NPI to make sure that negation is sentential):

(55) a. maa   qaabala   ʔaħad-un   Zaydan   (SA)
          NEG   meet.3MSG.PFV   one-NOM   Zayd-ACC
          'No one has met Zayd.'
          [$_{NegP}$ *maa* [$_{TP}$ [$_{vP}$ qaabala ʔaħad-un   Zaydan

      b. *maa   Zayd-un   qaabala hu   ʔaħad-un   (SA)
          NEG   Zayd-NOM   meet.3MSG.PFV-him   one-NOM

This ungrammaticality is expected if *maa* is the head of a NegP on top of TP. The clitic left dislocated NP Zaydan cannot occupy a position between NegP and TP, hence it cannot intervene between *maa* and the verb. However, if *maa* is in the CP layer, there is nothing to prevent Zaydan from intervening between *maa* and the verb. Indeed, a clitic left dislocated NP can precede and follow contrastive focus *maa* (Moutaouakil 1991: 276–277).

(56) a. al-kitaab-u   maa   allaftu-hu   bal   sˁaħħaħtu-hu (SA)
          DEF-book-NOM   NEG   write.1SG.PFV-it   but   correct.1SG.PFV-it
          'I haven't written this book; I have only corrected it.'
          [$_{FP}$ al-kitaab-u [$_{FocusP}$ maa [$_{VP}$ allaftu-hu   bal   sˁaħħaħtu-hu

      b. maa   al-kitaab-u   allaftu-hu   bal   sˁaħħaħtu-hu (SA)
          NEG DEF-book-NOM   write.1SG.PFV-it   but   correct.1SG.PFV-it
          'I haven't written this book; I have only corrected it.'
          [$_{FocusP}$ maa [$_{FP}$ al-kitaab-u [$_{VP}$ allaftu-hu   bal   sˁaħħaħtu-hu

When it does not have a contrastive focus interpretation, *maa* is a sentential negative marker that can license NPIs. But when it has a contrastive focus interpretation, *maa* cannot license NPIs. Similar contrasts are in Moutaouakil (1991: 274–275):

(57) a. maa qaabaltu   ʔaħad-an   (SA)
         NEG meet.1SG.PFV   one-ACC
         'I have not met anyone.'

   b. *maa l-baariħata   qaabaltu   ʔaħadan bal al-yawma (SA)
       NEG   DEF-yesterday meet.1SG.PFV   one-ACC but DEF-today

   c. *maa qaabaltu   ʔaħadan l-baariħata   bal al-yawma (SA)
       NEG   meet.1SG.PFV one-ACC DEF-yesterday but DEF-today

Accordingly, the contrastively focused *maa* cannot license the NPI because it is buried inside the focused constituent *l-baariħata*, and hence fails to c-command the NPI. The ungrammaticality is reduced to failure to properly license the NPI via either of the two configurations: c-command and the Spec-Head configurations (cf. Benmamoun 1997, 2006; Alqassas 2015, 2016). The following is an illustration:

(58)

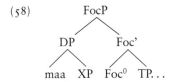

On the other hand, the non-contrastively focused *maa* is either under the head of the NegP or the head of a Focus projection (FocP) where it can c-command the NPI, hence the grammaticality. The following is an illustration:

(59)

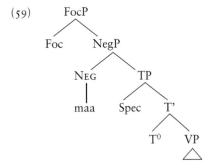

4.3 NCI licensing

Earlier syntactic analyses of NSIs, which treated NPIs and NCIs as a single class, introduced a range of theoretical licensing mechanisms in an attempt to consolidate the behavior of these two types of elements. The major syntactic accounts are the NPI approach, the NQ approach, and the lexical ambiguity approach. This section introduces these analyses for historical perspective. A more recent syntactic account of NCIs relies on syntactic agreement. This account will be introduced and discussed later.

4.3.1 *The NPI approach*

This approach treats NCIs as NPIs that do not contribute a negative reading to the sentence (Laka 1990; Ladusaw 1992). As such, NCIs are 'non-strict' NPIs which do not always require the presence of a sentential negative marker. These non-strict NPIs, such as preverbal nominal NPIs, are licensed by an 'empty negative morpheme' heading a functional projection ΣP; they move to a preverbal position (the specifier of ΣP) in order to identify this null negative morpheme preceding the verb (Spanish: Laka 1990: 107).

(60) a. *(No) vino   nadie.   (Spanish)
          not   came   anybody
          'Nobody came.'

      b. Nadie (*no)   vino.   (Spanish)
          nobody no   came
          'Nobody came.'

The challenge for this analysis is that preverbal (and prenegative) NCIs in some languages cannot be licensed by covert negation (Benmamoun 1997: 273):

(61) ħətta waħəd   *(ma)-dʒa   (MA)
      NCI   one   NEG-come.3MSG.PFV
      'No one came.'

In this MA example, we see that the NCI *ħətta waħəd* requires the negative marker when it is preverbal. If preverbal NCIs can be licensed by a covert negative operator, this account incorrectly predicts that the NCI can be licensed without the negative marker.

4.3.2 *The NQ approach*

An alternative approach treats NCIs as inherently negative universal quantifiers which must be licensed in the specifier of a NegP (a requirement known as the 'NEG-Criterion,' see Zanuttini 1991; Haegeman and Zanuttini 1996). This analysis essentially treats NCIs as negative operators. This approach is advantageous in that it can account for the ability of NCIs to occur without negation preverbally and to stand alone as negative fragment answers (since NCIs are inherently negative, there is no need for a negative marker). The only requirement for NCIs in this account is that they occur in a Spec-Head relation with Neg^0.

This analysis faces the challenge of explaining why the NCI, as an inherently negative element, still requires a negative marker when postverbal. Moreover, this analysis has to explain why the combination of the postverbal NCI and negative marker does not result in a double negation reading. To explain the co-occurrence of postverbal NCIs and the negative marker, Zanuttini (1991) proposes that postverbal NCIs cannot move to Spec/NegP at LF – a licensing requirement – because NegP is above TP, which acts as a barrier. When a negative marker heads the NegP, however, TP's barrierhood is circumvented. To account for the failure of the negative marker + NCI to yield a double negation reading, Haegeman and Zanuttini (1996: 139) posit an LF process called NEG-factorization:

(62) $[\forall x\neg][\neg] = [\forall x]\neg$

This process guarantees that the two instances of negation are interpreted as one single negation yielding a concord reading. However, this analysis does not explain why the negative marker cannot co-occur with preverbal NCIs (Zeijlstra 2004; Penka 2011).

4.3.3 *The lexical ambiguity approach*

This approach assumes that the asymmetry in the behavior of non-strict NCIs is due to the lexical ambiguity of these words (Herburger 2001). Postverbal NCIs require the negative marker because they are NPIs, whereas preverbal NCIs do not require the negative marker because they are NQs. In other words, this approach posits that NPIs and NQs are distinct but homophonous lexical items in non-strict NC languages. Herburger supports this analysis with data showing that a preverbal NCI can license a postverbal NCI without inducing a double negation reading (a phenomenon known as 'negative spread'). The following is an illustrative example from JA:

(63)   wala-ħada   štara   ʔayy ʔiši   (JA)
       NCI-one   buy.3MSG.PFV any thing
       'No one bought anything.'

The preverbal NCI in (29) functions as an NQ. It produces a sentential negation reading even though there is no negative marker in the sentence. The postverbal NCI, on the other hand, functions as an NPI, since it does not contribute a negative reading. If it did contribute a negative reading, the sentence would exhibit a double negation, which is not the case.

Proponents of this analysis must explain why the NPI-type NCI cannot be preverbal, while the NQ-type NCI cannot be postverbal. Herburger reduces these distributional constraints to independent principles for Spanish NCIs. Herberger argues that NPI-type NCIs cannot be preverbal because regular Spanish NPIs cannot be preverbal. Conversely, Herburger derives the postverbal position of NQ-type NCIs pragmatically, arguing that a preverbal NQ structure would assert the existence of an event without providing a theme. In fact, Herburger contends that such sentences are possible under the right conditions, as in the following example:

(64) temen   que   el bebe sen   aitista   se   pasa   (Spanish)
      fear   that   the baby is.SBJV autistic clitic spends
      el   timpo mirando at nada
      the   time   looking at nothing
      'They fear the baby is autistic. He spends his time looking at nothing.'

Herburger gives the following representation for this sentence:

(65) e [look(e) and Agent(baby,e) and [thing(x) and Theme(x,e)]]

This analysis faces several challenges. First, regular NPIs can be licensed in interrogative and conditional environments. If postverbal NCIs were indeed NPIs we would incorrectly predict that they, too, should be able to be licensed in non-negative contexts such as interrogative and conditional sentences. Second, if preverbal NCIs were NQs we would incorrectly predict that the MA NCI *hatta*-phrases in preverbal position should not require the negative marker.

4.3.4 NCI analyses in Arabic

As with NPIs, the syntactic dependency between NCIs and negation can be established by licensing relations via structural configurations such as c-command and Spec-Head relations (Benmamoun 1996, 1997, 2006; Ouali and Soltan 2014).

The syntactic dependency between determiner NCIs and negation in MA is instantiated as a requirement for determiner NCIs to be c-commanded by negation when postverbal and to exist in a Spec-Head relationship with negation when preverbal (Benmamoun 1997). The NCI *hetta* in MA must co-occur with negation when postverbal. Benmamoun (1996, 1997) argues that the NCI, similar to the NPI ḥada, is licensed by negation under c-command.

(66) *(ma)-dʒa   hatta wəld   (MA)
      NEG-come.3MSG.PFV   NCI boy
      *'Any boy didn't come.' (Benmamoun 1996: 49)

As with the NPI subject in (28), the NCI in (66) is the subject of the sentence. It is merged in Spec-VP and moves to Spec-TP. The negative marker is the head of a NegP projection on top of VP. The verb moves to the negative head, forms a complex V+NEG, and they both move through T and land in a functional projection above TP, placing negation in a position c-commanding the NCI subject in Spec-TP.

(67)

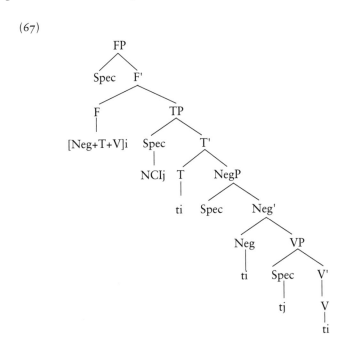

As for the preverbal NCI *ħatta waħad* in MA, Benmamoun argues that it is licensed under a Spec-Head relationship with negation.

(68) ħətta   waħəd   ma-dʒa   (MA)
      even   one   NEG-come.3MSG.PFV
      *'Anyone didn't come.' (Benmamoun 1997: 273)

Unlike the postverbal NCI *wala hada*, the preverbal NCI is not c-commanded by negation. Negation is in T, and the NPI is above it in Spec-TP. How, then, can negation license the NCI? If the Spec-Head configuration is sufficient to license NCIs in MA, and if the NCI subject is in Spec-TP, the complex head [verb+negation] occupying T should license the NCI. Benmamoun argues for this analysis, giving evidence from the contrast below (Benmamoun 1997: 281):

(69) a. ħətta ktab   ma-qrat-u   səlwa   (MA)
          even book   NEG-read.3FSG.PFV-it   Salwa
          'Salwa didn't read any book.'

      b. * ħətta ktab   səlwa   ma-qrat-u   (MA)
          even book   alwa   NEG-read.3FSG.PFV-it
          'Any book, Salwa did not read it.'

In both examples, the NCI is an NP dislocated from the VP-internal object position. However only the second example, where the subject intervenes between the dislocated NCI and negation, is ungrammatical. In a language like MA, where dislocated objects are grammatical, we expect both examples in (69) to be licit, on a PAR with the following dislocated NP objects:

(70) lə-ktab   (səlwa)   ma-qrat-u   (səlwa)   (MA)
      DEF-book   Salwa   NEG-read.3FSG.PFV-it   Salwa
      'Salwa didn't read any book.'

Nonetheless, there is an argument for LF licensing in JA. The so-called 'never-words' in JA, which are adverbial NCIs, can be focus-fronted. Alsarayreh (2012) argues that these words are licensed at LF under c-command by negation.

(71) a. ʔaħmad   ma-biħibb-iš   l-tˤayyarah   (JA)
          Ahmad   NEG-like.3MSG.IPFV-NEG   DEF-plane
          ʔabadan/bilmarrah
          ever/ at all
          'Ahmad doesn't like planes at all.'

      b. ʔabadan/bilmarrah   ʔaħmad   ma-biħibb-iš   (JA)
          ever/   at all   Ahmad   NEG-like.3MSG.IPFV-NEG
          l-tˤayyarah
          DEF-plane
          'Ahmad doesn't like planes at all.'

These examples show that the NPI can be focus-fronted to a position above the subject. Clearly, this element is not c-commanded by negation overtly, but is also not in a Spec-Head relation with negation. The preverbal subject may be in Spec-TP or in Spec-CP, but either way, the adverbial NCI cannot occupy Spec-TP (where it could enter into a Spec-Head relationship with negation). For these reasons, Alsarayreh argues that these NCIs are licensed at LF by reconstruction to their postverbal position where they are c-commanded by negation.

So far, this section has shown that the current contributions to NCI licensing converge on the conclusion that NCIs from different lexical categories are licensed at different levels of representation. Determiner NCIs, for instance, cannot be licensed covertly, while adverbial NCIs can.

In addition to the question of overt/covert licensing, the syntactic configuration for NCI licensing is also at issue. Recall Benmamoun's (1997) conclusion that both c-command and the Spec-Head relation are valid licensing configurations between NCIs and negation in MA. In addition to these possibilities, the behavior of the NCI *bagi* 'yet' in MA (and the NPI *ʕammər* in MA) led Benmamoun (2006) to propose a third licensing configuration: the head-complement configuration. To see how this possibility unfolds, let us first look at the distribution of the NCI *bagi* relative to negation. As with the NPI *ʕammər* in MA, *bagi* 'yet' displays head-like properties, it carries subject-agreement, as in (72), and permits the intervention of the subject between itself and negation, as in (73).

(72) a. nadya   baq-a   ma-ʒat   (MA)
         Nadia   yet-FSG   NEG-come.3FSG.PFV
         'Nadia hasn't come yet.'

     b. lə-wlad   baq-yin   ma-ʒaw   (MA)
         DEF-children   yet-PL   NEG-come.3MPL.PFV
         'The children haven't come yet.'

(73) baqi   ʕumar   ma-ʒa   (MA)
     yet   Omar   NEG-come.3MSG.PFV
     'Omar hasn't come yet.'

The task here is to determine the precise syntactic configuration under which this NCI is licensed. First, covert licensing of *bagi* is ruled out because of the incorrect prediction it makes (cf. (39)). Covert licensing via reconstruction of this NCI to a position c-commanded by negation is also presumably not possible, since there is no evidence that this NCI was ever postverbal (and hence in the c-command domain of negation) in the first place. Covert licensing under c-command is also ruled out, since this NCI is not c-commanded by negation, and overt licensing in Spec/NegP is challenged by the fact that the subject can intervene between the NCI and negation. Accordingly, Benmamoun proposes that *bagi*, similar to the NPI *ʕammər*, is licensed via the head-complement relation. He analyzes the NCI as a head that selects NegP as its complement. Consistent with the analysis of the NPI *ʕumr* in JA in (Alqassas 2015, 2016), I analyze the NCI *baʕd* as an adverb that heads its own phrase but it does not project a clausal projection.

The NCI *baʕd* in JA, the NCI equivalent of the MA *bagi*, can occur postverbally. Therefore, it is possible to argue that this NCI is licensed under reconstruction to a postverbal position c-commanded by negation (Alqassas 2015, 2016). Under such an analysis, the licensing of this NCI in JA would pattern with the adverbial NCIs in JA. Alternatively, it is possible to argue that this NCI always originates in a postverbal position, where it is licensed by negation under c-command, while its surface preverbal position is the result of subsequent movement (Alqassas 2015). In this case, licensing of *baʕd* in JA would resemble NPI licensing in Hindi.

(74)   a.   ma-saafar-iš   baʕdo   (JA)
            NEG-travel.3MSG.PFV-NEG   yet-him
            'He hasn't traveled yet.'

       b.   baʕd-o   ma-saafar-iš   (JA)
            yet-him   NEG-travel.3MSG.PFV-NEG
            'He hasn't traveled ye+t.'

Level of representation and licensing configuration are not the only points of interest in NCI licensing. Another issue concerns the contrast between preverbal determiner NCIs in JA, which cannot co-occur with negation as in (75), and the equivalent elements in MA, which must co-occur with negation as seen in (76). Additionally, it remains unclear how these preverbal NCIs in JA are licensed in the absence of an overt licenser like negation.

(75)   a.   *(ma)-ʔadʒa   wala-ħada   (JA)
            NEG-come.3MSG.PFV   NCI-one
            'No one came.'

       b.   wala-ħada   (*ma)-ʔadʒa   (JA)
            NCI-one   NEG-come.3MSG.PFV
            'No one came.'

       c.   *(maa)-saafar   wala-waaħad   (QA)
            NEG-travel.3MSG.PFV   NCI-one
            'No one traveled.'

       d.   wala-waaħad   (*maa)-saafar   (QA)
            NCI-one   NEG-travel.3MSG.PFV
            'No one traveled.'

(76)   a.   *(ma)-dʒa   ħatta   wəld   (MA)
            NEG-come.3MSG.PFV   NCI   one
            'Anyone didn't come.' (Benmamoun 1996: 49)

       b.   ħatta waħəd   *(ma)-dʒa   (MA)
            NCI one   NEG-come.3MSG.PFV
            'Anyone didn't come.' (Benmamoun 1997: 273)

The issue here is how the preverbal NCI gets licensed in the absence of the negative marker. This NCI is treated as a lexically ambiguous expression in Egyptian (Ouali and Soltan 2014) and Palestinian Arabic (Hoyt 2005a), in other words as two homophonous words in the lexicon. The postverbal homophone is an NCI, while the preverbal one is a negative quantifier. Ouali and Soltan (2014) develop a lexical ambiguity analysis within a syntactic agreement approach to NC along the line of Zeijlstra (2004, 2008). The NCI carries a formal feature [uNeg] that it checks against the formal feature [iNeg] carried by the negative marker. This licensing relation takes place via the syntactic operation Agree. Ouali and Soltan adopt a generalized version of Baker's (2008) Agree:

(77)   A functional head F agrees with XP, XP a maximal projection, only if
    (i)   F c-commands XP (the c-command condition).
    (ii) There is no XP such that F c-commands YP, YP c-commands XP and YP has phi-features (the locality condition).
    (iii) F and XP are contained in all the same phases (e.g., full CP) (the phase condition).
    (iv) XP is made active for agreement by having an unchecked formal feature (the activity condition).

Following Zeijlstra's (2008) analysis of Negative Concord (NC) as a syntactic agreement phenomenon, they propose that the NCI enters the derivation specified for an uninterpretable negation feature [uNeg] that seeks agreement with an interpretable negation feature [iNeg]; this Agree relation is necessary in order for licensing to take place and the derivation to converge at LF. Consider the derivations below for example (76)a:

(78)   [NEG$_{[iNeg]}$ *(ma)-dʒa   [NCI$_{[uNeg]}$ ħətta wəld]]
         |_____ Agree _____|

This analysis explains how the presence of two negative expressions in the same phrase fails to produce a double negation reading. The NCI has a formal, rather than a semantic, negation feature that does not contribute a negative interpretation at LF. This account also explains the syntactic dependency between the NCI and negation.

The syntactic agreement approach provides no direct explanation for why a preverbal NCI in a language like JA cannot co-occur with the negative marker. To account for such cases, Zeijlstra postulates the existence of an abstract negative operator $Op_\neg$ that carries an interpretable negation feature [iNeg] and occupies the Spec/NegP position. Below is the derivation for the JA example in (75)b above:

(79)   [NegP *Op¬*$_{[iNeg]}$ [FP NCI$_{[uNeg]}$ wala-ħada   [TP T (*ma$_{[iNeg]}$)-ʔadʒa]]]

The abstract negative operator licenses the NCI. The presence of a negative marker makes an NC reading impossible. However, this analysis is challenged by the preverbal and postverbal NCIs in MA, which require the presence of a negative marker, as in (76) above.

Zeijlstra suggests that the negative markers in such a language always carry an uninterpretable negation feature [uNeg], hence the need for an abstract negative operator to license both the negative marker and the NCI. The derivations for preverbal and postverbal NCIs in MA under Zeijlstra's system are shown in (80)a and (80)b, respectively.

(80)   a.   [NegP *Op¬*$_{[iNeg]}$ [NCI$_{[uNeg]}$ ħətta waħəd   [NEG$_{[uNeg]}$ *(ma)-dʒa]]]
       b.   [NegP *Op¬*$_{[iNeg]}$ [NEG$_{[uNeg]}$ *(ma)-dʒa [NCI$_{[uNeg]}$ ħətta waħəd   ]]]

The negative operator here is required in order to license the negative marker and the NCI, since both carry uninterpretable negation features [uNeg]. The parametric difference under this system is that the negative marker carries an uninterpretable negation feature [uNeg] in strict NC languages like MA, but an interpretable one [iNeg] in non-strict NC languages like JA.

Ouali and Soltan (2014) depart from this idea, proposing instead that the negative marker always carries an [iNeg], and that the parametric difference between Egyptian Arabic (EA) (which is similar to JA) and MA lies in the feature specification of the NCI. The NCI in a strict NC language like MA is always specified for with a [uNeg] feature. This feature, in turn, is licensed by the negative marker, which carries the [iNeg] feature. The NCI in non-strict NC languages like EA and JA, on the other hand, enters the derivation underspecified for the [NEG] feature. Since the [iNeg] feature is more economical (inasmuch as it does not require licensing), the NCI is assigned the [iNeg] feature in the preverbal position. Therefore, an NC reading is impossible when the negative marker co-occurs with the preverbal NCI in JA. Below is the derivation for (75)b:

(81)   [FP wala-ħada$_{[iNeg]}$ [TP [*v*P ʔadʒa]]]

However, under Ouali and Soltan's (2014) system, the NCI must be assigned the [uNeg] feature in postverbal position in a language like JA, because the negative marker, which carries [iNeg], is required for negation to scope over the TP.[4] A sentence which contains both a postverbal NCI specified for [iNeg] and a negative marker (which always carries [iNeg]) cannot have an NC reading. The following is the derivation for (75)a:

(82)   [NegP NEG$_{[iNeg]}$ ma [*v*P ʔadʒa   wala-ħada$_{[uNeg]}$]]

There is evidence in JA, however, that even the preverbal *wala* fails to contribute a negative interpretation when preceded by a negative constituent (Alqassas 2015: 125):

(83)   maʕumrhuuš$_{[iNEG]}$ wala-ħada$_{[uNEG]}$ zaar   el-batra   (JA)
       never   NCI-person   visit.3MSG.PFV   DEF-Petra
       'Never has anyone visited Petra.'

Under the multi-locus analysis developed in this monograph, it is possible to explain the behavior of the NCI wala-NP. If this NCI always carries a [uNeg] feature, an element that carries an [iNeg] feature can license it. When the NCI is postverbal, this element is the negative marker. When the NCI is preverbal, a negative compound like *maʕumrhuuš* 'never' is also expected to license it since it c-commands it, yielding a concordant reading (cf. Alqassas 2015 for details). But when the NCI is preverbal and there is no negative expression preceding it, a last resort insertion of a covert negative operator can license the NCI.

The interesting question is why the negative marker cannot license the preverbal NCI, as evident from the fact that a negative marker does not co-occur with the preverbal NCI. Alqassas (2015) gives evidence that the NCI wala-NP in preverbal position is a constituent that is base generated in the left periphery of the clause (the CP layer). In other words, it is higher than the NegP that dominates TP. Consequently, negation neither c-commands it nor does it enter into a Spec-Head relation with it. Therefore, the NCI must be licensed by a covert negative operator. The following is an example and its derivation for illustration:

(84)   a.   wala-ħada   zaar   el-batra   (JA)
            NCI-person   visit.3MSG.PFV   DEF-Petra
            'No one has not visited Petra.' (= Everyone visisted Petra.)

       b.   [NegP *Op*¬$_{[iNeg]}$ [wala-ħada$_{[uNEG]}$ zaar   el-batra

If this analysis is on the right track, we predict the following. If the preverbal NCI wala-NP co-occurs with a negative marker or negative compound that is lower than the NCI, the result should be a double negation reading. This prediction is borne out below:

(85)   a.   wala-ħada $_{[uNEG]}$ maa$_{[iNEG]}$ zaar   el-batra   (JA)
            NCI-person   NEG   visit.3MSG.PFV   DEF-Petra
            'No one has not visited Petra.' (= Everyone visisted Petra.)

       b.   wala-ħada $_{[uNEG]}$ maʕumrhuuš$_{[iNEG]}$ zaar   el-batra (JA)
            NCI-person   never   visit.3MSG.PFV   DEF-Petra
            'No one has never visited Petra.' (= Everyone visisted Petra.)

This syntactic agreement analysis of NC is in line with recent analyses for the same phenomenon in European languages (cf. Penka 2011). The syntactic agreement analysis advocated here is based on the idea that a covert negative operator is a last resort mechanism available in the language to license NCIs that are located higher than TP in the syntactic structure. Such cases of NCI behavior and their analysis support the multi-locus analysis of negation. By allowing negation to project in multiple positions in the syntactic structure, it is possible to account for the distributional puzzles and negative readings (concordant versus double negation readings) of NCIs in relation to negative markers and negative compounds.

Notes

1. For a more detailed overview of NSIs in Arabic, see Alqassas 2018.
2. The English NPIs *anything* and *anyone* can be licensed in negative and non-negative polarity environments, including questions:

   (i) I can't see anything/anybody.
        Can you see anything/anybody?

   It is worth pointing out that *anything* and *anyone* can appear in non-polarity environments, as in:

   (ii) Children believe anything adults say.
        Children like anyone who is nice to them.

   These instances of *any* are not NPIs but free choice *any* (FC any) (cf. Dayal 2004).
3. This assumption is motivated by two observations. First, there is cross-linguistic evidence that NPIs can be licensed in Spec/NegP (Progovac 1993; Haegeman 1995). Second, the availability of the Spec-Head relationship as a licensing configuration for the Moroccan NCI *hetta*+NP motivates the assumption that this configuration is available for NPIs.
4. This is based on the assumption that semantic interpretation of negation requires taking scope over tense phrase (TP) (Zanuttini 1991; Ladusaw 1992), and on Herburger's (2001) pragmatic principle arguing against such structures.

5

Distribution of the negation strategies

5.1 Jordanian and Egyptian negative markers

This section explores the explanatory power of the multi-locus analysis of negation in accounting for the distributional contrasts between two negation strategies in Jordanian Arabic (JA) and Egyptian Arabic (EA). These two strategies are the use of the discontinuous marker *ma...š* and the non-discontinuous marker *miš*. I claim the distribution of these strategies follows from analyzing bipartite negation as a low negation occupying a position below TP. Following Benmamoun (2000), I assume that the discontinuous pattern is a result of predicate merger with negation in which the predicate undergoes head movement to the negative head for feature checking. I argue that this movement is tied to the person feature of the predicate, giving rise to discontinuous negation. I also depart from Benmamoun's (2000) idea that with non-discontinuous negation the subject NP fulfills the checking requirement of the negative head. Instead, I argue that a covert copular head fulfills the checking requirement as a last-resort mechanism when the predicate lacks the person feature.

(1) a. ma-ʕind-huu-š   sayyaara   (JA)
        NEG-have-him-NEG   car
        'He does not have a car.'

     b. es-sayyaara miš ʕind-o   (JA)
        DEF-car.fs   NEG have-him
        'The car is not with him.'

I also argue that EA does not have this checking requirement and that, aside from with perfective verbs, predicate merger with negation is an optional post-syntactic operation. Assuming that perfective verbs undergo V-to-T movement (Benmamoun 2000; Soltan 2007), the obligatory merger between perfective verbs and negation is due to minimality constraints. Specifically, the verb must move into the negation head on its way up to the tense head to avoid minimality violations. All other contexts in EA, unlike in JA, tolerate non-discontinuous negation (cf. with imperfective verbs, with fronted prepositional predicates).

(2) a. miš   ba-saafir   kətiir   (EA)
          NEG ASP-travel.1SG.IPFV   much
          'I do not travel much.' (Soltan 2011: 259)

     b. ? miš ʕand-ii   ʕarabiyyah   (EA)
          NEG at-me   car
          'I don't have a car.' (Soltan 2011: 259)

(3) a. *miš   ba-saafir   kθiir   (JA)
          NEG ASP-travel.1SG.IPFV   much
          'I do not travel much.'

     b. *miš   ʕind-o   sayyaara   (JA)
          NEG have-him   car

Further evidence supporting this analysis comes from the following contrasts between JA and EA:

(4) a. wallahi   ma-*(ani)   ʕaarif   (JA)
          by God   NEG-*(COP) know.AP
          'By God, I don't know.'

     b. wallahi   ma-(ana)   ʕaarif   (EA)
          by God   NEG-(COP) know.AP
          'By God, I don't know.'

The fact that the copular pronoun is required in JA but not in Cairene Egyptian Arabic (CEA) is crucial. This will be analyzed in this chapter as a difference in the feature structure of negation in JA and CEA. This chapter puts forward an analysis along the lines of Benmamoun (2000) but revised in light of the new data from JA and CEA, suggesting that negation in JA has a checking requirement while in EA it does not.

This section will focus primarily on bipartite sentential negation, which involves the use of the proclitic *ma-* and the enclitic -*š* (see (5) below) in JA as well as in two dialects of EA, namely CEA and Sharqeyyah Egyptian Arabic. The greater part of this section will focus on JA since bipartite negation in JA can be realized in a number of ways, including discontinuous negation (see (5) below), independent negation (see (11) below), and enclitic negation (see (10) below); and because many of the distributional facts regarding the negative markers in JA are shared by the dialects of EA. Thus the JA facts suffice as the empirical basis for the theoretical analyses presented here. Moreover, the JA data are a contribution that broadens the empirical basis for analyzing the syntax of negation in Arabic as a whole.

Analyses of negation, both cross-linguistically and in Arabic specifically, consider the interaction of negative markers with the head movement of a verb, the locus of negation in the hierarchical structure, and the syntactic status of negative markers. In Arabic, the distribution of two patterns of bipartite negation (discontinuous and independent negation) overlap within the same dialect and across dialects. To explain their distribution, there is a syntactic account that reduces the distributional contrasts in Arabic to syntactic head movement with the locus of negation below TP (Benmamoun 2000; Aoun et al. 2010). Another analysis puts forward a morphological account that reduces it to morphological head movement with the locus of negation above TP (Soltan 2011). The syntactic account depends on categorical features to drive head movement of the verb to negation. This presents the empirical challenge of explaining, for example, why movement is optional in CEA imperfective verbs but obligatory in JA imperfective verbs. The solution is generally to assume that a categorical feature can be either strong or weak within the same context in one dialect in a way that differs from another dialect, but this kind of explanation significantly weakens the explanatory power of the analysis.

With respect to the morphological analysis, a challenge arises on somewhat similar grounds. The morphological analysis cannot explain why the morphological merger with negation is optional for CEA imperfective verb forms but obligatory for CEA perfective verb forms as well as JA imperfective and perfective verb forms. Formulating morphological rules for these empirical facts will result in rather stipulative and idiosyncratic rules that lack explanatory power. I argue instead for a hybrid analysis that builds on both of these analyses. Significantly, I claim obligatory merger is syntactic while optional merger is morphological.

As for the head status of the negative markers, the proclitic has been analyzed as a head of the negative projection, but the analysis of the enclitic is controversial. One analysis treats it as a specifier of NegP (Ouhalla 1993), another as a head in the negative projection (Benmamoun 2000; Aoun et al. 2010), and a third treats the enclitic as a head in a separate projection (Hoyt 2007; Soltan 2011). To address this, I first revisit the status of the enclitic negative marker -*š* in JA. As a dialect that allows the enclitic to appear without the proclitic in certain contexts, for example with imperative verbs and imperfective verbs carrying the aspectual prefix *ba*-, JA has been reported as a dialect in which the enclitic can be a source of negative force. This provides evidence supporting the argument that analyzes it as part of the negative projection (Aoun et al. 2010). Based on empirical facts from JA, I claim enclitic negation involves phonological deletion of *ma* when negating a labial-initial predicate. I provide empirical and theoretical arguments against analyzing enclitic negation as an adverb or a head of NegP. Instead, I argue in favor of analyzing it as a head of a separate projection distinct from the negative projection. I refer to this separate projection as the negative agreement projection AgrPolP.

I first introduce facts regarding various forms of negation in the dialects. Discontinuous negation in JA, enclitic (-*š* by itself) negation in JA, independent negation in JA, and both patterns of negation in EA are discussed in the following section. I then explain previous analyses of *ma* and -*š* in Arabic, and revisit one previous analysis of -*š* and argue against analyzing it as Spec/NegP or a NEG head. Instead I propose to analyze it as the head of an agreement projection (AgrPolP) selected by the NegP projection. The analysis I develop in this chapter explains the distribution of discontinuous and independent negation in JA. This chapter also discusses the theoretical implications of the analysis.

5.1.1 *Discontinuous negation* ma. . .-š *and* la. . .-š *in JA*

In many Arabic dialects, including JA and EA, sentential negation consists of two negative elements which appear as a discontinuous morpheme, as in examples (5)a–b.[1] The first element is *ma*, which usually appears as a proclitic on the verb as in (5).[2] The second element is -*š*, which shows up as an enclitic on the verb as in (5). Even when the verb carries a prefix like the aspectual particle *ba-* and/or a suffix as in subject agreement morphology or object clitics, the negative marker *ma* appears as the leftmost morpheme and -*š* appears as the rightmost morpheme, as in (5)b.

(5)   a.   *(ma)-ʔakal-iš   (JA)
            NEG-ate.3MSG.PFV-NEG
            'He did not eat.'

      b.   (ma)-b-aʕrif-humu-š   (JA)
            NEG-ASP-know.1SG.IPFV-them-NEG
            'I don't know them.'

In addition to negating perfective and imperfective verbs carrying the aspectual particle *ba-* (b-imperfect) in (5), the use of the discontinuous negation [*ma*. . .-*š*] can also be found in sentences that have subjunctive verbs (e.g., (6)), imperfective verbs not carrying aspectual *ba-*,[3] the pseudo-verbal predicate *badd* (8)a, possessive prepositions (8)b–d, the existential preposition *fi* (8)e, and copular pronouns (9). Therefore, one might conclude that this form of negation can negate all kinds of verbal predicates. However, the form of negation used for negative imperatives in JA is [*la*. . .-*š*] rather than [*ma*. . .-*š*].

(6) a. bafad⁽d⁽il   ?inn-ak   *(ma)-truuḥ-iš   (JA)
         prefer.1SG.IPFV   COMP-you   NEG-go.2MSG.IPFV.SBJV-NEG
         'I prefer that you don't go.'

     b. mišaan   *(ma)-truuḥ-iš   (JA)
         COMP   NEG-go.2MSG.IPFV.SBJV-NEG
         'So that you don't go.'

(7) a. kunt   *(ma)-tnaam-iš   (JA)
         COP   NEG-sleep.2MSG.IPFV.SBJV-NEG
         'You used not to sleep.'

     b. bageet   *(ma)-tnaam-iš   (JA)
         COP   NEG-sleep.2MSG.IPFV.SBJV-NEG
         'You used not to sleep.'

(8) a. ma-bad-naa-š   nruuḥ   (JA)
         NEG-want-1PL-NEG   go.1PL.IPFV.SBJV
         'We do not want to go.'

     b. ma-ʕinda-naa-š   sayyaara   (JA)
         NEG-have-us-NEG   car
         'We do not have a car.'

     c. ma-maʕ-naa-š   masʕaari   (JA)
         NEG- have-us-NEG   money
         'We do not have money.'

     d. ma-lee-naa-š   ?aʕdaa?   (JA)
         NEG-have-1PL-NEG   enemies
         'We do not have enemies.'

     e. ma-fii-naa-š   ḥeel   (JA)
         NEG- in-us-NEG   strength
         'We do not have the strength.'

(9) a. ?ani   m-anii-š   taʕbaan   (JA)
         I   NEG-I-NEG   tired
         'I am not tired.'

     b. la-truuḥ-iš   (JA)
         NEG-2.go.IMP-NEG
         'Don't go.'

5.1.2 *Enclitic negation: the negative marker -š in JA*

While the canonical form of negation uses the two elements *ma* and *-š*, the use of *-š* alone (without *ma* or *la*) is equally plausible in many grammatical environments. This use can be found when the negated predicate is a present tense verb (10)a, with the past tense copula *bageet* (10)b, with the pseudo-verbal predicate *badd* (10)c, *maʕ* (10)d, and *fi* (10)e, and the negative imperative verbs (10)f.

(10) a. b-aʕrif-iš   (JA)
             ASP-know.1SG.IPFV-NEG
             'I don't know.'

       b. wagtha   bageet-iš   aʕrif   (JA)
          at that time be.1SG.PFV-NEG know.1SG.PFV
          'Lit. At that time, I was not knowing.'

       c. bad-naa-š   nruuħ   (JA)
          want-1PL-NEG go.1PL.IPFV
          'We do not want to go.'

       d   maʕ-naa-š   masʕaai   (JA)
          have-us-NEG   money
          'We do not have money.'

       e. fii-naa-š   ħeel   (JA)
          in-us-NEG   strength
          'We do not have the strength.'

       f. truuħ-iš   (JA)
          go.2MSG.IMP-NEG
          'Don't go.'

5.1.3 *Independent negation: the negative marker* miš *in JA*

JA also has the independent negative marker *miš*. This negative marker appears in sentences with the future aspectual particle *rayeħ/raħ*, the progressive aspectual participle *gaaʕid*, and the verbless sentences that do not have a possessive reading, as in (11), (12), and (13) respectively:

(11) miš   rayeħ   ʔazuur   l-batra   (JA)
      NEG   FUT   visit.1MSG.IPFV DEF-Petra
      'I am not going to visit Petra.'

(12) miš   gaaʕid   b-amzaħ   (JA)
      NEG   PROG   ASP-joke.1MSG.IPFV
      'I am not joking.'

(13) ?ani   miš   zaʕlaan   (JA)
      I   NEG   upset.ms
      'I am not upset.'

5.1.4 *Negation in Egyptian*

Negation in EA does not allow use of the enclitic negative marker alone
without the proclitic. Therefore, this language will not be discussed when
analyzing this aspect of JA negation. In sentential negation, however, this
dialect has both negative markers as can be seen below:[4]

(14) a. maa-saafir-t-iš   (EA)
          NEG-travel.PFV-1SG-NEG
          'I did not travel.' (Soltan 2011: 257)

      b. maa-ba-saafir-š   kətiir   (EA)
          NEG-ASP-travel.1SG.IPFV-NEG   much
          'I don't travel much.' (Soltan 2011: 259)

Unlike in JA, independent negation is an option in CEA when negating
imperfective verb forms. Moreover, CEA differs from JA by allowing independent negation with prepositional predicates hosting a subject clitic:[5]

(15) a. miš   ba-saafir   kətiir   (EA)
          NEG   ASP-travel.1SG.IPFV   much
          'I do not travel much.' (Soltan 2011: 259)

      b. ? miš   ʕand-ii   ʕarabiyyah[6]   (EA)
          NEG   at-me   car
          'I don't have a car.' (Soltan 2011: 259)

Sharqeyyah, another Egyptian dialect, is different from all of these dialects in that it allows independent negation with perfective verb forms.
The below example is from Soltan (2011: 262):[7]

(16) ?anaa   miš   ləʕib-t   (Sharqeyyah)
      I   NEG   play.1SG.PFV
      'I did not play.'

5.1.5 *Previous analyses of bipartite negation in Arabic*

Bipartite negation in Arabic involves the use of the two negative markers
ma and *-š* as in (17). The negative marker *ma* has been analyzed as a head
of NegP lower than tense phrase (TP) in Ouhalla (1993), Bahloul (1996),
Benmamoun (2000), and Aoun et al. (2010). The main reason for analyzing

ma as a head of NegP is that while some dialects use both *ma* and *-š*, most dialects use *ma* by itself for sentential negation (Aoun et al. 2010).

(17) ma-b-aʕirf-iš   (JA)
      NEG-ASP-know.1SG.IPFV-NEG
      'I don't know.'

The status of *-š*, however, is debatable. One analysis treats it as an adverb similar to French *pas* (Ouhalla 1990, 1993), treating it as a specifier of NegP on a PAR with other analyses of *pas* in French (cf. Pollock 1989; Moritz and Valois 1994). Another analysis treats it as part of *ma*, such that *ma. . .-š* is a discontinuous morpheme (a circumfix) under Neg⁰ (Bahloul 1996; Benmamoun 2000; Aoun et al. 2010). Ouhalla proposes that *ma* is the head of negation and *-š* is its specifier, as illustrated in (18).

(18)

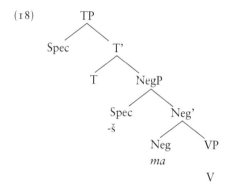

This second analysis derives the proclitic nature of *ma* by generating it in the head position of NegP below TP. This allows the verb to merge with it before moving to T, as illustrated in (19). Presumably, the enclitic nature of *-š*, on the other hand, is derived simply by cliticizing onto the complex *ma* +V.

(19)

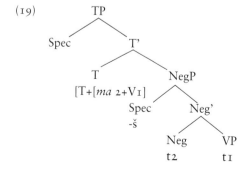

As pointed out by Aoun et al. (2010), the Spec-Head analysis captures the lack of a double negation reading which would be induced by an analysis where each head has a separate projection. However, Aoun et al. (2010) argue against the Spec-Head analysis and adopt Benmamoun's (2000) analysis, where both *ma* and *-š* are one discontinuous morpheme under the same Neg⁰ without having two separate projections for *ma* and *-š*, as in (20):

(20)

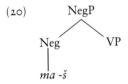

The following are their arguments against Ouhalla's analysis. First, since non-verbal predicates such as *zaʕlaan* in (21) do not move to the head of NegP, it is not clear why we do not get the incorrect word order [-š ^*ma*] under Ouhalla's analysis, in which -š should be linearized before *ma* since it is in Spec/NegP.

(21) ʔani miš zaʕlaan   (JA)
      I   NEG upset
      'I am not upset.'

Second, the fact that *ma* and *-š* appear as *miš* in constituent negation, as in (22)a, makes it plausible to analyze *ma* and *-š* as one morpheme under the head of NegP. Following Zanuttini (1991), it is assumed here that constituent negation does not project a NegP. Third, the negative marker -š can be used by itself for sentential negation in Jordanian Arabic, as in (22)b.

(22) a. miš   kull tˤ-tˤullaab   hoon   (JA)
          NEG   all   DEF-students here
          'Not all the students are here.'

      b. b-aʕirf-iš   (JA)
          ASP-know.1SG.IPFV-NEG
          'I don't know.'

Under this analysis, the obligatory discontinuous negation with perfective verbs can be reduced to the V-to-T movement of the perfective verb in a structure where, since NegP is between TP and VP, the verb must move to and merge with the negation head to avoid minimality violations.

Recall that negation circumscribes the imperfective verbs in JA as in (2)b but does not have to do so in CEA as in (2)a. Benmamoun (2000) accounts for this using feature checking and the availability of checking configurations as options for the dialects. According to this approach, negation has a [+D] EPP feature that can be checked either via head adjunction of the verb to negation or via the subject in Spec/NegP. For MA, the only option is head adjunction, but in EA the subject can check that feature. JA here patterns with MA.

This analysis can capture a wide range of negation facts in many dialects. Yet it is still not clear why only one checking configuration is available in certain environments but both configurations are available in other environments within the same dialect. Furthermore, it is not clear why only one configuration is available in a certain environment of a certain dialect while the two configurations are available in that same environment of a different dialect. I argue that a version of this feature checking analysis is necessary for developing an analysis that can predict the distribution of the two negation patterns within and across the dialects.

In addition to analyzing -š as an adverb in Spec/NegP and analyzing it as a head in NegP, there is an analysis that treats -š as a head in a separate projection (that head is the inflectional projection I^0 in Hoyt's 2007 analysis of Palestinian Arabic and Neg^0 in Soltan's 2011 of EA), while *ma* is the head of a negative projection on top of TP.[8]

Soltan 2011 proposes a split NegP analysis for bipartite negation in EA. The marker -š is analyzed as a separate head in a NegP projection while *ma* is a head of the negative projection PolP, the source of negative interpretation. Both functional projections of these negative markers are on top of TP, in line with the analysis of negation above TP in Diesing and Jelinek (1995). This analysis is expected to make possible the formulation of a morphological algorithm that can explain the distribution of independent and discontinuous negation in a wide range of contexts across the Arabic dialects.[9] Below is the algorithm:

(23)   a.   In contexts where NEG is adjacent to a hosting head *H*, *H* moves to NEG and then to Pol, and the circumfixal *maa-H-š* pattern arises.

       b.   Otherwise, NEG incorporates into Pol, giving rise to the *miš* pattern.

This analysis reduces all cases of discontinuous negation to the presence of a hosting head adjacent to -š. This head moves to -š and to *ma* at PF, presumably at the linear level. This analysis is predicated on three crucial assumptions. First, to derive the discontinuous negation entirely at PF, -š and *ma* must also be separate heads to allow the hosting head to merge with each negative marker from the right direction, specifically the left edge of -š and right edge of *ma-*. Second, both negative markers must be above TP to avoid head movement in cases of V-to-T movement of perfective verbs, and to avoid violating Head Movement Constraint in Sharqeyyah as in (24) and child language structures (where independent negation precedes the perfective verb) based on anecdotal and observational evidence from Egyptian children's speech (cf. Omar 1967). Finally, according to EA syntax, the negative markers must also be adjacent to a hosting head lower in the structure to block merger with participles and the marker of future aspect.

(24)　ʔanaa　miš　ləʕib-t　　　　　　　　　　　　　　　(Sharqeyyah)
　　　I　　　NEG　play.1SG.PFV
　　　'I did not play.' (Soltan 2011: 262)

It is not clear how the imperfective verb in EA has the option not to merge with -š at PF, given that, similar to the perfective verb, the imperfective verb is a suitable host and is adjacent to negation at the PF linear level. However, I argue that a version of this analysis is necessary to explain the distribution of negation patterns in Arabic.

Notice that, in these previous analyses, the negative marker *miš* has been analyzed as the result of merging the negative markers *ma* and -š with each other when the predicate does not move into the negative head merging with it, whether this is a syntactic merger through head movement and incorporation (Benmamoun 2000; Aoun et al. 2010) or a PF merger (Soltan 2011).

5.1.6 Enclitic negation and the status of -š in JA

In this section, I argue that the enclitic negative marker is a negative agreement clitic heading its own projection (AgrPolP) and dominated by the NegP headed by *ma*. To begin with, I maintain the standard analysis of sentential negation in Arabic which assumes that negation projects a NegP (Ouhalla 1990, 1993; Benmamoun 2000; Aoun et al. 2010, among others).[10] Previous analyses of *ma* and *la* assume that they are bound morphemes (proclitics) in dialects which have bipartite negation such as JA, Moroccan Arabic, and EA. In these dialects, the morpheme *ma* is analyzed as a proclitic because it is phonologically weak and adjacent to the predicate it negates. Phonological weakness is manifested by the fact that *ma* is a weak syllable which consists of a consonant and a short vowel [ma]. Moreover, phonological weakness is manifested by the fact that *ma* is unstressed or at least does not carry sentential stress, as in (25).[11]

(25)   a.   ma-`b-aʕirf-iš   (JA)
              NEG-ASP-know.1SG.IPFV-NEG
              'I don't know.'

       b.   la-`truuḥ-iš   (JA)
              NEG-ASP-go.2MSG.IMP-NEG
              'Don't go.'

As for adjacency, the negative marker *ma* must be adjacent to the predicate it negates when -*š* is present. Consider (26) and (27) where NPs
cannot intervene between *ma* and the predicate:

(26)   a.   ʔaḥmad   ma-`b-iʕirf-iš   (JA)
              Ahmad   NEG-ASP-know.3MSG.IPFV-NEG
              'Ahmad doesn't know.'

       b.   *ma   ʔaḥmad   `b-iʕirf-iš   (JA)
              NEG   Ahmad   ASP-know.3MSG.IPFV-NEG

(27)   a.   ʔaḥmad   la-`truuḥ-is   (JA)
              Ahmad   NEG-go.2MSG.IMP-NEG
              'Don't go, Ahmad.'

       b.   *la   ʔaḥmad   `truuḥ-iš   (JA)
              NEG   Ahmad   go.2MSG.IMP-NEG

Therefore, it is reasonable to assume that *ma* and *la* are proclitics in JA
based on the fact that they are phonologically weak and adjacent to the
predicate.

As for the syntactic status of the morphemes *ma*, *la*, and -*š*, *ma* and *la*
have been analyzed as heads of a NegP projection. The morpheme -*š* has
been analyzed as a specifier in Spec/NegP (Ouhalla 1990) and as a head
which forms a discontinuous morpheme with *ma* (Benmamoun 2000). I
follow the standard analysis of *ma* and *la* as heads of a NegP projection
in JA (Ouhalla 1993; Bahloul 1996; Benmamoun 2000; Aoun et al. 2010,
among others). I give further arguments for this analysis from the tests
for the syntactic status of negative words. First, *ma* and *la* block V-to-T
movement because of the Head Movement Constraint. Assuming that
past tense verbs in Arabic move to T (Benmamoun 2000; Aoun et al.
2010), if *ma* is a head we can expect it to block V-to-T movement. This
expectation is borne out in (28)b–c where negation cannot follow the
verb regardless of how the negative markers *ma* and -*š* are ordered:

(28)   a.   ma-šuft-iš   (JA)
              NEG-see.1SG.IPFV-NEG
              'I did not see.'

b. *šuft-iš-ma   (JA)
    see.1SG.IPFV-NEG-NEG

c. *šuft   miš   (JA)
    see.1SG.PFV   NEG

More importantly, the fact that *ma* is a proclitic suggests that the verb incorporates with *ma*. In other words, this is a head-to-head movement. The negative marker *la* is used in negative imperatives in JA. It has been assumed that imperative verbs move to a higher projection (TP or CP) to check an IMP feature. If this analysis is on the right track, and if *la* is a head, we can then predict that the verb cannot cross over *la*. This is borne out in (29)b–c where the imperative verb cannot cross over *la* (regardless of the order of *la* and *iš*) but it incorporates with it instead, as in (29)a.

(29) a. la-truuħ-iš   (JA)
          NEG-go.2MSG.IMP-NEG
          'Don't go.'

      b. * truuħ-iš-ma   (JA)
          go.2MSG.IMP-NEG-NEG

      c. *truuħ   miš   (JA)
          go.2MSG.IMP   NEG

Second, *ma* and *la* cannot be used in the *why not* construction. Remember that according to this test, negative markers which fail this test are syntactic heads. Consider these examples which show that *ma* and *la* fail this test:

(30) a. *leeš   la ?   (JA)
          why   NEG
          'Why not.'

      b. *leeš   ma ?   (JA)
          why   NEG
          'Why not.'

It should be pointed out that the negative adverb which can PASS the *why not* test is *laʔ(a)* (31)b rather than *la*. While *la* and *laʔ(a)* are related historically, it is still reasonable to argue that they now have different statuses syntactically: a head and an adverb, respectively. This adverb is only used as a negative interjection when answering a yes/no question, as in (31)a below:

(31) a. badd-ak   tsaafir ?   la?(a),   ma-badd-iš   (JA)
          want.IPFV-you   travel.2MSG.IPFV   no,   NEG-want.1SG.IPFV-NEG
          'Do you want to travel?'   'No, I don't want to.'

      b. leeš   la?(a) ?   (JA)
          why   no
          'Why not?'

As for -š, I argue in favor of analyzing it as a separate head, thus main-
taining both Ouhalla's analysis that it is separate and Benmamoun's
analysis that it is a head. The syntactic status tests suggest analyzing it as
a head rather than an XP. There are arguments, however, against analyzing it as part of the head *ma*. Therefore, I propose that -š is a head of a
separate projection: an agreement projection AgrPol[0].[12]

First, since -š is postverbal, we cannot be certain whether the verb
can move across it or not. But one can argue that the verb moves
through it and incorporates with it. This would nicely explain the fact
that -š is an enclitic which appears on the verb (or verbal complex). A
similar argument was made for the head status of *n't* in English and *ne*
in French based on their clitic status. The enclitic -š fails the *why not*
test by virtue of being a clitic rather than a free morpheme like *not* and
pas. Therefore, the fact that neither of the negative markers *ma*, *la*, or
-š can PASS the *why not* test explains the use of the adverb *la?(a)* in (31)
b and suggests that all three markers are syntactic heads rather than
adverbs.

Another argument against analyzing -š as an adverb can be advanced if
we compare -š with French *pas*. Unlike French *pas*, -š cannot be the realization of a negative operator for sentential negation. This is clear from
the fact that -š is not in complementary distribution with any n-word
(negative words such as NCIs) in JA as in:

(32)   ma-šuft-iš   wala-ħada   (JA)
       NEG-see.1SG.PFV   no-one
       'I did not see anyone.'

In French, the enclitic *pas* is argued to be the realization of the negative operator in Spec/NegP. The negative adverb *pas* is adjoined to VP
and moves to Spec/NegP (Zeijlstra 2004). When a negative constituent
is in the sentence, it is base generated in Spec/*v*P and has to move to
Spec/NegP to form a compound with the negative operator, as in (33)
a. Then, the negative marker *pas* has to be absent since it cannot move
to Spec/NegP which is already occupied by the negative constituent.
Therefore, if *pas* is used in a sentence which has an n-word, a double
negation reading arises, as in (33)b (from Zeijlstra 2004: 260):

(33) a. personne   ne   mange   (French)
          N-body   NEG   eats
          'Nobody eats.'

      b. personne   ne   mange   pas   (French)
          N-body   NEG   eats   NEG
          'Nobody doesn't eat.'

In contrast, -*š* in JA, as in the above example in (32), can co-occur with n-words without causing any double negation reading. This observation leads us to the conclusion that -*š* is not a realization of the negative operator. Consequently, there are no grounds for analyzing it as a negative adverb occupying the Spec/NegP position on a PAR with French *pas*, as assumed by Ouhalla (1990, 1993, 2002).[13]

I now turn to the arguments against analyzing -*š* as part of *ma*. First, the negative marker -*š* can appear with a negative marker other than *ma*, namely *la*. There are three options for negating imperative verbs in JA: using *la* (34)a alone, using -*š* (34)b alone, or using both *la* and -*š* (34)c.

(34) a. laa   truuħ   (JA)
          NEG   go.2MSG.IMP
          'Don't go.'

      b. truuħ-iš   (JA)
          go.2MSG.IMP-NEG
          'Don't go.'

      c. la-truuħ-iš   (JA)
          NEG-go.2MSG.IMP-NEG
          'Don't go.'

If -*š* is part of *ma*, then we expect -*š* to be part of *la* too since -*š* is used with both. The problem is that -*š* can never show up with *la* as a continuous morpheme. If -*š* is part of *la*, it is not clear why this would not be allowed. However, the continuous morpheme '*la* -*š*' does not exist (cf. (35)a–(35)b). Notice that the continuous morpheme *miš* as well as the discontinuous *ma*. . .-*š* do exist in negative imperatives which express cautioning, as in (36).

(35) a. miš   truuħ   (JA)
          NEG   go.2MSG.IMP
          'Don't go.'

      b. *liš   truuħ   (JA)
          NEG   go.2MSG.IMP
          'Don't go.'

(36) a. miš   truuħ   (JA)
          NEG   go.2MSG.IMP
          'Lit. You shouldn't go.'

      b. miš   ma-truuħ-iš   (JA)
          NEG   NEG-go.2MSG.IMP-NEG
          'Lit. You shouldn't not go.'

Second, Benmamoun's analysis of -š as a head of NegP is partly motivated by the observation that -š appears alone to negate verbs in one
dialect of JA (namely, the dialect discussed in this book). However,
a deeper look at the distribution of the -š alone construction shows
that this is empirically challenged. In fact, -š appears alone only when
the negated predicate is a present tense verb (10)a, the past tense
copula bageet (10)b, the pseudo-verbal predicate badd (10)c, maʕ
(10)d, and fi (10)e, or the negative imperative verbs (10)f (examples
are in section 5.1.2 above). On the other hand, -š cannot appear alone
in perfective verbs (which never carry the labial-initial prefix ba-) as in
(5)a, subjunctive verbs (again never carrying aspectual ba-) as in (6),
imperfective verbs not carrying aspectual ba- (y-imperfect), or non-
labial-initial possessive prepositions like ʕind 'have' and li 'have' in
(8)b and (8)d.
    Setting the negative imperative aside, one could argue that the absence
of ma is due to a phonological deletion of an underlyingly present ma
since -š can only be alone when the predicate is labial-initial. Indeed,
Blau (1960: 198) proposed that ma is deleted because it is similar to the
b- prefix which denotes the imperfect indicative in Levantine Arabic and
EA. In other words, this deletion is a case of haplology. Lucas (2009)
maintains that 'this type of phonetic reduction is most likely to happen
with the most frequently occurring lexical items, which have been
abundantly demonstrated to favor rapid and reduced articulation' (cf.
Schuchardt 1885; Bybee and Hopper 2001: 10–13; Bybee 2003) (cited
in Lucas 2009).
    However, the fact that -š can appear alone in negative imperatives in
Palestinian Arabic motivated Lucas (2009: 265) to develop an analysis
in which -š is the source of negative interpretation and ma is not covert
in syntax when -š is used alone. Lucas reports that ma is optional with
b-imperfective verbs, labial-initial pseudo-verbs, and, implicitly, with
imperatives.[14] He also reports that ma is obligatory with labial-initial and
non-labial-initial perfective verbs, as well as non-labial-initial pseudo-
verbs. His proposal is that the -š alone construction in Palestinian Arabic
was triggered by the phonetic reduction to zero of ma, but only in the
context of the highest frequency labial-initial verbs, the most frequent
of which would have been the pseudo-verbs (e.g., the pseudo-verbal

predicate *badd* (10)c, *maʕ* (10)d, and *fi* (10)e). Under this analysis, a sequence of two bilabials collapses into one diachronically. He also reports this very same phonological process taking place synchronically in Modern Aramaic (Khan 1999).

Lucas (2009) thus claims that the phonological deletion analysis is not enough to explain all the cases in which -*š* can appear alone. Specifically, he reports that -*š* can show up alone in the imperative despite the fact that the imperative verb is never labial-initial. Therefore, Lucas argues that children reanalyzed the phonetic deletion of *ma* in pseudo-verbs as the absence of *ma* from the syntactic representation, in which case -*š* became inherently negative and is used alone in negation. After this reanalysis, the use of -*š* alone extends to other non-past verb forms, such as the b-imperfect and the imperative. But this can hardly be the case, given that, similar to the discussion of JA above, in Palestinian Arabic the -*š* alone construction is impossible with non-past verbs which are non-labial-initial (e.g., subjunctive verbs in (37), and imperfective verbs not carrying aspectual *ba-* (y-imperfect) in (38)). This can only be explained by viewing deletion as phonological but not syntactic, which is to say, *ma* is present in the syntactic derivation. Crucially, at least the presence of *ma*, in (38)b, or aspectual *ba-*, in (38)c, is required to make the sentence grammatical. Using both *ma* and *ba-* is also allowed (38)d.[15]

(37) mišan   *(ma)-tnaam-iš   (JA)
      COMP   (NEG)-sleep.2MSG.IPFV-NEG
      'So that you don't sleep.'

(38) a. wagtha   kunt   aʕrif   (JA)
          at that time be.1SG.PFV know.1SG.IPFV
          'At that time, I knew.'

      b. wagtha   kunt   *(ma)-ʕirf-iš   (JA)
          at that time be.2S.PFV   (NEG)-know.1SG.IPFV-NEG
          'At that time, I did not know.'

      c. wagtha   kunt   *(ba)-ʕirf-iš   (JA)
          at that time be.1SG.PFV (ASP)-know.1SG.IPFV-NEG
          'At that time, I did not know.'

      d. wagtha   kunt   ma-ba-ʕirf-iš   (JA)
          at that time be.1SG.PFV NEG-ASP-know.1SG.IPFV-NEG
          'At that time, I did not know.'

      e. wagtha   ma-kunt-iš   (b)-aʕrif   (JA)
          at that time NEG-be.1SG.PFV-NEG   ASP-know.1SG.IPFV
          'At that time, I did not know.'

These facts are not the only arguments that support this phonological deletion analysis of the -š alone construction. Below, I provide one more argument supporting the phonological deletion analysis as the explanation for the -š alone construction in b-imperfective verb forms, in addition to providing a different phonological deletion analysis for the -š alone construction in negative imperatives, which are never labial-initial. As for the b-imperfective verbs, positing a phonological deletion rule which deletes *ma* from pseudo-verbs at some stage based on the frequency of their use raises the question as to why this rule would not apply to b-imperfective verbs, given that some of these b-imperfective verbs must be as frequent as pseudo-verbs. The following verbs are among the Swadesh hundred word list of basic/core vocabulary that is generally not subject to historical borrowing: 'drink,' 'eat,' 'sleep,' 'see,' 'hear,' 'know,' 'fly,' 'lie,' 'sit,' 'stand,' 'walk,' 'come,' 'swim,' 'give,' 'say,' 'die,' and 'kill' (Campbell 2004). That these verbs are core vocabulary implies that they are frequently used and important. Therefore, phonological reduction must have applied to the present indicative 'b-imperfect' when negated with the n-word *ma* just as with labial-initial pseudo-verbs. How could this rule be purely phonological if it does not apply to these frequent verbs when they are used in the b-imperfective verb form?

Additionally, we still have yet to explain how -š can appear alone in negative imperatives despite the fact that neither *la* nor the imperative verb is labial-initial (cf. (34)b). It is possible to argue for that phonological deletion to explain the use of the enclitic negative marker by itself in negative imperatives, which are never labial-initial. In the phonological deletion scenario, it is possible that *la* is deleted because it has an alveolar consonant which is followed by another alveolar consonant. There is evidence that this rule operates in other constructions in JA, but admittedly the deletion is slightly different and offers inconclusive or weak evidence. Consider the example in (39) in which the word-final alveolar consonant [l] in the noun *tˤuul* is deleted when followed by the alveolar-initial noun *nhaar*. Another example is the deletion of the definite article *l-* (another alveolar consonant) in nouns that have a [l] word initially as in *lħaaf* 'blanket' and *lsaan* 'tongue' as in (40).[16]

(39) a. tˤuul   nhaar-oh   y-ištaɣil   (JA)
          length   daytime-his   3MSG-work.IPFV
          'He's working all day long.'

      b. tˤuu-nhaar-oh   y-ištaɣil   (JA)
          length-daytime-his   3MSG-work.IPFV
          'He's working all day long.'

(40) a. li-lħaaf   →   lħaaf   (JA)
          DEF-blanket   blanket
          'The blanket.'   'The blanket.'

      b. li-lsaan   →   lsaan   (JA)
          DEF-tongue   tongue
          'The tongue.'   'The tongue.'

The imperative verb always carries the prefix [t-], the second person marker. Therefore, the frequent use of the imperative might allow the phonetic reduction of *la* to zero. But the deletion in these examples is a deletion of an alveolar consonant rather than a whole syllable, while the presumed deletion of the negative *la-* would be a deletion of the whole syllable containing the alveolar consonant [t] and the vowel [a]. Therefore, there is no conclusive evidence as to whether imperative verbs are truly negated by the enclitic by itself or by a covert proclitic negative marker *la-*.

A special use of imperatives in JA provides evidence that what's deleted in the negative imperative is the negative marker *la* rather than *ma*. Negative imperatives in Arabic can also be used to express 'cautioning' rather than 'prohibition.' In example (41)a, the imperative verb is negated by the negative word *miš*. This marked use of the negative *miš* expresses the marked use of the imperative (to express cautioning rather than prohibition). In example (41)b, the negative imperative appears to be double negated. However, interpretation of the first negative *miš* shows that it is negating a covert modal (like 'should'). Therefore, it is hypothesized that this negative marker *miš* is in a higher clause, allowing the use of discontinuous negation with the imperative *ma-truuħ-iš*. It is important to note that it is not grammatical to use -*š* by itself when the negative imperative has *ma* rather than *la* as the proclitic. This would be in contradiction with Lucas's claim about Palestinian Arabic if the same facts hold for Palestinian Arabic.

(41) a. miš   truuħ   (JA)
          NEG   go.2MSG.IMP
          'Lit. You shouldn't go.'

      b. miš   ma-truuħ-iš   (JA)
          NEG   NEG-go.2MSG.IMP-NEG
          'Lit. You shouldn't not go.'

      c. *miš   truuħ-iš   (JA)
          NEG   go.2MSG.IMP-NEG
          'Lit. You shouldn't not go.'

Notice that this phonological deletion analysis predicts that -*š* cannot appear alone in negative imperatives of the dialects which use *ma* instead

of *la* along with -*š*.[17] This prediction is borne out. In EA, negative imperatives do not allow the deletion of *ma*, as in (42):

(42)   *(ma-)truuḥ-ši   (EA)
       NEG-go.2MSG.IMP-NEG
       'Don't go.'

Based on the syntactic tests and arguments presented in this section, I
propose that -*š* is an agreement morpheme which occupies a head position in an AgrPolP projection (agreement polarity). The lack of negative
interpretation can be captured by having -*š* carry an uninterpretable
NEG feature that gets valued and deleted by entering into an agreement process with the interpretable NEG feature carried by *ma*. This is a
schematic illustration:

(43)

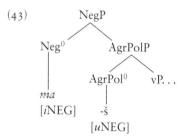

5.1.7 Discontinuous and independent negation in JA

In this section, I argue that head movement of the verb or the predicate
to the negation head is motivated by the need to check the formal feature
[D] of the negative head against the subject agreement morpheme of the
verb or predicate. This argument is based on the observation that when
the predicate (inflected preposition) does not have subject agreement, a
discontinuous negation pattern is impossible in JA. Therefore, I depart
from Benmamoun (2000) in that the subject NP here does not fulfill the
checking requirement of negation. Instead, head movement is the only
checking possibility. The verb or non-verbal predicate can always check
the D feature of NEG by head-to-head movement (V-to-NEG or Pred-
to-NEG). In the case of non-verbal predicates, I argue that a last-resort
copular pronoun (overt or covert) co-indexed with the subject (overt
subject or covert *pro*) fulfills that checking requirement, resulting in
either the independent negation *miš* or *ma*-COP-*iš*. As such, independent
negation and discontinuous negation of the verb or non-verbal predicate
are in complementary distribution and not in free variation.[18]

Before moving to the argument for feature checking as the source of the two negation patterns, I will lay out the structure and locus of NegP that I adopt. In the previous section I argued that *ma* heads NegP while -*š* heads a negative agreement projection AgrPolP. Recall that various arguments were put forward in Chapter 2 to support the claim that bipartite negation is lower than TP and that this type of negation is the default, i.e, the unmarked option. The following is the schematic representation:

(44)

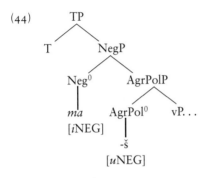

If negation is below TP, it is possible to argue that the auxiliary is below TP and negation can either precede or follow the auxiliary. But if negation is above TP, we would have to posit two positions for negation, one below TP to explain how the imperfective verb can host negation and one above TP to explain how the auxiliary can host negation. However, positing two positions for discontinuous negation does not have an independent motivation.

As for the proclitic nature of *ma*, it is plausible to suggest that the verbal complex moves to the head of NegP and incorporates with *ma*. I assume, following Benmamoun (2000) and Soltan (2007) that the perfective verb moves to T. Therefore, the verb moves through AgrPol⁰ and Neg⁰ and picks up both -*š* and *ma* respectively on its way to T⁰. Since subject agreement morphemes are closest to the verb in Arabic, I assume that AgrP is on top of TP, following Baker's (1985) mirror principle in which morphological derivations reflect syntactic derivations and vice versa. Similarly, since the aspectual *ba*- prefix is next closest to the verb, the Asp projection is on top of the AGR projection. The following is a schematic representation:

(45)

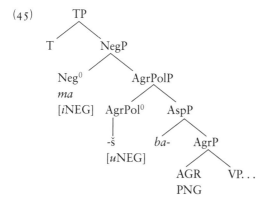

What, then, drives the verb movement to negation? Assuming that the imperfective verb does not move to T in Arabic, and assuming that categorical features drive movement (Benmamoun 2000), a straightforward answer to this question lies in the fact that the negation marker carries a feature that needs to be checked. This feature is referred to as the D feature in Benmamoun (2000). But what is this D feature exactly? To answer this question, let us first look at the following minimal pair verbless sentences with prepositional predicates. In all of the examples in (46) and (47), the predicate is inflected with Person/Number/Gender (PNG). But in (46)a, the PNG inflections of the prepositional predicate are construed as the subject, while in (47)a, the subject is the definite NP *es-sayyaara* 'the car,' a feminine singular noun.

(46) a. ma-ʕind-huu-š   sayyaara   (JA)
          NEG-have-him-NEG   car.FS
          'He does not have a car.'

      b. *miš ʕind-uh   sayyaara   (JA)
          NEG   have-him   car.FS

(47) a. es-sayyaara   miš   ʕind-o   (JA)
          DEF-car. FS   NEG   have-him
          'The car is not with him.'

      b. *es-sayyaara   ma-ʕind-huu-š   (JA)
          DEF-car.FS   NEG-have-him-NEG

Accordingly, the data suggests that continuous negation can only occur when the predicate carries PNG inflections that display agreement with the subject. Therefore, I propose a revised version of Benmamoun's proposal. Under Benmamoun's proposal, either the subject itself or the subject agreement inflections carried by the verb or non-verbal predicate can check the D feature of negation. The revised version I suggest is that only the person feature of the pronominal agreement of the verb or predicate can check the D feature. Cases where the non-verbal predicate is negated by *miš* will be analyzed as structures with a covert copular pronoun that has the person feature which can license the D feature of negation. This movement is not possible for adjectival and nominal predicates because agreement inflections do not include the person feature. See the examples below. The adjective does not carry any person specification and thus can modify both the first and the second person subject pronouns.[19]

(48) a. ?ani miš za$laan   (JA)
          I   NEG upset.ms
          'I am not upset.'

      b. ?inte miš za$laan   (JA)
          you   NEG upset.ms
          'You are not upset.'

So far, the system here can generate the JA perfective, imperfective, inflected prepositions and copular pronouns. In all of these cases, the verbal and non-verbal predicates merge with negation and all carry subject PNG inflections. The structures in (49), (50), (51), and (52) illustrate the derivations for a perfective verb, an imperfective verb, a non-verbal prepositional predicate, and a copular pronoun, respectively.

(49) $[_{TP}$ Neg^0 VERB Agr^0 AgrPol^0 T^0 $[_{NegP}$ <Neg^0 verb Agr^0 AgrPol^0> $[_{AgrPolP}$ <verb Agr^0 AgrPol^0> $[_{AgrP}$ <verb Agr^0> $[_{VP}$ <verb>...]]]]]

(50) [TP T^0 $[_{NegP}$ Neg^0 Asp^0 VERB Agr^0 AgrPol^0 $[_{AgrPolP}$ <Asp^0 verb Agr^0 AgrPol^0> $[_{AspP}$ <Asp^0 verb Agr^0> $[_{AgrP}$ <verb Agr^0> $[_{VP}$ <verb>...]]]]]]

(51) [TP T^0 $[_{NegP}$ Neg^0 PREP Agr^0 AgrPol^0 $[_{AgrPolP}$ <PREP Agr^0 AgrPol^0> $[_{AgrP}$ <PREP Agr^0> $[_{PP}$ <PREP>...]]]]]

(52) [TP T^0 $[_{NegP}$ Neg^0 AUX Agr^0 AgrPol^0 $[_{AgrPolP}$ <aux Agr^0 AgrPol^0> $[_{AgrP}$ <aux^0 Agr^0> $[_{AuxP}$ <aux^0> $[_{AP}$ ADJ...]]]]]

Recall that discontinuous negation can be realized on either the past tense copula *kaan* or on the imperfective verb that follows the copula as in (38) above. In cases where negation is realized on the copula, the derivation is similar to that in (52). But when negation is realized on the imperfective verb, the auxiliary must be higher than negation. In an analysis where NegP is on top of TP, it is not possible to generate negation on the imperfective verb lower than the auxiliary. The derivation in (53) corresponds to example (38):

(53) $[_{TP}$ T $[_{AuxP}$ Aux $[_{NegP}$ Neg^0 VERB Agr^0 AgrPol^0> $[_{AgrPolP}$ <verb Agr^0 AgrPol^0> $[_{AgrP}$ <verb Agr^0> $[_{VP}$ <verb>...]]]]]

We now turn to JA verbless sentences and future tense (where *miš* is with a null copula). Here we see that *miš* is conditioned by the distribution of the copular pronoun. But the copula is not pronounced in *miš*. This makes sense if the copular pronoun is needed syntactically (to check the D feature) when the verb/inflected preposition cannot move to it (as in the JA future), or when the verb/inflected preposition is not there to begin with as in verbless sentences with nominal and adjectival predicates. This means that *miš* involves the insertion of the copular pronoun as a last resort. First, the independent negative marker is a negative copula that is made of the two negative markers and a null copular pronoun that fulfills the checking requirement of the negative marker when the predicate cannot do so. This necessarily means that the negative copula with an overt copular pronoun should have the same distribution as the independent negative marker *miš*. This is borne out in JA. Consider the contrasts below:

(54) a. es-sayyaara miš ʕind-o (JA)
            DEF-car   NEG have-him
            'The car is not with him.'

     b. es-sayyaara ma-hii-š ʕind-o (JA)
            DEF-car   NEG-COP-NEG have-him
            'The car is not with him.'

     c. *miš ʕind-o sayyaara (JA)
            NEG have-him car
            'He does not have a car.'

     d. *ma-huu-š ʕind-o sayyaara (JA)
            NEG-COP-NEG have-him car
            'He does not have a car.'

Similarly, in verbless sentences with adjectival predicates the negative marker *miš* and the negative copula *ma-ni-š* are interchangeable:

(55) a. ʔani m-anii-š taʕbaan (JA)
           I   NEG-I-NEG tired
           'I am not tired.'

b. ?ani   miš   taʕbaan   (JA)
   I   NEG-I-NEG   tired
   'I am not tired.'

So, we can safely say that there is no overlap between the independent negative marker and the discontinuous negative marker, except when the copular pronoun is the head that checks the D feature of negation as a last resort. In other words, discontinuous negation and independent negation are both instances of bipartite negation, but when a copular pronoun is the head merging with negation it has the option of not getting pronounced at the phonological component. Therefore, the derivation for a sentence like (54)a is as in (56) where, since the preposition does not have a subject agreement inflection, the copular pronoun (aux) is inserted as a last resort:

(56) $[_{TP}$ T^0 $[_{NegP}$ Neg^0 AUX Agr^0 $AgrPol^0$ $[_{AgrPolP}$ <aux Agr^0 $AgrPol^0$> $[_{AgrP}$ <aux^0 Agr^0> $[_{AuxP}$ <aux^0> $[_{PP}$ PREP...]]]]]]

If this analysis of *miš* as a negative copula is correct, we expect to find the overt copular pronoun sandwiched by the negative markers in sentences that have the future aspectual particle *rayeh/rah*, and the progressive aspectual participle *gaʕid*. This is borne out in JA:[20]

(57) ma-an-iš   raayeh ?azuur   l-batra   (JA)
      NEG-COP-NEG   FUT   go.1SG.IPFV   DEF-Petra
      'I am not going to visit Petra.'

(58) ma-an-iš   gaaʕid bamzah   (JA)
      NEG-COP-NEG   PROG   joke.1SG.IPFV
      'I am not joking.'

Again, the fact that the verb does not move through the participle to negation makes the copular pronoun the only option for negation to check the D feature. Evidence for lack of verb movement can be found in the following example where the adverb can intervene between the participle and the verb:

(59) miš   raayeh dayman   ?azuur   l-batra
      NEG   FUT   always   go.1SG.IPFV   DEF-Petra
      'I am not going to always visit Petra.'

If this analysis is on the right track, the ungrammaticality of (54)d can be reduced to the use of the copular pronoun for checking the negation D feature when the prepositional predicate carries subject agreement.

5.1.8 *Discontinuous and independent negation in CEA and Sharqeyyah*

Imperfective verb forms in CEA optionally merge with the negative markers. Under an approach which treats the merger as a syntactic merger motivated by a strong D feature on negation, it is possible to explain the lack of merger by assuming that CEA has both a strong D feature that drives verb movement to negation and a weak D feature that can be checked without verb movement to negation. This sort of explanation provides an easy solution for CEA; however, the strong versus weak feature division has its explanatory power only when it can be used to explain cross-linguistic or cross-dialectal variation. If even a single dialect has both features, the theory of strong versus weak feature division is significantly weakened. Therefore, I propose that CEA does not have any feature checking requirement for negation across the board. This would then mean that all cases of discontinuous negation in CEA are not caused by the need to check any feature of negation. This proposal thus requires a description of the rules governing the distribution of discontinuous negation and independent negation in CEA. The challenge here is that, as Soltan (2011) points out, both forms of negation overlap. This also makes it difficult to formulate a syntactic analysis, or even a morphological analysis along the lines of Soltan (2011), as I will show below. However, it is possible to explain the CEA negation facts using Soltan's morphological approach if we follow the analysis proposed in this chapter in which negation is lower than tense and CEA negation does not have any feature checking requirement for negation. Below I argue for this proposal and support it with empirical contrasts between CEA and JA.

The challenges presented by the CEA distribution of discontinuous negation and independent negation render a morphological analysis too weak to predict when merger with negation is obligatory as opposed to when it is optional. We know that the imperfective verb form optionally merges with negation while the perfective verb form obligatorily merges with negation. It is not clear how this can be produced by a morphological rule. In other words, a morphological rule should have the host merge with negation either optionally in all contexts or obligatorily in all contexts, given that in all of these contexts there is an element (verbal or non-verbal predicate) that can host negation. Otherwise, the morphological operation reflects idiosyncratic cases and there is no morphological generalization that can predict the distribution of discontinuous negation and independent negation.

I believe that Soltan's morphological analysis is useful, and indeed can explain the distribution of negation forms in CEA provided that we have the locus of the discontinuous negative markers below TP. Having negation below TP reduces the obligatory merger between perfective verbs and negation to the well-known theoretical consensus that perfective verbs move to T. Therefore, if negation is between TP and VP, and if the perfective verb has to move to T, the only option for the perfective verb is to move to the negation heads, picking them up on its way to T. This is in agreement with Benmamoun's (2000) and Aoun et al.'s (2010) analyses of negation below TP. With an explanation for the obligatory merger between perfective verb forms and negation, we can reformulate Soltan's morphological operation into one where having the right host (verbal or non-verbal predicate) for negation results into an optional merger with negation. This leads to the following implication for the CEA morphological rule. Whenever discontinuous negation is possible, independent negation must be possible. This is because the morphological operation is optional. In the case of perfective verb forms this implication does not hold, not because it is an exception but because discontinuous negation in this context is not produced by the morphological operation. Instead it is produced by the V-to-T movement of perfective verbs, where the locus of negation between V and T provides the right circumstances for negation to find a host via an incidental syntactic movement.

We can thus rewrite Soltan's formula for the morphological operation as a morphological operation in CEA rather than for all Arabic dialects as follows:

(60)   a.   In contexts where AgrPol is adjacent to a hosting head *H*, *H* may move to AgrPol and then to NEG, and the circumfixal *ma-H-š* pattern arises.

   b.   Otherwise, AgrPol incorporates into NEG, giving rise to the *miš*-pattern.

This modified version of Soltan's morphological rule finds more support from an empirical observation reported in Soltan (2011). Recall this modified version yields the implicational rule that whenever there is discontinuous negation we expect to find continuous negation (unless syntax incidentally provides a host, as in the perfective verb's movement to tense).[21] Inflected prepositions merge with negation in CEA. We can observe that, although it is less preferred, CEA allows independent negation in this context. However, the equivalent structure in (54)c is ungrammatical in JA. In (61) the perfective verb moves through the subject agreement head, then through the negation heads and stops in T.

The derivations in (62) are for CEA imperfective verb forms. In (62) a the imperfective verb moves to subject agreement and no further syntactic movement is needed, given that the imperfect does not move to T. Then the negative marker in AgrPol merges with the NEG head at the morphological level, giving rise to independent negation. In (62)b the imperfective verb merges with both negative markers at the morphological level, resulting in the discontinuous negation pattern.

(61) $[_{TP}$ Neg^0 VERB Agr^0 AgrPol^0 T^0 $[_{NegP}$ <Neg^0 verb Agr^0 AgrPol^0> $[_{AgrPolP}$ <verb Agr^0 AgrPol^0> $[_{AgrP}$ <verb Agr^0> $[_{VP}$ <verb>...]]]]]

(62)   a.   miš   ba-saafir   kətiir   (EA)
            NEG   ASP-travel.1SG.IPFV   much
            'I do not travel much.' (Soltan 2011: 259)
            Option 1: $[_{TP}$ T $[_{NegP}$ NEG $[_{AgrPolP}$ AgrPol $[_{AgrP}$ VERB Agr^0 $[_{VP}$
            <verb>...]]]]]

       b.   maa-ba-saafir-š   kətiir   (EA)
            NEG-ASP-travel.1SG.IPFV-NEG   much
            'I don't travel much.' (Soltan 2011: 259)
            Option 2: $[_{TP}$ T $[_{NegP}$ NEG $[_{AgrPolP}$ AgrPol $[_{AgrP}$ VERB Agr^0 $[_{VP}$
            <verb>...]]]]]

This analysis for CEA does not view independent negation in CEA as involving a negative marker that has a null copular pronoun. This explains why independent negation is possible with the CEA imperfective verbs but not possible with those in JA. If this analysis is on the right track, we should be able to find empirical contrasts between CEA verbless sentences and their counterparts in JA. Consider the following contrast from inflected prepositions between the JA example in (54)c and the CEA example below:

(63)   ʔ miš   ʕand-ii   ʕarabiyyah   (EA)
       NEG   at-me   car
       'I don't have a car.' (Soltan 2011: 259)

The fact that independent negation is possible in CEA even when the inflected preposition carries the subject agreement inflections gives empirical support for the claim that there is no feature checking requirement, and that merger with negation is an optional morphological operation. Further evidence supporting this analysis comes from the following contrasts between JA and CEA:

(64)   a.   wallahi   ma-*(ani)   ʕaarif   (JA)
            by God   NEG-*(COP) know.AP
            'By God, I don't know.'

       b.   wallahi   ma-(ana)   ʕaarif[22]   (CEA)
            by God   NEG-(COP) know.AP
            'By God, I don't know.'

Recall that the negative marker in JA requires the copular pronoun, but the negative marker in CEA does not. Notice here that the CEA example without the copular pronoun does not have any constituent carrying subject agreement clitics. Remember that if negation in CEA had a D formal feature that needed to be checked, and if the subject NP could satisfy this checking requirement, we would incorrectly predict the CEA example to be ungrammatical. This strongly suggests that negation in JA has a checking requirement while in CEA it does not.[23]

Now we move to a challenge presented to this analysis by the fact that the Sharqeyyah dialect in Egypt allows independent negation with perfective verb forms. This is a challenge specifically for an analysis that has the locus of NegP lower than TP. If the perfective verb must move to T, why does it not precede or merge with negation? I think that this observation gives support, rather than challenge, to the analysis in this chapter. The observation from this dialect is considered a challenge based on the premise that the locus of negation is uniform in all the dialects. However, micro-variation studies show that negation can have multiple positions across the different varieties of the same language (Zanuttini 1997a, 1997b) and even within the same dialect (Ramchand 2001). Therefore, one can argue that negation in Sharqeyyah is on top of TP, which is the same position Soltan claims generalized for all the Arabic dialects.

Under this cross-dialectical approach to the locus of negation, it is possible to reduce the distribution of negation forms in Sharqeyyah to an optional morphological rule that allows the host to merge with negation optionally even in the case of perfective verb forms. Assuming negation is higher than TP in the Sharqiyya example, the perfective verb, which is in T, does not have to move to negation in narrow syntax.[24]

We now have a system which reduces dialectal variation in the distribution of the discontinuous and independent negation patterns to the availability of V/Pred-to-NEG movement in narrow syntax, the availability of V/Pred-to-NEG movement at PF, and the locus of negation below TP or above TP. However, these options are in a system constrained in a manner that gives us the power to predict when, within and across the dialects, a certain pattern is optional and when it is obligatory. Specifically, head movement in narrow syntax produces an obligatory discontinuous negation, whereas head movement at PF produces an optional discontinuous negation. The combination of these mechanisms is what produces the complicated cross-dialectal negation landscape.[25]

Table 5.1 summarizes the properties of negative markers in JA, CEA, and Sharqeyyah. The variation in the distribution of the two negation patterns (discontinuous versus independent negation) is the result of strength of the categorial feature, locus of negation, and the availability of a morphological merger rule.

Table 5.1 Morphosyntactic properties of negation in JA, CEA, and Sharqeyyah

PROPERTIES	DIALECTS		
	JA	CEA	Sharqeyyah
Syntactic merger	yes	no[1]	no
NegP below TP	yes	yes	no
Morphological merger	no	yes	yes

[1] Recall that the CEA perfective verbs merge with negation in narrow syntax, not for the purpose of checking any negation feature but to avoid minimality violations when undergoing V-to-T movement.

5.1.9 *Theoretical implications: head movement and negation locus*

The locus of head movement and the locus of negation are controversial in the literature. For head movement, the debate is whether it takes place in the syntax proper (narrow syntax) (Roberts 2010), post-syntactically at PF (i.e., the morphological component) (cf. Boeckx and Stjepanovic 2001; Chomsky 2001), or in both components with certain types of head movement in syntax and other types at PF/morphology (Embick and Noyer 2001). In this text I follow a version of the last approach. I propose that languages (and dialects of the same language) differ in whether they allow movement of the same head to occur in narrow syntax, at PF, or in both components of the grammar. Similarly, there is a debate over the locus of negation regarding whether the locus of negation is a parametric choice that is based on the order of inflectional morphology and negative markers relative to the verb (Ouhalla 1991), or whether language may opt for any position of negation (Zanuttini 1997; Ramchand 2001; Zeijlstra 2004, 2008). I argue that this last approach is crucial for the analysis I develop to explain the distribution of negation patterns in the Arabic dialects.

Head movement and the locus of negation have been central to previous analyses of negation patterns cross-linguistically, particularly in English and French. The syntactic status of the negative marker, either as a head or an XP, is significantly related to head movement (Pollock 1989, 1993; Laka 1990; Haegeman 1995; Potsdam 1997). There are two main tests to help decide whether the negative marker is a negative head (X^0) or a negative adverb (Spec-XP). These tests are the head movement test (Zanuttini 2001) and the Why Not test (Merchant 2001).

Zeijlstra (2004: 153) shows how Zanuttini (2001) takes the blocking of head movement in French as a test to argue that the negative marker *ne* is a head. In (65)a we see how the clitic *la* is able to move from its position before the infinitive phrase to the position before the finite verb *fait*. However, in (65)b, the movement of this clitic to a position higher than *ne* is not possible. The ungrammaticality of this movement is generally interpreted as the inability of the clitic *la* to move across the head *ne* (i.e., head movement constraint, Travis 1984).[26]

(65)   a.   Jean   la$_i$ fait   manger   t$_i$ à Paul   (French)
           Jean   it   makes   eat   it   to Paul
           'Jean makes Paul eat it.'

       b.   *Jean   l$_i$'a   fait   ne   pas
           Jean   it.has   made   NEG   NEG
           manger t$_i$ à l'enfant   (French)
           eat   it   to DEF-kid
           'Jean has made the child not eat it.'

       c.   Jean   ne   l$_i$'a   pas   fait   manger t$_i$ à Paul   (French)
           Jean   NEG   it.has   NEG   made   eat   it   to Paul
           'Jean hasn't made Paul eat it.'

Another example of blocking head movement taken from Zanuttini and cited in Zeijlstra is the blocking of verb movement in the Italian dialect Paduan. In (66)a, the verb can move from its position to C^0 in yes/no questions. This movement is not possible in negative interrogatives as in (66)b. This can be explained if (following Zanuttini) we assume that the negative marker is a head and thus blocks the V-to-C movement.

(66)   a.   vien-lo?   (Paduan)
           comes-he?
           'Is he coming?'

       b.   *vien-lo   no?   (Paduan)
           comes-he   NEG   ?
           'Isn't he coming?

A third example of blocking head movement is from the long clitic-climbing in Romance languages. In the Italian example in (67)a, the clitic can move from its position as the complement of a nonfinite verb *vedere* to a position higher than the finite verb *vuole*. This movement, however, is not possible in (67)b, the negative counterpart of (67)a. This contrast can be explained if we assume that the negative marker *non* is a head which blocks the movement of the clitic, according to Zanuttini. Examples in (67) are from Italian cited in Zeijlstra (2004: 153).

(67) a. Gianni li   vuole   vedere   (Italian)
       Gianni them   wants   see
       'Gianni wants to see them.'

     b. *Gianni li   vuole   non   vedere   (Italian)
        Gianni   them   wants NEG   see
        'Gianni doesn't want to see them.'

Notice that in these cases it is V-to-T movement and clitic-climbing, both of which take place in narrow syntax, which are used as tests of the head status of the negative markers and to understand their word order facts. A second test for the status of negative markers is Merchant's (2001) Why Not test. It is argued that the wh-word 'why' in the Why Not construction is an XP which adjoins to the negative marker. This implies that the negative marker has to be an XP in order for the wh-word to adjoin to it. Zeijlstra's illustration is in (68):

(68) [YP [XP why] [YP not]]

In Italian and Greek, on the other hand, the failure of the negative marker to PASS the Why Not test identifies it as a head:

(69) a. *perche   non?   (Italian)
         why   NEG
         'Why not?'

     b. *giati   dhen?   (Greek)
        why   NEG
        'Why not?'

With regard to English *not* and *n't*, Zeijlstra agrees with Haegeman's (1995) conclusion that English *not* is a specifier and English *n't* is a syntactic head.[27] Zeijlstra points out that the original analysis (cf. Laka 1990; Pollock 1993) was that the negative marker blocks the movement of the verb from V to T in English. This analysis assumes that T must be filled. Thus, in (70)a, the problem is that T is not filled by the verb. But in (70) b the problem is that the verb that moved across the negative marker is a head, thus violating the Head Movement Constraint (Travis 1984).

(70) a. *John not know the answer
     b. *John know not the answer

This analysis considers Do-support to be a last resort in order to fill the T head when verb movement is blocked by the negative marker, as in:

(71) John does not know the answer

However, Zeijlstra argues that English verbs can move across the negative marker *not*. He gives the following examples:

(72) a. John has not been ill
      b. John is not ill

Notice that there is a contrast in the position of the verb *to be* in (72). In (72) a, the verb *to be* is to the right of the negative marker while it is to the left in (72)b. Zeijlstra considers this as evidence that the verb *to be* is base generated in a position lower than the negative marker in (72)b and moves to a position higher than the negative marker *not*, which is to say it moves across *not*. Accordingly, Zeijlstra rejects Do-support as an argument for analyzing *not* as a head which blocks V-to-T movement in English. He also takes the fact that *not* passes the *why not* test as evidence for the XP status of *not*.

It has been argued that the weaker form of *not*, *n't*, is a head (Haegeman 1995; and Zanuttini 1991 and Pollock 1993 cited in Zeilstra 2004). Zeiljstra reports the following examples to show the contrast in the behavior of *not* and *n't*. In (73)a, the negative marker *n't* has to move to C with the finite verb 'has,' while *not* in (73)d cannot do so. This contrast can be explained if we assume that *n't* is a head but *not* is an adverb.

(73) a. Hasn't John left?
      b. *Has John n't left?
      c. Has John not left?
      d. *Has not John left?

In a language such as French, which has two negative markers for sentential negation, the preverbal marker *ne* is analyzed as X^0 but the postverbal *pas* is analyzed as an XP. The preverbal marker blocks V-to-T movement, as in (74)a. In (74)b, the verb moves to Neg^0 and picks up *ne* before it lands in T^0. On the other hand, *pas* does not block head movement because it is in Spec/NegP, i.e., it is an XP.

(74) a. *John aime ne pas Marie
      b. John n'aime pas Marie

Moreover, *pas* passes the Why Not test, while *ne* does not. This suggests that *pas* is an XP and *ne* is not, as in (75):

(75) a. pourquoi pas ?   (French)
          why   NEG ?
          'Why not?'

      b. *pourquoi ne ?   (French)
          why   NEG?

The analysis in this chapter contributes to two cross-linguistic theoretical debates. The first issue is whether these kinds of head movement all take place at PF (that is to say, are morphological) (cf. Boeckx and Stjepanovic 2001; Chomsky 2001), all take place in narrow syntax (Roberts 2010), or whether some take place in narrow syntax and some at PF (Embick and Noyer 2001). The second issue is whether the locus of negation is a parametric choice that is based on the order of inflectional morphology and negative markers relative to the verb (Ouhalla 1991) or whether negation can have multiple positions in the same language (Zanuttini 1997; Ramchand 2001; Zeijlstra 2004, 2008).

As for the first debate, the analysis here suggests that head movement can be syntactic and morphological, thus in line with Embick and Noyer's 2001 approach. I claim, however, that the same head movement (rather than different types of head movement) can take place both in syntax and in morphology. Furthermore, the choice between syntactic movement and morphological movement is behind the variation in the distribution of discontinuous and independent negation within the context of imperfective verbs and non-verbal predicates. In other words, it is the availability of head movement in the syntactic and morphological components as options for the grammar that produces the complex cross-dialectal distribution of the negation patterns. A certain dialect specifies whether head movement takes place at one or both components of the grammar. But it does so by working within the limits of the system. For example, in a language where syntactic head movement occurs, we do not expect to find morphological head movement in the same syntactic environments (e.g., in JA).[28] Moreover, in a language where negation is above TP and morphological head movement occurs, we expect to find both patterns of negation in all environments (e.g., Sharqeyyah). The other advantage for this analysis is its ability to predict that syntactic head movement of the predicate to negation is not optional, which is to say that a certain dialect will either exclusively have it or not have it, while the morphological head movement is optional. Furthermore, morphological head movement is limited by being optional across the board in all environments of the same dialect, rather than being optional in certain environments and obligatory in others.

As for whether or not the locus of negation is a parametric choice, the analysis in this chapter is in line with the approach stating the locus of negation may be different cross-dialectally. The position of negation interacts with V-to-T movement of perfective verb forms and with optional morphological head movement. With negation lower than TP, perfective verb forms have to merge with the negative markers on their way up to T, hence the obligatory discontinuous negation with perfective verbs in CEA. With negation above TP, syntax feeds morphological head movement in a dialect that has that head movement (Sharqeyyah), thus producing optional merger between negation and the predicate that hosts it in all kinds of environments. On the other hand, V-to-T movement of the CEA perfective verbs in narrow syntax makes PF movement of these verbs apply vacuously.

The analysis in this section is consistent with the results of the head movement and the Why Not tests. It is also consistent with the fact that -*š* is not a realization of the negative operator, given that it can co-occur with NPIs without causing any double negation reading. It also captures the fact that -*š* is not inherently negative, given that it fails to negate subjunctive and nonfinite verbs without *ma* and fails to negate imperatives expressing cautioning without *ma*, cases that were not reported in previous literature. This evidence is in addition to the failure of -*š* to negate all other non-labial-initial predicates as reported previously in the literature as well as in this book. These facts were established by reporting observed restrictions on these environments and by extending the phonological deletion analysis of *ma* when it negates labial-initial predicates to *la* when it negates the always-alveolar-initial negative imperatives (acknowledging that the evidence is weak evidence). This analysis is also consistent with the fact that -*š* is a clitic that attaches to the verb (or verbal complex). Analyzing -*š* as a head makes it plausible to claim that the verb incorporates with it via head movement, in accordance with similar arguments made for the head status of *n't* in English and *ne* in French. This analysis thus captures the enclitic nature of -*š*, given that the predicate can undergo head movement and incorporate with -*š* in AgrPolP^0. Finally, this analysis nicely captures the fact that in the absence of predicate merger with the negative markers, the discontinuous morpheme *ma. . .-š* is linearized as [*ma^-š*], hence giving rise to the independent negative marker *miš*.

5.2 Standard Arabic negative markers

This section focuses on SA, reducing the dichotomy in the behavior of *maa* on the one hand and *laa* and its variants on the other hand to the proposal that *maa* is higher than TP, while *laa* is lower than TP. I argue that, thanks to the multi-locus analysis of negation, *laa* can carry the tense marker giving rise to the past tense negative marker *lam* and the future negative marker *lan*, or it can merge with the copular head giving rise to the negative copula *laysa*. The relevant SA data is not included here because of space limitations.

Lam and *lan* are tensed variants of *laa*, and carry past and future tense by virtue of being located between T and V (Benmamoun 1992; Ouhalla 1993; Aoun et al. 2010). In these cases, the verb cannot carry the tense feature because negation intervenes and verb movement to T would cause a minimality violation. Hence, imperfective verbs in SA cannot carry tense, and thus negation carries it instead. This analysis assumes that imperfective verbs do not move to T, while perfective verbs do (Benmamoun 2000):

(76)

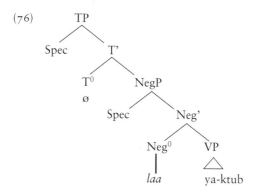

(77)

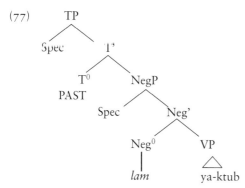

(78)

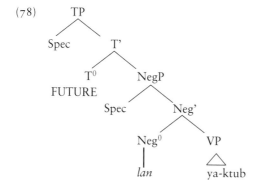

(79)

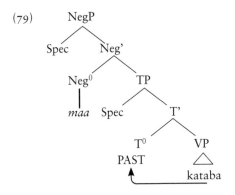

(80)

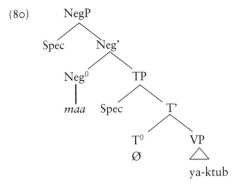

One advantage of analyzing *maa* and *lam* at different positions is that we can have a straightforward explanation for why *maa* can precede perfective and imperfective verbs while *laa*, *lam*, and *lan* can only precede imperfective verbs. By analyzing negation as two distinct categories, one higher than tense and another lower, we can classify the negative markers in SA into two types: the high negative *maa*, and the low negative *laa* and its tensed variants *lam* and *lan*.

Being lower than tense, *laa* is the default negative marker and is used with present tense. It can carry the past tense producing *lam*, can carry the future tense producing *lan*, and can also carry the copula *ays* producing the negative copula *laysa* (cf. Ouhalla 1993 for similar claims).

Recall that there is evidence spporting the idea that *maa* is a negative marker in a NegP above TP while *laa/lam/lan* are in a NegP projection below TP. These types of negation exhibit contrasts in compatibility with nonfinite verbs. Specifically, there are distributional contrasts with respect to negating verbs which occur after the complementizer *ʔan*):

(81) a. ʔuriid-u   ʔan   laa   tadxul-a   (SA)
         I-want-IND   that NEG   enter.2MSG.IPFV-SBJV
         'I want you not to enter.' (Fassi Fehri 1993: 172)

b. *ʔuriid-u   ʔan   maa   tadxul-a   (SA)
   want.1SG.IPFV.IND   that   NEG   enter.2MSG.IPFV-SBJV

Notice that the embedded verb *tadxul-a* cannot carry tense:

(82) a. ʔaradt-u   ʔan   laa   tadxul-a   (SA)
        want.1SG.PFV.IND   that   NEG   enter.2MSG.IPFV-SBJV
        'I wanted you not to enter.'

     b. *ʔaradt-u   ʔan   laa   daxalta   (SA)
        want.1SG.PFV.IND   that   NEG   enter.2MSG.PFV

and its subject can be case marked by the matrix verb:

(83) a. ʔuriid-u   ʔan   yadxulu   (SA)
        want.1SG.IPFV.IND   that   enter.3MPL.IPFV.SBJV
        'I want them to enter.'

     b. ʔuriid-u-hum   ʔan   yadxulu   (SA)
        want.1SG.IPFV.IND-them   that   enter.3MPL.IPFV.SBJV
        'I want them to enter.'

Recall that all of this follows from a multi-locus analysis which distinguishes between *maa* and *laa* by positing two different structural positions as follows (representations are repeated from previous chapters for convenience):

(84) a. [TP [AspP [vP [VP WANT [NegP   laa [AspP [vP [VP
     b. [TP [AspP [vP [VP WANT [*NegP maa [AspP [vP [VP

Each of the three negative markers in SA – specifically sentential *maa*, *laa*, and its tensed variants *lam/lan*, and focused *maa* – occupy a different position in the clause structure. The sentential negative marker *maa* is the head of NegP above TP. The negative markers *laa*, *lam*, and *lan* are heads of a NegP below TP.

As for *maa*, recall that when it does not have a contrastive focus interpretation, *maa* is a sentential negative marker that can license NPIs. But when it has a contrastive focus interpretation, *maa* cannot license NPIs and is thus regarded as a separate marker, referred to here as contrastive focus *maa*.

(85) a. maa   qaabaltu   ʔaħad-an   (SA)
        NEG   meet.1SG.PFV   one-ACC
        'I have not met anyone.'

b.   *maa   l-baariħata   qaabaltu   ʔaħadan
     NEG   DEF-yesterday   meet.1SG.PFV   one-ACC
     bal   al-yawma   (SA)
     but   DEF-today

c.   *maa   qaabaltu   ʔaħadan   l-baariħata
     NEG   meet.1SG.PFV   one-ACC   DEF-yesterday
     bal   al-yawma   (SA)
     but   DEF-today

When *maa* is used for sentential negation without a contrastive focus interpretation, it can occur in embedded clauses preceding the verb (Fassi Fehri 1993: 167), suggesting that there is no requirement for it to be in root clauses and thus it can intervene between the complementizer and the verb. Recall that this is consistent with analyzing it as the head of a NegP between CP and TP. Crucially in example (86)b below, we are not coordinating two CPs but rather two TPs. Negation must thus be part of the lower conjoined TP.

(86)   a.   zaʕama   ʔan   maa   ħadaθa   šayʔ-un (SA)
            pretend.3MSG.PFV   that   NEG   happen.3MSG.PFV   thing-NOM
            'He pretended that nothing has happened.'
            [TP [VP zaʕama [CP ʔan [NegP maa [TP [VP ħadaθa   šayʔ-un

       b.   zaʕama   ʔanna-hu   qaʕada   wa   (SA)
            pretend.3MSG.PFV   that-him   sit.3MSG.PFV   and
            maa   btasama
            NEG   smile.3MSG.PFV
            'He pretended that he sat and has not smiled.'
            [TP [VP zaʕama [CP ʔanna-hu [TP [VP qaʕada wa [NegP maa [TP
            [VP btasama

Given these empirical contrasts between *maa* which is associated with contrastive focus and maa which is not, it follows that we should restrict Ouhalla's (1993) analysis of *maa* as focused negation in FocP to the special use of *maa* with a contrastive reading, as when *maa* negates preposed NPs and PPs (Moutaouakil 1993; Ouhalla 1993).

(87)   maa   riwaayat-an   ʔallafat   (SA)
       NEG   novel-ACC   write.PFV.3FSG
       Zaynabu   (bal qasiidat-an)
       Zaynab   (but poem-ACC)
       'It is not a novel that Zaynab has written (but a poem).' (Ouhalla
       1993: 227)

(88)

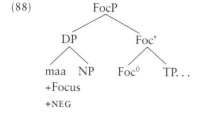

To conclude, this section shows that the sentential negative marker *maa* occupies a position higher than TP and does not interact with the tense head at the morphological level. On the other hand, the negative marker *laa* occupies a position below TP and interacts with tense morphologically. The lower NegP is a projection that intervenes between TP and VP. The negative marker which occupies the head position of this lower NegP – namely *laa*, displays form of the negative varaints *lam* 'did not' and *lan* 'will not'. By virtue of being above TP, *maa* can precede the subject of verbless sentences while *laa* and its variants *lam* and *lan* cannot do so. The fact that *maa* cannot negate non-finite verbs while *laa* can do so is consistent with the analysis of *maa* as a marker that dominates TP while *laa* dominates VP. The distinct analyses put forward for *maa* that is associated with contrastive focus and *maa* that is not are supported by NSI facts. This contrastively focused *maa* is a negative that cannot license NPIs and can be followed by a (clitic) left dislocated NP or a preposed PP, while the unmarked *maa* (the one not associated with contrastive focus) can license NPIs. The following schematic representation, repeated from Chapter 3 for convenience, reflects the multi-locus reality displayed by the empirical distribution of the negative markers in SA:

(89)   [FocusP CONTRASTIVE FOCUS MAA [NegP PRESUPPSOTIONAL/
        EMPHATIC MAA [TP [NegP UNMARKED NEGATION LAA/LAM/
        LAN [*v*P . . .

Notes

1. The use of *ma. . .-š* for expressing sentential negation is attested in the modern Arabic dialects. It is found in the North African and Levantine dialect regions, as well as in Yemen and Oman. For further information, see Cowell (1964), Woidich (1968), Holes (1995), Brustad (2000), among others.

2. All the examples in this chapter are from Jordanian Arabic unless otherwise indicated.

3. The present indicative verb is also called the b-imperfect because it always carries the prefix *ba-*. The imperfective verb that does not carry this

prefix (such as negative imperative and infinitive verb forms) is called the y-imperfect (cf. Lucas 2009).

4. See also the same phenomenon in Morrocan Arabic.

    (i)   ma-qra-š   l-wəld   (MA)
           NEG-read.3MSG.PFV-NEG   the-boy
           'The boy didn't read.' (Aoun et al. 2010: 96)

    (ii)   Omar ma-ta-y-šrəb-š   (MA)
           Omar NEG-ASP-3MSG-drink.IPFV-NEG
           'Omar does not drink.' (Benmamoun 2000: 83)

5. Moroccan Arabic patterns with JA in this respect:

    (i)   *Omar ma-ši   ta-y-šrəb   (MA)
           Omar   NEG-NEG ASP-3MSG-drink.IPFV

    (ii)   *maši ʕand-ii   sayyara   (MA)
           NEG   at-me   car
           'I don't have a car.' (Benmamoun 2000: 83)

6. Soltan 2011 marks this example with a question mark to indicate that this negation pattern occurs less preferably in this context compared to in the context of imperfective verbs. The point here, Soltan's point per se, is that it is a possibility (although less preferable).

7. Moroccan Arabic is different from the other dialects discussed here in that nominal and adjectival predicates can host negation in verbless sentences.

    (i)   Omar ma-ši   muʕallim   (MA)
           Omar   NEG-NEG teacher
           'Omar is not a teacher.' (Benmamoun 2000: 46)

    (ii)   huwa   ma-fəllah-š   (MA)
           he   NEG-farmer-NEG
           'He is not a farmer.' (Aoun et al. 2010: 101)

    (iii) a. ʕomar ma-ši   mridˤ   (MA)
               Omar NEG-NEG ill
              'Omar is not ill.' (Aoun et al. 2010: 41)

          b. ʕomar ma-mridˤ-š   (MA)
               Omar NEG-ill-NEG
              'Omar is not ill.' (Aoun et al. 2010: 41)

8. When analyzing negation in PA, Hoyt (2007) entertains the idea that -š could be the head of I^0. There are two reasons for placing -š as the head of I^0. The first is based on the assumption that the verb is in I^0 (V-to-I/T movement). The second is based on the assumption that *ma* is in a functional projection on top of IP. The latter assumption is based on the observation that *ma* appears as a proclitic on elements that are preverbal as in the subject NPI *ħada* in (i), the adverbial NPI *ʕumr*. Consider the illustrative examples from JA below. Under the multi-locus analysis of this book, these examples may support the idea

that negation can be above TP but they do not constitute grounds for rejecting the idea that negation can project below TP. Nonetheless, one might argue that negation is the spell-out of a negative feature specified at the NP *hada* and the adverb *ʕumr*, respectively. The negative indefinite is analyzed as a pronoun of negation in Awwad (1987), Mohammad (1998), and Brustad (2000). In a similar fashion, the negative adverb can be treated as a negative compound that does not branch in syntax (cf. Alqassas 2015 for this analysis).

(i)   ma-had-aaš   zaar   el-batra   (JA)
      NEG-INDEF.PRON-NEG   visit.3MSG.PFV   DEF-Petra
      'No one visited Petra.'

(ii) ma-ʕumr-h-uuš   zaar   el-batra   (JA)
      NEG-ever-3MSG-NEG   visit.3MSG.PFV   DEF-Petra
      'He never visited Petra.'

Hoyt (2007) also gives examples from a Palestinian variety that has negation preceding the existential preposition *fii* and the inflected prepositions (possessive prepositions) Such cases are ungrammatical in JA (cf. examples below):

(i)   *ma-fii-h-š   kaan   masʕaari   bi-l-bank   (JA)
      NEG-exist-3MSG-NEG   COP.3MSG.past   money   in-DET-bank
      'There was no money in the bank.'

(ii) *ma-maʕ-i-š   kaan   masʕaari   (JA)
      NEG-have-I-NEG   COP.3MSG.past   money
      'I did not have money.'

Such examples can only be produced under some performance related conditions, be it 'distractions, shifts of attention and interest, and errors ... false starts, deviations from rules, changes of plans in mid-course ...' (Chomsky 1965: pp. 3–4). In other words, these two instances of negation should not be the critical empirical observation that drives the analysis of sentential negation in the language.

9. The separate functional head for -š is claimed to better account for the complementary distribution between -š and the NPI *ʕumr*. It provides a syntactic position that can be targeted for deletion. This can be compared to the discontinuous head analysis in which it is hard to target -š and can also be compared to the specifier position that theoretically does not block NPIs from occupying other (multiple) specifier positions of the same functional head.

10. This assumption is also supported by cross-linguistic evidence that Negative Concord (NC) languages project a NegP. Zeijlstra's (2004) conclusion was that languages which have NC also have a NegP projection. Example (i) shows that JA is an NC language. The negative constituent consisting of *wala-hada* 'no-one' obligatorily co-occurs with the negative marker.

(i)   ma-šuft-iš   wala-ħada   (JA)

NEG-see.1SG.PFV-NEG   no-one

'I didn't see anyone.'

11. I use the notation (`) to mark sentential stress.

12. Agreement here involves agreement in negative features and not phi-features as will be clear from the analysis that follows.

13. Another argument for the head status of -*š* (as well as *ma* and *la*) comes from the standard analysis that negative affixes and weak and strong negative particles are syntactic heads, whereas negative adverbs are maximal projections (cf. Zanuttini 1997a, 1997b, 2001; Rowlett 1998; Merchant 2001; Zeijlstra 2004, 2008), the negative marker -*š* is expected to be a head rather than an XP. While treating -*š* as a head may be unproblematic, I show that treating it as part of *ma* is problematic.

14. Lucas (2009: 249) reports one example in which the imperative is negated with -*š* by itself. He does not report whether Palestinian Arabic uses *ma* in the imperative. JA uses *la* along with -*š* in addition to -*š* by itself.

15. While the tense of the overall clause in these examples is past, it is important to note that what is negated is the imperfective verb rather than the past tense auxiliary *kunt*.

16. Another relatively similar deletion rule in all Arabic dialects as well as in SA is the assimilation of /l/ when followed by a coronal initial word as in (*al-dub* → *a-ddub* 'the bear'). The difference here is that the deletion involves compensation by geminating the coronal.

17. Of course, if a certain dialect uses -*š* alone to negate imperative verbs and does not use *la* to negate the imperative, one can confidently say that this dialect has partially progressed to a stage where -*š* is the source of negative interpretation.

18. This is not the case for negation in EA, as I explain later.

19. For the MA examples in which adjectival and nominal predicates can merge with negation, I do not think the there is syntactic head movement of the predicate. I think it is merely a morphological merger that takes place in the PF component.

20. All instances of negated copular pronouns are more likely to be attested in the speech of older speakers. It is more common these days to not pronounce the pronoun.

21. This approach of finding a host for the clitic at PF and only incidentally in narrow syntax is a prominent approach in distributed morphology and has been followed by many authors (Marantz 1984, 1988; Halpern 1992; Schutze 1994; Embick and Izvorski 1996; Embick and Noyer 2001; among others). Notice, however, that I adopt a modified version of this approach. My approach is that language may opt for providing a host for the clitic in either narrow syntax or PF. This is supported by the empirical evidence from distribution of negation patterns in JA and CEA, explaining the parametric

choices in JA and CEA. Crucially, however, syntactic movement and morphological movement are in complementary distribution when available
in the same language, as will be shown for MA. This is supported by the
empirical evidence regarding how negation patterns are distributed in JA
and CEA.

22. Thanks are due to Abbas Al-Tonsi, Mahmoud Al-Ashiri, and Yehia Mohamed
    for providing judgment. See also Al-Tonsi et al. (1987: 107) for a similar
    example.

23. It is possible to find support for idea that the predicate does not move to the
    negation head in CEA due to lack of a checking requirement, while JA has
    that checking requirement. Interestingly, EA is also a wh-in situ language,
    unlike JA. So it is not surprising to find a contrast between CEA and JA in
    negation too. CEA, similar to Coptic, is an in situ language. The contrasts
    between JA and CEA can then be looked at as contrasts in movement. JA
    has movement while CEA does not. I thank Abbas Benmamoun for pointing
    out the possible correlation between my analysis and the fact that CEA is
    influenced by Coptic, as an in situ language.

24. There is not much known about this dialect, and we do not know why
    this type of negation in Sharqiyya might be higher than TP. But it is pos-
    sible that there are semantic or pragmatic differences between perfective
    verbs negated by the discontinuous morpheme *ma...š* and perfective verbs
    negated by *miš*.

25. These mechanisms are perhaps enough to explain the distribution of
    Moroccan Arabic negation patterns. Moroccan Arabic is a dialect that
    resembles JA and differs from CEA in that it does not allow independ-
    ent negation with imperfective verb forms. Therefore, one can claim that
    Moroccan Arabic has the same feature checking requirement, which is
    Benmamoun's (2000) original idea and adopted in this book. However
    Moroccan Arabic differs from both JA and CEA in that it allows more cases
    of discontinuous negation. The position I take here is to propose that it is a
    morphological operation in Moroccan Arabic that produces those cases of
    discontinuous negation in verbless sentences, where nominals and adjectives
    can host negation. Examples are from Aoun et al. (2010: 101).

(i) a. huwa   ma-fəllaḥ-š   (MA)
         he   NEG-farmer-NEG
         'He is not a farmer.'

(ii) b. huwa   ma-tˤwil-š   (MA)
         he   NEG-tall-NEG
         'He is not tall.'

The morphological rule simply specifies that these are suitable hosts
for negation in that dialect. As predicted earlier, this rule is optional in
Moroccan Arabic since independent negation is also possible in these cases
(Benmamoun 2000: 46).

(i)   a.   Omar   ma- ši   muʕallim   (MA)
             Omar   NEG-NEG   teacher
             'Omar is not a teacher.'

(ii)   b.   Omar   ma-ši   mridˤ   (MA)
             Omar   NEG-NEG   sick
             'Omar is not sick.'

Recall that the availability of a checking requirement for negation in JA was the explanation for why prepositional predicates carrying subject agreement inflections must merge with negation. If Moroccan Arabic has the same checking requirement, we predict that independent negation should be ungrammatical in this same context. This prediction is borne out in the following example:

(i)   *maši   ʕand-ii   sayyara   (MA)
        NEG   at-me   car
        'I don't have a car.'

26. Examples (7a–b) are from Kayne (1989), cited in Zeijlstra (2004: 153), (7c) is from Zeijlstra (2004).

27. Languages in which the negative element is a head can express the same concept as 'why not' (e.g., Italian *perque no?*).

28. However, we may find it in other environments as in discontinuous negation with nominal and adjectival modifiers in Moroccan Arabic (cf. Benmamoun 2000).

6

The Jespersen Cycle of negation

6.1 Syntactic variation and change in Jordanian Arabic negation[1]

This chapter explores the dynamic interaction between syntax and phonology behind the complex variation in negation strategies in Jordanian Arabic (JA) discussed in this book as well as an unexpected change-in-progress in their distribution counter to the direction of the Jespersen Cycle (JC). This chapter discusses the free variation and mutual exclusivity of the negation strategies from a diachronic perspective within the JC of negation. The primary focus is on the limited distribution of enclitic negation (stage III negation in JC) and the ongoing spread of single negation (stage I negation in JC) in pragmatically marked contexts. This analysis sheds light on the interplay between the Internal Language (I-Language) and External Language (E-Language) of a speaker with respect to the locus of negation as either below TP or above TP.

Recall that JA has all three stages of the JC. The following are illustrative examples for each stage.

In stage I, negation is expressed by one element.

(1) maa   b-aʕrif   (JA)
     NEG   ASP-know.1SG.IPFV
     'I don't know.'

In stage II this element weakens and a new element is introduced to reinforce the first element.

(2) ma-b-aʕrif-iš   (JA)
     NEG-ASP-know.1SG.IPFV-NEG
     'I don't know.'

In stage III the first element is dropped and the new element becomes the only marker of negation.

(3) b-aʕrif-iš   (JA)
     ASP-know.1SG.IPFV-NEG
     'I don't know.'

The synchronic analysis of negation as able to occupy a position below
TP or above TP provides two important findings in support of Lucas's
(2009, 2010) JC reconstruction of -š as an NPI adverb *šayʔ/ʔiši* 'at all.'[2]
The three major categories of negation (single, bipartite, and enclitic)
can represent the three stages of the cycle (I, II, and III, respectively).
They co-exist synchronically but in different syntactic and pragmatic
contexts.

Second, the incompatibility between single negation and -š reveals the
inner workings of the cycle. Being syntactically adjacent to the verb, the
lower marker *ma* weakens morphologically, hence the need for *ʔiši/-š* as
a reinforcer. However, since *maa* is higher and not adjacent to the verb,
we do not expect it to weaken or give rise to the need for -š, resulting in
incompatibility between single negation and -š.

6.2 Negation strategies in Jordanian Arabic

Discussion in this book of the negation strategies in JA has focused
primarily on the Hourani dialect which has bipartite negation as the
canonical strategy.

(4) a. ma-b-aʕrif-iš   (Hourani)
         NEG-ASP-know.1SG.IPFV-NEG
         'I don't know.'

     b. ma-ʕrift-iš   (Hourani)
         NEG-know.1SG.PFV-NEG
         'I didn't know.'

Single negation is the non-canonical strategy associated with syntactically and semantically marked contexts. Therefore the two negation
strategies are mutually exclusive and give rise to the following distributional contrasts:

(5) a. wallah   maa   b-isaamḥ-ak   (JA)
         by-God   NEG   ASP-forgive.3MSG.IPFV -you
         'By God, he will not forgive you.' (adapted from Alqassas
         2015: 114)

     b. *wallah   ma-b-isaamiḥ-k-iš   (JA)
         by-God   NEG-ASP-forgive.3MSG.IPFV -you

(6) a. ʕumr-o   maa zaar   el-batra   (JA)
         NPI-ever-his NEG visit.3MSG.PFV   DEF-Petra
         'He has never visited Petra.'

     b. *ʕumr-o   ma-zaar-iš   el-batra   (JA)
         NPI-ever-his NEG-visit.3MSG.PFV-NEG   DEF-Petra
         'He has never visited Petra.'

Under the JC of negation, the expectation is that enclitic negation gradually becomes more commonplace as single negation dies out. However, there is evidence of a change-in-progress in the Hourani dialect of JA showing that single negation is spreading into unmarked contexts in which bipartite negation is expected. To understand why this change is taking place, we need to consider the possible extra-linguistic reasons in addition to the internal linguistic reasons that could be driving this change.

As for the extra-linguistic factors, it is important to consider the influence of dialect contact in this context. Single negation is available in the Ammani variety as the canonical strategy:

(7) a. maa b-aʕrif   (Ammani)
         NEG ASP-know.1SG.IPFV
         'I don't know.'

     b. maa ʕrift   (Ammani)
         NEG know.1SG.PFV
         'I didn't know.'

This creates a variationist context in which single negation and bipartite negation are mutually exclusive in the I-Language of a Hourani speaker, but the two negatives are in free variation from the perspective of the E-Language. According to Lightfoot (2006), I-Language is an internal system of an individual. The E-Language is language out there with its range of variation in the community of practice, not representing any internal system of an individual. The availability of single negation as a free variant has the potential to drive the spread of single negation. This chapter, however, argues that single negation is spreading primarily due to linguistic reasons.

The following section discusses the distributional limitations on enclitic negation to show that enclitic negation involves phonological deletion of the proclitic negative marker *ma-* rather than a genuine stage III negation. This is with the exception of negative imperatives which exhibit a genuine stage III negation. I then continue to discuss the effect of pragmatically ambiguous contexts in expanding the distribution of stage III negation.

6.3 Stage III negation in Jordanian Arabic: phonological deletion

The use of the enclitic negative marker in Levantine Arabic is analyzed in the literature in two different ways. Some analyze it as a by-product of the phonological reduction of the proclitic negative marker *ma-* (cf. Blau 1960; Lucas 2009, 2010 for Palestinian Arabic). Others analyze it as a genuine stage III negation where the enclitic marker is inherently negative (Wilmson 2014).

The negative marker *ma-* gets deleted when it is followed by a labial-initial predicate as a result of the phonological process known as 'haplology.' The negative marker *ma-* is a labial morpheme and attaching it to a labial-initial predicate creates a bilabial clash. In JA, there is distributional evidence to support the idea that stage III negation (the use of the enclitic by itself) is the result of phonological deletion of *ma-*. Consider the following contrasts showing the grammaticality of enclitic negation in labial-initial predicates and the ungrammaticality of enclitic negation in non-labial-initial predicates:

(8) a. b-aʕrif-iš   (JA)
ASP-know.1SG.IPFV-NEG
'I don't know.' (imperfective verb)

b. maʕ-naa-š   masʕaari   (JA)
have-us-NEG   money
'We do not have money.' (prepositional predicate)

c. fii-naa-š   ħeel   (JA)
in-us-NEG   strength
'We do not have the strength.' (prepositional predicate)

d. bad-naa-š   nruuħ   (JA)
want-we-NEG   go.1PL.IPFV
'We do not want to go.' (pseudo-verb)

(9) a. *(ma-)ʕrift-iš   (JA)
(NEG)know.1SG.PFV-NEG
'I didn't know' (perfective verb)

b. *(ma-) ʕinda-naa-š   sayyaara   (JA)
(NEG) have-us-NEG   car
'We do not have a car.' (prepositional predicate)

c. *(ma-) il-naa-š   ʔaxu   (JA)
(NEG) have.we-NEG   brother
'We do not have a brother.' (prepositional predicate)

There is supporting evidence that a bilabial clash is the trigger for enclitic negation. Consider the following case in which stage III negation is acceptable with the labial-initial perfective copula *baga* in the speech of older Hourani speakers, but stage III is not acceptable with the non-labial-initial perfective copula *kaan* (cf. Alqassas 2012 for details of this study).

(10)   a.   *(ma-)   kunt-iš   bi-l-beit   (JA)
              (NEG)   COP.1SG.PFV-NEG   at-DEF-home
              'I was not at home.'

      b.   (ma-)   bageet-iš   bi-l-beit   (JA)
              (NEG)   COP.1SG.PFV-NEG   at-DEF-home
              'I was not at home.'

There is yet more evidence that supports the phonological deletion of *ma-* in such contexts. JA has evidence from phonological weakening in the speech of older subjects: *ma* → *ʔa* in all environments. Presumably, this stage was an intermediary stage laying the ground for *ma-* deletion at later stages and producing the synchronic phenomenon of enclitic negation in labial-initial contexts. Figure 6.1 shows higher acceptability of *ma-* reduction into *ʔa-* for older Hourani speakers (cf. Alqassas 2012 for details).

Therefore, it is reasonable to conclude that phonological deletion feeds the transition from stage II (bipartite negation) into stage III (enclitic negation).

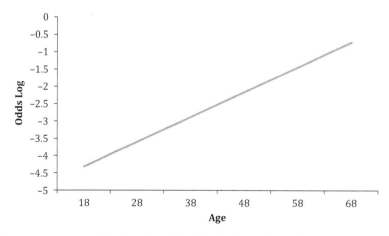

Figure 6.1 *ma-* weakening into *ʔa-* in labial-initial predicates

The challenge, however, is to explain why stage III negation is possible in negative imperatives, which are negated by the prolitic *la-* and the enclitic *-š*, with no bilabial clash. Neither the proclitic marker nor the imperative verb is labial. The proclitic marker is alveolar-initial and the imperative verb is always prefixed with the second person morpheme *t-*.

(11) (la)-t-ruuḥ-iš   (JA)
      (NEG)-2go.IMP-NEG
      'Don't go.' (negative imperative)

Could this be an alveolar clash that results in the deletion of the whole monosyllabic morpheme *la-*? It is possible to entertain this idea because there are cases of alveolar deletion in JA. Recall the following cases:

(12) a.   tˤuul   nhaar-oh   y-ištayil   (JA)
           length   daytime-his   3MSG-work.IPFV
           'He's working all day long.'

      b.   tˤu-nhaar-oh   y-ištayil   (JA)
           length-daytime-his   3MSG-work.IPFV
           'He's working all day long.'

The word-final alveolar consonant [l] in the noun *tˤuul* is deleted when followed by the alveolar-initial noun *nhaar*.

Recall also the deletion of the definite article *l-* (another alveolar consonant) in nouns that have a [l] word initially as in *lḥaaf* 'blanket' and *lsaan* 'tongue.'

(13) a.   l-ilḥaaf   →   ilḥaaf   (JA)
           DEF-blanket   blanket
           'the blanket'   'the blanket'

      b.   l-ilsaan   →   ilsaan   (JA)
           DEF-tongue   tongue
           'the tongue'   'the tongue'

A relatively similar deletion rule is the assimilation of /l/ when followed by a coronal initial word as in (al-dub → a-ddub 'the bear'). In this case, however, the deletion also involves a compensation by geminating the coronal.

Crucially all of these cases involve the deletion of an alveolar consonant, whereas the presumed deletion of the negative marker *la-* would constitute a case in which the whole monosyllabic morpheme *la-* is deleted. Accordingly, we conclude that at the very least the evidence is weak, since nowhere else in the language do we see deletion of alveolar-initial syllables.

Thus negative imperatives, which are non-labial-initial imperfective verbs, might be evidence of a genuine syntactic change to stage III negation as opposed to a phonological deletion of *la-*. Not all imperfective verbs in JA allow enclitic negation, however. Consider the following examples in which the subjunctive verb, which is also imperfective, does not allow enclitic negation:[3]

(14) ʕašaan   *(ma)-t-ruuḥ-iš   (JA)
      so that   *(NEG)-2MSG-go.SBJV-NEG
      'So that you go.' (subjunctive)

6.4 Stage III in Jordanian Arabic: syntactic change

So far it is reasonable to conclude that negation in JA has partially changed into stage III negation. That is, only negative imperatives seem to have a genuine stage III negation. In JA, an imperative verb that is negated by the enclitic negative marker by itself may be inherently negative and does not have a dependency relation on a covert proclitic negative marker as a result of phonological deletion.

Accordingly, one can conclude that stage III negation is a process which is currently in progress in JA. Nonetheless, given that there are forces which promote stage III negation, such as the phonological deletion of *ma-* in labial-initial predicates in addition to the use of stage III in negative imperatives, it is intriguing to ask why stage III negation is limited in distribution.

This question becomes more intriguing once we consider empirical facts from child language acquisition and the history of the development of the enclitic negative marker. First, there is evidence that stage III negation is used across the board in child data. Consider the following illustrative examples showing enclitic negation used in labial and non-labial-initial predicates (cf. Abu El-Haija 1981 for data from JA children) iš:

(15) b-aʕrif-iš   (JA)
      ASP-know.1SG.IPFV-NEG
      'I don't know.'

(16) ʕrift-iš   (JA)
      know.1SG.PFV-NEG
      'I didn't know.'

(17) t-ruuḥ-iš   (JA)
      2-go.IMP-NEG
      'Don't go.'

Moreover, stage II negation (the development of the enclitic suffix as a negative marker) first emerged sometime between the eighth to the eleventh centuries (Lucas 2007: 414). Considering these elements, we would expect stage III negation to be widespread, and we might expect a complete change into stage III negation in the future at which point single negation will not be used at all.

The obvious answer as to why a complete shift to stage III negation (at which point single negation is dropped) is not possible in JA lies in the fact that stage I negation (single negation) is mutually exclusive with stage II negation (bipartite negation). Therefore, acquiring stage I negation as the negation strategy associated with syntactically and semantically marked contexts leads to a situation where the distribution of bipartite negation and enclitic negation cannot be across the board. Crucially, however, there is evidence showing that contexts that are ambiguous in markedness (that is to say, they can have either a marked or unmarked interpretation) allow the use of single negation even when the sentence has an unmarked reading. Recall that rhetorical questions give us one context in which single negation is obligatory and bipartite negation is ungrammatical. The outcome of this restriction is that a question that has bipartite negation will be interpreted as an interrogative question (an unmarked interpretation), whereas a question that has single negation will be interpreted as a rhetorical question:

(18) leeš   inbaariħ   ma-dʒaab-hin-iš   (JA)
      why   yesterday   NEG-bring.3MSG.PFV-them-*NEG
      'Why didn't he bring them yesterday?' (interrogative)
      #'Why didn't he bring them yesterday!' (rhetorical)

(19) leeš   inbaariħ   maa   dʒaab-hin   (JA)
      why   yesterday   NEG   bring.3MSG.PFV-them
      'Why didn't he bring them yesterday!' (rhetorical)
      'Why didn't he bring them yesterday?' (interrogative)

However, a question which has single negation can also be interpreted as an interrogative question. Such cases do not involve stylistic shifting into the Ammani dialect which uses *maa* by itself as the unmarked negative marker.

Consider the following example in which single negation and bipartite negation are in free variation when construing the question as an interrogative. Again, the use of single negation to construe an interrogative question in this context does not involve style-shifting:

(20) miin   ma-dʒaab-hin-iš   (JA)
      who   NEG-bring.3MSG.PFV-them.F-NEG

'Who didn't bring them?' (interrogative)
#'Who didn't bring them?' (rhetorical)

(21) miin   maa   dʒaab-hin   (JA)
      who   NEG   bring.3MSG.PFV-them.fem
      'Who didn't bring them?' (rhetorical)
      'Who didn't bring them?' (interrogative)

Accordingly, it is possible to reconstruct the following micro-steps for the ongoing spread of stage I negation in JA:

(22) Steps for the spread of stage I negation after becoming marked
      (i)   Stage I negation is marked and used in rhetorical questions
      (ii) Stage I negation is less marked and used in sentences ambiguous between a rhetorical and interrogative reading
      (iii) Stage I negation gradually becomes more acceptable in unmarked environments

The spread of stage I negation (single negation) is also attested in JA in contexts that are unmarked. This raises the question of a possible contact-induced change. Recall that stage I negation (single negation) is found in SA and urban JA of the Ammani variety. Alqassas (2012) investigated the possible effect of college education, gender, and age to test such a hypothesis. The study considered the distribution of negation in various phonological and syntactic environments using a grammaticality judgment and preference task. The results show that, when all predictors were entered simultaneously, only age was a significant predictor of the stylistic spread of stage I negation as measured by its use in unmarked contexts.

These results suggest that the use of stage I negation in unmarked contexts might be a gradual change-in-progress associated with the spread of stage I negation in contexts of ambiguous markedness.

Table 6.1 Variables simultaneously in the equation

		B	S.E.	Wald	df	Sig.	Exp(B)
Step 1[a]	Coll Ed	.616	.524	1.379	1	.240	1.851
	Age-centered	−.044	.016	7.678	1	.006	.957
	Gender	−1.002	.534	3.519	1	.061	.367
	Constant	−.319	.435	.537	1	.464	.727

Note: variable(s) entered on step 1: Coll Ed, Age-centered, Gender.

To summarize, the idea that mutual exclusivity contributes to the spread of stage I negation is supported by empirical evidence from heritage language acquisition. There is evidence of a correlation between Primary Linguistic Data (PLD) and accuracy in judging sentences involving mutual exclusivity between Negative Polarity Items (NPIs) and enclitic negation. In judging the grammaticality of sentences that have single negation in the context of NPIs, adult Egyptian heritage speakers have lower accuracy than adult native EA speakers (Albirini and Benmamoun 2015). In contrast, the same heritage speakers show higher accuracy when judging sentences designed to assess their acquisition of unmarked negation in Egyptian (bipartite negation) despite the impoverished input that heritage learners generally have.

This suggests that rich PLD (or having adequate exposure to PLD) is more critical for the acquisition of mutual exclusivity than it is for acquiring the locus of negation, suggesting that mutual exclusivity is acquired after unmarked negation.

As for the interplay between I-Language and E-Language, Lightfoot (2006) shows that E-Language changes are subtle and take time to spread, creating two co-existing systems and sometimes causing an I-Language change. I-Language changes can also lead to E-Language change. A new I-Language for a child presents other children with a new E-Language composed of both the old and the new I-Language input (Lightfoot 2006).

Restricting single negation to marked contexts is a development that came after the emergence of stage II bipartite negation (Lucas 2007, 2010). This is an I-Language feature that must have spread fast and still remains a feature today. The use of single negation in sentences that are ambiguous between an unmarked and a marked interpretation is an E-Language change. This change must have taken a long time to develop, and causes the spread of single negation elsewhere.

The ongoing spread of single negation in unmarked contexts exhibits the characteristics of an I-Language change-in-progress for the following reasons. First, the rate of spread is significantly fast when comparing co-existing generations in a short period of time. Second, social factors show no significant correlation with the change-in-progress that favors single negation. Third, the spread of single negation in subtle contexts (ambiguous contexts) is an E-Language feature that can explain its spread in unmarked contexts as an I-Language change.

As for what this means under the multi-locus analysis of negation in this book, single negation is only above TP before the change from single-locus to multi-locus *maa*. Single negation is both above TP and below TP after the change. This also means that the negative marker *maa* is gradually overtaking the function of bipartite negation as the unmarked type of negation, which predicts a change in the reverse direction with respect to the JC of negation in JA.

6.5 Conclusion

This chapter investigated syntactic change in one of the most variable categories in JA, namely negation. Internal factors (both syntactic and pragmatic) block the spread of stage III negation using the enclitic negative marker by itself, the new marker from a JC perspective, despite phonological factors spreading stage III. Pragmatic ambiguity as a trigger for change in the spread of single negation in subtle contexts (ambiguous contexts) is an E-Language feature, explaining its spread in unmarked contexts. The ongoing spread of single negation in unmarked contexts is an I-Language change-in-progress from single-locus to multi-locus distribution for the negative marker *maa*.

Notes

1. The ideas in this chapter benefitted from comments I received from the audience of the Georgetown University Roundtable (GURT) on Languages and Linguistics held in March 2017, organized by David Lightfoot. I thank David and the audience for the opportunity to present and improve these ideas.
2. Contra Wilmsen's 2014 reconstruction of -š as an interrogative pronoun.
3. This is presumably the case in Palestinian Arabic too.

7

Summary and conclusions

This chapter summarizes the central points argued for in the analyses chapters. The multi-locus analysis of negation provides a solid ground for investigating other syntactic categories such as the syntax of adverbs, subjects, tense, and the left periphery. The ability to explain the syntactic behavior of these categories (their co-occurance restrictions, semantic ambiguities, and subtle interpretational contrasts) leads us to a significantly better understanding of key issues related to the nature of subjects in syntactic theory, the movement of adverbs (XPs, syntactic adjuncts), and head movement of verbal and non-verbal predicates. Moreover, the multi-locus analysis of negation gives us insights into the syntactic licensing of a vital category of words, Negative Sensitive Items (NSIs), that have not received enough attention in the literature on Arabic. The syntactic licensing of these categories in Arabic bears on key theoretical issues in the cross-linguistic studies of negation and NSIs. Such issues include the syntactic licensing configurations for these items, the feature of structure/specifications of these items, and the availability of syntactic agreement in the context of negation.

Chapter 2 laid the ground for a multi-locus analysis for negation in Arabic. The chapter set out the background assumptions in the syntax of Arabic related to negation. Key issues were discussed including the previous analyses of negation, the position of the preverbal subjects, adverbial syntax, and the syntax of tense and aspect. The multi-locus analysis is initially motivated by key distributional contracts between the NegP protection below tense phrase (TP) and the one above TP in relation to the position of adverbs and subjects in the syntactic structure. Further support for this analysis is supplemented by the availability of complementizer deletion in certain contexts of negation, particularly with higher negation (use of *maa* by itself), and the availabity of certain negative markers such as *laa* and its variats *lam* and *lan* in the context of modals *qad* and *sawfa* in Arabic. The conclusion is that these modals and the higher negative compete to select a TP, hence their incompatibility with each other, and the compatibility between these modals and the lower negative.

Chapter 3 focuses on the semantic and pragmatic effects associated with the various positions of negation. The idea that the two negatives are located in different positions in the syntactic structure made it possible to probe the possible subtle semantic effects each negative has. Indeed, it is possible to find a contrast in the scope readings of each negative when construed with time adverbials. The higher negative (*maa* by itself) scopes over the time variable of tense, and thus has a wide scope interpretation of the temporal interpretation of the event and does not allow for a narrow scope interpretation of the event where the event can take place during a subset of the time period specified by tense or the time adverbial. The lower negative (e.g., bipartite negation in Jordanian Arabic (JA)), scopes over the event variable of the verb and allows for a narrow scope reading where the event could take place during the period of time specified by tense, hence the event can escape the scope of negation. An advantage for this analysis is that now we have an explanation for the correlation between the higher negative and adverbs of time that express categorical negation such as *qad* 'ever' in Qatari Arabic (QA) and *ʕumr* 'ever' in JA. The latter is a by-product of the former.

Similar contrasts can be found between the various negative markers located in different syntactic positions. Particularly, presuppositional readings for negative statements can arguably be explained by a difference in the position of negation (higher in the TP) as opposed to the non-presuppositional interpretations associated with the lower NegP below TP.

Chapter 4 introduces the key contrasts between two major NSI categories and shows the explanatory adequacy of a multi-locus analysis of negation to account for the mutual exclusivity between certain NSIs on the one hand and bipartite negation on the other. The chapter lays out the theoretical background of NSI licensing as this is necessary to develop an analysis for NSIs based on the multi-locus analysis of negation. This chapter extends this analysis to the QA and Standard Arabic (SA) data giving further evidence that the different positions of negation have different effects on NPI licensing. By virtue of the multi-locus analysis, it is possible to reduce the behavior of the NPIs to whether the NPI is properly licensed via one of the two licensing confugurations: the c-command by negation or being in Spec-Head relation with negation. The mutual exclusivity between the NPI *ʕumr* 'ever' and the enclitic negative marker is an epiphenomenon of the availabity of two negatives: a lower negative (NegP below TP) realized as bipartite negation, and a higher negative (NegP above TP) realized as single negation.

Chapter 4 also discusses the interaction between higher negation and determiner NCIs (*wala*-NP). The analysis of *wala*-NP in JA has implications for the syntactic agreement analyses of the cross-linguistic phenomenon of Negative Concord (NC). The empirical facts from JA favor a syntactic agreement analysis of NC along the lines of Penka (2011).

Particularly, this NCI in *preverbal* position can be licensed by a negative compound that dominates it in the syntactic structure, i.e., c-commands it. Moreover, the insertion of a covert negation operator is a last resort mechanism to license this NCI when this NCI is merged (base generated) in the CP layer and neither a negative marker nor a negative compound is able to enter into a licensing configuration with the NCI. Accordingly, a multi-locus analysis of negation is necessary to allow the negative operator to be inserted in the left periphery of the clause. The multi-locus analysis can also explain why a contrastively focused *maa* is incompatible with Negative Polarity Items (NPIs) in SA, while the unmarked *maa*, with no contrastive focus interpretation, can license NPIs. Under the multi-locus analysis, the former *maa* is buried inside the focused constituent (DP, AdvP) located in a Focus projection in the CP layer, hence this *maa* does not c-command the NPI and fails to license it. The unmarked *maa*, however, is located in a NegP projection above TP whereby it co-commands the NPI and properly licenses it.

In Chapter 5, two patterns of bipartite negation (discontinuous and independent negation) in Arabic were analyzed, specifically with reference to the JA and Egyptian (Cairene and Sharqeyyah) dialects. Previous analyses explain the distribution of these two patterns either through a syntactic account (Benmamoun 2000; Aoun et al. 2010) or a morphological account (Soltan 2011). I show that the distributional overlap between these two patterns of negation within the same dialect and across dialects is a challenge for both analyses, since neither analysis can predict where a certain pattern is obligatory and where it is optional. Furthermore, the distribution of these patterns looks idiosyncratic from a descriptive perspective. Building on these two analyses, I instead develop an analysis that explains their distribution across and within each of these dialects in a principled way through both syntactic and morphological rules. I base my analysis on a version of the approach in which head movement can take place in narrow syntax or at PF/morphology (cf. Embick and Noyer 2001), as well as the approach in which cross-dialectal variation in the locus of negation is a priori, given that a certain language may opt for any position of negation (cf. Zanuttini 1997a, 1997b; Ramchand 2001; Zeijlstra 2004). Significantly, I argue that the obligatory discontinuous pattern is produced by syntactic verb movement to negation or the tense head, while optional discontinuous negation is the result of an optional morphological head movement. Thus, cross-dialectal variation is the result of an interaction between the locus of negation, V-to-T movement, feature checking of the negative marker, and morphological merger.

Based on empirical and theoretical evidence, I argued that the JA enclitic negative marker is not inherently negative in the bipartite negative marker *ma...-š* (contra Lucas 2009 and Aoun et al. 2010).

Accordingly, I argue for analyzing it as a separate head of a negative agreement projection, AgrPolP. Regarding -š as a head of an agreement projection rather than an adverb in Spec/NegP or a head of NegP is consistent with: (i) the fact that -š is not the realization of the negative operator (that is to say, it can co-occur with n-words without causing any double negation reading); (ii) the fact that -š is not inherently negative and cannot be used by itself (without *ma*) to negate subjunctive and y-imperfective verbs or with imperatives expressing cautioning (as well as all other non-labial-initial predicates); (iii) the fact that -š can only appear alone in the environments that allow phonological deletion of the negative markers *ma*; and (iv) the fact that -š can appear with two different negative markers, namely *ma* and *la*, and yet we do not have the sequence *la*. . .-š as a continuous morpheme on PAR with *miš*. I also entertain the idea that the negative marker *la*- in JA negative imperatives negated by -š by itself might involve a covert *la*- deleted phonologically, since the imperative verb is always prefixed with the alveolar-initial person clitic [t-] and the marker *la*- is also alveolar-initial, suggesting another case of haplology resembling the bilabial clash between *ma*- and labial-initial predicates. I also showed that this presumed deletion in negative imperatives is based on weak and inconclusive evidence.

The fact that -š is a clitic that attaches to the verb (or verbal complex) makes it plausible to claim that the verb incorporates with it via head movement. Indeed, similar arguments are made for the head status of *n't* in English and *ne* in French. It is also shown that all three negative markers *ma*, *la*, and -š fail the *why not* test as would be predicted if they are not syntactic adverbs (XPs).

As for SA, the sentential negative marker *maa* is above TP (it selects TP) and thus does not interact with tense. This explains why perfective and imperfective verbs can follow it. On the other hand, since it is below TP, *laa* interacts with tense giving rise to *lam* and *lan*, which explains why verbs following them are imperfective. Additionally, since it is above TP (selecting TP), the sentential negative marker *maa* can precede the subject of verbless sentences and the preverbal indefinite subject pronoun *ʔaħada*. However, being below TP, *laa* cannot precede the subject of verbless sentences and can form the lexical compound *laa-ʔaħada* functioning as a negative indefinite subject.

The sentential negative marker *maa*, being above TP, cannot negate nonfinite verbs, which suggests that these verbs do not have a TP. However since it is below TP, *laa* can negate nonfinite verbs. Finally, contrastive focus *maa* is a form of meta-linguistic negation/constituent negation in which *maa* is in a Focus projection FocP in a layered CP. This negative cannot license NPIs and can be followed by a (clitic) left dislocated noun phrase (NP) or a preposed prepositional phrase (PP).

Based on the analyses put forward for the SA negative markers, the following schematic representation illustrates the multi-locus nature of negation in SA:

[FocusP CONTRASTIVE FOCUS MAA [NegP PRESUPPSOTIONAL/EMPHATIC MAA [TP [NegP UNMARKED NEGATION LAA/LAM/LAN [*v*P . . .

Chapter 6 explored the multi-locus analysis from a diachronic perspective, taking into consideration a change-in-progress in JA negation. This chapter explores the idea that imperative verbs negated by -*š* by itself could be a genuine case of stage III negation (from a Jespersn Cycle (JC) perspective) which has the enclitic as the source of negative interpretation. The implications of this from the perpective of the JC of negation are also discussed. The chapter shows that the three stages of JC are attested in JA. There is also evidence of intermediary stages between stage I and stage II. The negative marker *ma-* is reduced into *ʔa-* in the speech of older speakers of JA and is acceptable by many younger speakers. This evidence favors a JC analysis of negation in JA (cf. Lucas 2009) where the enclitic negative marker developed as a reinforcer for the phonetically weakening negative marker ma-. As for the relevance of the multi-locus analysis to the JA data, there is evidence from the JA data that the position of negation in the syntactic structure is not a parametric choice between a NegP above TP or below TP. Given the findings of this study that stage I negation – single negation using *maa* by itself – is a negative marker located in a NegP above TP, while stage II negation – bipartite negation – is in a NegP below TP, and given that the two stages exist in JA, it follows that the two positions of negation are not a parametric choice. Interestingly, there is even evidence from JA that *maa* in JA is undergoing a change-in-progress from being a unilocus marker occupying the NegP position above TP to becoming a multi-locus marker marker that can also occupy the position of the NegP projection below TP.

Bibliography

Abu El-Haija, Lutfi (1981), 'The acquisition of the negation system in Arabic as spoken in Jordan', Ph.D. dissertation, The Pennsylvania State University.

Abusch, D. (1998), 'Generalizing tense semantics for future contexts', in *Events in Grammar*, ed. S. Rothstein, Dordrecht: Kluwer, pp. 13–35.

Abusch, D. (2004), 'On the temporal composition of infinitives', in *The Syntax of Time*, ed. J. Guéron and J. Lecarme, Cambridge, MA: The MIT Press, pp. 1–34.

Acquaviva, P. (1997), *The Logical Form of Negation: A Study of Operator-variable Structures in Syntax*, New York: Garland Publishing.

Al-Naadirii, Mohammad As'ad (2009), *Naḥw Al-Lugha Al-'arabiyya*, Beirut: Al-maktaba Al-assrya.

Al-Tonsi, A., L. Al-Sawi and S. Massoud (1987), *An Intensive Course in Colloquial Egyptian Arabic*, Cairo: Center for Arabic Studies, American University of Cairo.

al-Zamakhshari (1859), *Kitāb al Mufaṣṣal fī al-Naḥw*.

Albirini, A. and E. Benmamoun (2015), 'Factors affecting the retention of sentential negation in heritage Egyptian Arabic', *Bilingualism: Language and Cognition*, 18.3, pp. 470–489.

Alexiadou, A. (1994), 'Issues in the syntax of adverbs', Ph.D. dissertation, University of Potsdam.

Alexopoulou, T., E. Doron and C. Heycock (2004), 'Broad subjects and clitic left dislocation', in *Peripheries: Syntactic edges and their effects*, ed. D. Adger, C. de Cat and G. Tsoulas, Oxford: Oxford University Press, pp. 329–358.

Alqassas, A. (2012), 'The morpho-syntax and pragmatics of Levantine Arabic negation: a synchronic and diachronic analysis', Ph.D. dissertation, Indiana University.

Alqassas, A. (2015), 'Negation, tense and NPIs in Jordanian Arabic', *Lingua*, 156, pp. 101–128.

Alqassas, A. (2016), 'Temporal NPIs and NCIs as adverb phrases: the case of Jordanian Arabic', in *Perspectives on Arabic Linguistics XXVIII*, ed. Y. A. Haddad and E. Potsdam, Amsterdam/Philadelphia: John Benjamins Publishing Company.

Alqassas, A. (2018), 'Negative Sensitive Items', in *The Routledge Handbook of Arabic Linguistics*, ed. Elabbas Benmamoun and Reem Bassiouney, London: Routledge, pp. 104–131.

Alsarayreh, A. (2012), 'The licensing of negative sensitive items in Jordanian Arabic', Ph.D. dissertation, University of Kansas.

Alwer, E. (2003), 'New dialect formation: the focusing of -kum in Amman', in *Social Dialectology in Honour of Peter Trudgill*, ed. D. Britain and J. Cheshire, Amsterdam: Benjamins, pp. 59–67.

Andersen, H. (1973), 'Abductive and deductive change', *Language*, 49, pp. 765–793.

Anderson, S. R. (1992), *A-Morphous Morphology*, Cambridge: Cambridge University Press.

Aoun, J., E. Benmamoun and L. Choueiri (2010), *The Syntax of Arabic*, Cambridge: Cambridge University Press.

Austin, John (1962), *How to do Things with Words*, Oxford: Clarendon.

Awwad, Mohammad Amin (1987), 'Free and bound pronouns as verbs in rural Palestinian colloquial Arabic', *Journal of Arabic Linguistics*, 16, pp. 108–118.

Ayyoub, G. (1981), *Structure de la Phrase en Arabe Standard*. Third Cycle Thesis, Paris VIII-Vincenne, France.

Bahloul, R. (1996), 'Negation in French and Tunisian Arabic', in *Perspectives on Arabic Linguistics Vol. 8*, ed. M. Eid, Amsterdam: John Benjamins, pp. 67–83.

Baker, C. L. (1970), 'Double negatives', *Linguistic Inquiry*, 1, pp. 169–186.

Baker, M. (1985), 'The Mirror Principle and morphosyntactic explanation', *Linguistic Inquiry*, 16, pp. 373–415.

Baker, M. (2008), *The Syntax of Agreement and Concord*, Cambridge: Cambridge University Press.

Bakir, M. (1980), *Aspects of Clause Structure in Arabic*, Bloomington: Indiana University Linguistics Club.

Benmamoun, E. (1992), 'Inflectional and functional morphology: problems of projection, representation and derivation', Ph.D. dissertation, University of Southern California.

Benmamoun, E. (1996), 'Negative polarity and presupposition in Arabic', in *Perspectives on Arabic Linguistics VIII*, ed. M. Eid, Amsterdam: John Benjamins, pp. 47–66.

Benmamoun, E. (1997), 'Licensing of negative polarity items in Moroccan Arabic', *Natural Language and Linguistic Theory*, 15, pp. 263–287.

Benmamoun, E. (2000), *The Feature Structure of Functional Categories: A Comparative Study of Arabic Dialects*, Oxford: Oxford University Press.

Benmamoun, E. (2006), 'Licensing configurations: the puzzle of head negative polarity items', *Linguistic Inquiry*, 37.1, pp. 141–147.

Benmamoun, E. and R. Kumar (2006), 'The overt licensing of NPIs in Hindi', in *Yearbook of South Asian Languages and Linguistics 2006*, ed. R. Singh, Berlin: Mouton de Gruyter.

Benmamoun, E., M. Abunasser, R. Al-Sabbagh, A. Bidaoui and D. Shalash (2013), 'The location of sentential negation in Arabic varieties', *Brill's Journal of Afroasiatic Languages and Linguistics*, 5.1, pp. 83–116.

Bianchi, V. (1995), 'Consequences of antisymmetry for the syntax of headed relative clauses', Ph.D. dissertation, Scuola Normale Superiore, Pisa.

Blau, J. (1960), *Syntax des palästinensichen Bauerndialektes von Bīr-Zēt: auf Grund der "Volkserzählungen aus Palästina" von Hans Schmidt und Paul Kahle*, Walldorf, Hessen: Verlag für Orientkunde Dr. H. Vorndran.

Blau, J. (1965), *The Emergence and Linguistic Background of Judaeo-Arabic*, Oxford: Oxford University Press.

Blau, J. (1981), *The Emergence and Linguistic Background of Judaeo-Arabic*, Jerusalem: Ben Zvi Institute.

Blau, J. (2002), *A Handbook of Early Middle Arabic*, Jerusalem: Max Schloessinger Memorial Foundation.

Bobaljik, Jonathan David and Höskuldur Thráinsson (1998), 'Two heads aren't always better than one', *Syntax*, 1.1, pp. 37–71.

Boeckx, C. and S. Stjepanovic (2001), 'Head-ing toward PF', *Linguistic Inquiry*, 32.2, pp. 345–355.

Borer, H. (1995), 'The ups and downs of Hebrew verb movement', *Natural Language and Linguistic Theory*, 13, pp. 527–606.

Bošković, Ž. (1996), 'Selection and the categorial status of infinitival complements', *Natural Language and Linguistic Theory*, 14, pp. 269–304.

Bošković, Ž. (1997), *The Syntax of Nonfinite Complementation: An Economy Approach*, Cambridge, MA: The MIT Press.

Bowers, J. (1993), 'The syntax of predication', *Linguistic Inquiry*, 24, pp. 591–656.

Brown, S. (1999), *The Syntax of Negation in Russian: A Minimalist Approach*, Stanford, CA: CSLI Publications.

Brown, S. and S. Franks (1995), 'Asymmetries in the scope of Russian negation', *Journal of Slavic Linguistics*, 3, pp. 239–287.

Brustad, K. (2000), *The Syntax of Spoken Arabic: A Comparative Study of Moroccan, Egyptian, Syrian and Kuwaiti Dialects*, Washington, DC: Georgetown University Press.

Burrdige, K. (1993), *Syntactic Change in Germanic: Aspects of Language Change in Germanic, with Particular Reference to Middle Dutch*, Amsterdam: John Benjamins.

Burzio, L. (1986), *Italian Syntax*, Dordrecht: Reidel.

Bybee, J. (2003), 'Mechanisms of change in grammaticization: the role of frequency', in *Handbook of Historical Linguistics*, ed. R. Janda and B. Joseph, Oxford: Blackwell, pp. 602–623.

Bybee, J. and P. Hopper (eds) (2001), *Frequency and the Emergence of Linguistic Structure*, Amsterdam: John Benjamins.

Campbell, L. (2004), *Historical Linguistics: An Introduction*, Cambridge, MA: The MIT Press.

Chomsky, N. (1965), *Aspects of the Theory of Syntax*, Cambridge, MA: The MIT Press.

Chomsky, N. (1970), 'Remarks on nominalization', in *Reading in English Transformational Grammar*, ed. R. Jacobs and P. Rosenbaum, Waltham: Ginn, pp. 184–221.

Chomsky, N. (1989), 'Some notes on the economy of derivation', in *Functional Heads and Clause Structure, MIT Working Papers in Linguistics Vol. 10*, ed. I. Laka and A. Mahajan, Cambridge, MA: The MIT Press.

Chomsky, N. (1992), 'A minimalist program for linguistic theory', *MIT Occasional Papers in Linguistics 1*, Cambridge, MA: The MIT Press.

Chomsky, N. (1995), *The Minimalist Program*, Cambridge, MA: The MIT Press.

Chomsky, N. (2000), 'Minimalist inquiries, the framework', in *Step by Step: Essays on Minimalist Syntax in Honor of Howard Lasnik*, ed. R. Martin et al., Cambridge, MA: The MIT Press, pp. 1–52.

Chomsky, N. (2001), 'Derivation by phase', in *Ken Hale: A Life in Language*, ed. M. Kenstowicz, Cambridge, MA: The MIT Press, pp. 1–52.

Chomsky, N. (2004), 'Beyond explanatory adequacy', in *Structures and Beyond*, ed. A. Belletti, Oxford: Oxford University Press, pp. 104–131.

Cinque, G. (1999), *Adverbs and Functional Heads: A Cross Linguistic Perspective*, Oxford: Oxford University Press.

Collinder, B. (1969), *Survey of the Uralic Languages*, second revised edition, Stockholm: Almqvist & Wiksell.

Cormack, A. and N. Smith (2000), 'Head movement and negation in English', *Transactions of the Philological Society*, 98.1, pp. 49–85.

Cowell, M. (1964), *A Reference Grammar of Syrian Arabic*, Washington, DC: Georgetown University Press.

Dahl, Ö. (1979), 'Typology of sentence negation', *Linguistics*, 17, pp. 79–106.

Davidson, D. (1967), 'The logical form of action sentences', in *The Logic of Decision and Action*, ed. N. Rescher, Pittsburgh: University of Pittsburgh Press.

Davies, H. (1981), 'Seventeenth-century Egyptian Arabic: a profile of the colloquial material in Yusuf al-Sirbini's Hazz al-Quhuf fi Sarh Qasid abi Saduf', Ph.D. dissertation, University of California.

Dayal, V. (2004), 'The universal force of free choice *any*', *Linguistic Variation Yearbook*, 4, pp. 5–40.

Diesing, M. (1992), *Indefinites*, Cambridge, MA: The MIT Press.

Diesing, M. and E. Jelinek (1995), 'Distributing arguments', *Natural Language Semantics*, 3.2, pp. 123–176.

Embick, D. and R. Izvorski (1996), 'Participle-auxiliary word-orders in Slavic', in *Formal Approaches to Slavic Linguistics: The Cornell Meeting*, Ann Arbor, MI: Michigan Slavic Publications, University of Michigan, pp. 210–239.

Embick, D. and R. Noyer (2001), 'Movement operations after syntax', *Linguistic Inquiry*, 32.4, pp. 555–595.

Enc, M. (1991), 'On the absence of the present tense morpheme in English', MS thesis, University of Wisconsin.

Engels, E. (2012), *Optimizing Adverb Positions*, Amsterdam: John Benjamins.

Fassi-Fehri, A. (1993), *Issues in the Structure of Arabic Clauses and Words*, Dordrecht: Kluwer.

Fassi Fehri, A. (2000/2004), 'Temporal/aspectual interaction and variation across Arabic heights', in *The Syntax of Time*, ed. J. Lecame, Cambridge MA: The MIT Press, pp. 235–257.

Fassi Fehri, A. (2012), *Key Features and Parameters in Arabic Generative Grammar*, Amsterdam: John Benjamins

Ferguson, C. (1983), 'God wishes in Syrian Arabic', *Mediterranean Language Review*, 1, pp. 65–83.

Giannakidou, A. (1998), *Polarity Sensitivity as (Non)Veridical Dependency*, Amsterdam and Philadelphia: John Benjamins.

Giannakidou, A. (1999), 'Affective dependencies', *Linguistics & Philosophy*, 22, pp. 367–421.

Giannakidou, A. (2006), 'N-Words and negative concord', in *The Blackwell Companion to Syntax Vol. 3*, ed. M. Everaert et al., Malden: Blackwell.

Giannakidou, A. (2009), 'The dependency of the subjunctive revisited: temporal semantics and polarity', *Lingua*, 119, pp. 1883–1908.

Giannakidou, A. (2011), 'Negative and positive polarity items: licensing, compositionality and variation', in *Semantics: An International Handbook of Natural Language Meaning*, ed. C. Maineborn et al., Berlin: Mouton de Gruyter.

Giorgi, A. and F. Pianesi (1997), *Tense and Aspect: From Semantics to Morphosyntax*, Oxford: Oxford University Press.

Haegeman, L. (1995), *The Syntax of Negation*, Cambridge: Cambridge University Press.

Haegeman, L. (2002), 'Some notes on DP-internal negative doubling', in *Syntactic Microvariation*, ed. S. Barbiers, L. Cornips and S. van der Kleij, Amsterdam: Meertens Institute Electronic Publications in Linguistics 2, pp. 152–184.

Haegeman, L. and T. Lohndal (2010), 'Negative concord and (multiple) agree: a case study of West Flemish', *Linguistic Inquiry*, 41.2, pp. 181–221.

Haegeman, L. and R. Zanuttini (1991), 'Negative heads and the NEG criterion', *The Linguistic Review*, 8, pp. 233–251.

Haegeman, L. and R. Zanuttini (1996), 'Negative concord in West Flemish', in *Parameters and Functional Heads. Essays in Comparative Syntax*, ed. A. Belletti and L. Rizzi, Oxford: Oxford University Press, pp. 117–179.

Halle, M. and A. Marantz (1993), 'Distributed morphology and the pieces of inflection', in *The View from Building*, vol. 20, ed. K. Hale and S. J. Keyser, Cambridge, MA: The MIT Press, pp. 111–176.

Hallman, P. (2015), 'The Arabic imperfective', *Brill's Journal of Afroasiatic Languages and Linguistics*, 7, pp. 103–131.

Halpern, A. (1992), 'Topics in the placement and morphology of clitics', Ph.D. dissertation, Stanford University.

Harrell, R. (1962), *A Short Reference Grammar of Moroccan Arabic*, Washington, DC: Georgetown University Press.

Heim, I. (1982), 'The semantics of definite and indefinite noun phrases', Ph.D. dissertation, University of Massachusetts.

Heim, I. (1988), *The Semantics of Definite and Indefinite Noun Phrases*, New York: Garland.

Heim, I. (1994), *Comments on Absuch's theory of Tense*, Manuscript, Cambridge, MA: The MIT Press.

Herburger, E. (2001), 'Negative concord revisited', *Natural Language Semantics*, 9, pp. 289–333.

Hirschbühler, P. and M. Lahelle (1992/3), 'Le statut de *(ne) pas* en français contemporain', *Recherches Linguistiques de Vincennes*, 22, pp. 31–58.

Hoeksema, J. (1997), 'Negation and negative concord in Middle Dutch', in *Negation and Polarity: Syntax and Semantics*, ed. D. Forget, P. Hirschbühler, F. Martineau and M. Rivero, Amsterdam: John Benjamins, pp. 139–156.

Höhle, T. (1991), 'On reconstruction and coordination', in *Representation and Derivation in the Theory of Grammar*, ed. H. Haider and K. Netter, Kluwer: Dordrecht, pp. 139–197.

Holes, C. (1990), *Gulf Arabic*, London: Routledge.

Holes, C. (1995), *Modern Arabic: Structures, Functions and Varieties*, Washington, DC: Georgetown University Press.

Horn, Laurence R. (1985), 'Metalinguistic negation and pragmatic ambiguity', *Language*, 61, pp. 21–174.

Horn, Laurence R. (1989), *A Natural History of Negation*, Chicago: The University of Chicago Press.

Hornstein, N. (1995), *Logical Form: From GB to Minimalism*, Cambridge, MA: Blackwell.

Hoyt, F. (2005a), 'Negative concord in two dialects of Arabic', Manuscript, University of Texas, Austin.

Hoyt, F. (2005b), *Negative Concord and Restructuring in Palestinian Arabic*, Austin: University of Texas.

Hoyt, F. (2005c), *Sentential Negation Marking in Palestinian and Moroccan Arabic: A Study in Comparative Morphosyntax*, Austin: University of Texas.

Hoyt, F. (2007), 'An arabic wackernagel clitic? The morphosyntax of negation in Palestinian Arabic', in *Perspectives on Arabic Linguistics XX*, ed. M. Mughazy, Amsterdam: John Benjamins, pp. 105–134.

Hoyt, F. (2010), 'Negative concord in Levantine Arabic', Ph.D. dissertation, University of Texas.

Iatridou, S. (1990), 'About Agr(P)', *Linguistic Inquiry*, 21, pp. 551–577.

Jackendoff, R. (1969), 'An interpretive theory of negation', *Foundations of Language*, 5, pp. 218–241.

Jackendoff, R. (1972), *Semantic Interpretation in Generative Grammar*, Cambridge, MA: The MIT Press.

Jackendoff, R. (1977), 'X-bar-syntax: a study of phrase structure', *Linguistic Inquiry Monograph 2*, Cambridge, MA: The MIT Press.

Jackendoff, R. (1981), *Xbar Syntax: A Study of Phrase Structure*, Cambridge, MA: The MIT Press.

Jespersen, O. (1917), *Negation in English and Other Languages*, Copenhagen: Host.

Johnson, K. (1991), 'Object positions', *Natural Language and Linguistic Theory*, 9, pp. 577–636.

Johnstone, T. M. (1967), *Eastern Arabian Dialect Studies*, London Oriental Series 17, London: Oxford University Press.

de Jong, K. J. and B. A. Zawaydeh (1999), 'Stress, duration, and intonation in Arabic word-level prosody', *Journal of Phonetics*, 27, pp. 3–22.

Kayne, R. (1989), 'Notes on English agreement', *CIEFL 1*, pp. 40–67.

Kayne, R. (1992), 'Italian negative imperatives and clitic-climbing', in *Hommages à Nicolas Ruwet*, ed. L. Tasmowski-De Ryck and A. Zribi-Hertz, Ghent: Communication & Cognition, pp. 300–312. [Reprinted in Kayne (2000), *Parameters and Universals*, Oxford and New York: Oxford University Press.]

Kayne, R. (1994), *The Antisymmetry of Syntax*, Cambridge, MA: The MIT Press.

Kayne, R. (1998), 'Overt vs. covert movement', *Syntax*, 1, pp. 128–191.

Kemenade, V. (2000), 'Jespersen's Cycle revisited: formal properties of grammaticalization', in *Diachronic Syntax: Models and Mechanisms*, ed. S. Pintzuk, G. Tsoulas and A. Warner, Oxford: Oxford University Press.

Khan, G. (1999), *A Grammar of Neo-Aramaic: The Dialect of the Jews of Arbel*, Leiden: Brill.

Khan, G. (2004), *The Jewish Neo-Aramaic Dialect of Sulemaniyya and H: alabja*, Leiden: Brill.

Kitagawa, Y. (1986), 'Subjects in Japanese and English', Ph.D. dissertation, University of Massachusetts.

Koopman, H. and D. Sportiche (1991), 'The position of subjects', *Lingua*, 85.2/3, pp. 211–258.

Kouloughli, D. E. (1988), 'Renouvellement énonciatif et valeur aoristique: à propos de l'opposition maa/lam en arabe', *Langues Orientales Anciennes, Philologie et Linguistique*, 1, pp. 49–72.

Kuroda, S.-Y. (1988), 'Whether we agree or not: a comparative syntax of English and Japanese', *Lingvisticæ Investigationes*, 12, pp. 1–47.

Laanest, A. (1966), 'Izhorskii iazyk', in *IAzyki Narodov SSSR, Tom 3, Finno-Ugorskiei Samodiiskie Iazyki*, ed. V. I. Lytkin, Moscow: Nauka, pp. 109–111.

Ladusaw, W. (1977), 'The scope of some sentence adverbs and surface structure', in *Proceedings of NELS 8*, ed. M. J. Stein, Amherst: GLSA University of Massachusetts, pp. 97–111.

Ladusaw, W. (1979), 'Polarity sensitivity as inherent scope relations', Ph.D. dissertation, University of Texas.

Ladusaw, W. (1988), 'Adverbs, negation, and QR', in *Linguistics in the Morning Calm 2, Selected Papers from SICOL-1986*, ed. H. Haghoe, Seoul: The Linguistic Society of Korea, pp. 481–488.

Ladusaw, W. (1992), 'Expressing negation', in *Proceedings of SALT II*, ed. C. Baker et al., Cornell, NY: Cornell Linguistic Circle.

Laka, I. (1990), 'Negation in syntax: on the nature of functional categories and projections', Ph.D. dissertation, Massachusetts Institute of Technology.

Lasnik, H. (1975), 'On the semantics of negation', in *Contemporary Research in Philosophical Logic and Linguistic Semantics*, ed. D. J. Hockney, Dordrecht: Reidel.

Lebeaux, D. (1990), 'Relative clauses, licensing and the nature of the derivation', in *Proceedings of NELS Vol. 20*, University of Massachusetts, MI: GLSA, pp. 318–332.

Lightfoot, D. (2006), *How New Languages Emerge*, Cambridge: Cambridge University Press.

Lightfoot, D. (2017), 'Discovering new variable properties without parameters', *Linguistic Analysis* (Special Edition, edited by Simin Karimi and Massimo Piattelli-Palmarini, *Parmeters: What are they? Where are they?*), 41.3–4, pp. 409–445.

Linebarger, M. C. (1980), 'The grammar of negative polarity', Doctoral dissertation, Massachusetts Institute of Technology. [Reproduced by the Indiana University Linguistics Club, Indiana, 1981.]

Linebarger, M. C. (1981), *The Grammar of Negative Polarity*, Bloomington: Indiana University Linguistics Club.

Linebarger, M. C. (1987), 'Negative polarity and grammatical representation', *Linguistics and Philosophy*, 10, pp. 325–387.

Lucas, C. (2007), 'Jespersen's Cycle in Arabic and Berber', *Transactions of the Philological Society*, 105, pp. 398–431.

Lucas, C. (2009), 'The development of negation in Arabic and Afroasiatic', Ph.D. dissertation, University of Cambridge.

Lucas, C. (2010), 'Negative -š in Palestinian (and Cairene) Arabic: present and possible past', *Brill's Annual of Afroasiatic Languages and Linguistics*, 2.1, pp. 165–201.

Marantz, A. (1984), *On the Nature of Grammatical Relations*, Cambridge, MA: The MIT Press.

Marantz, A. (1988), 'Clitics, morphological merger, and the mapping to phonological structure', in *Theoretical morphology*, ed. M. Hammond and M. Noonan, San Diego, CA: Academic Press, pp. 253–270.

Martin, R. (1996), 'A minimalist theory of PRO and control', Ph.D. dissertation, University of Connecticut.

Martin, R. (2001), 'Null case and the distribution of PRO', *Linguistic Inquiry*, 32, pp. 141–166.

McCarthy, J. (1979), 'Formal approaches in Semitic phonology and morphology', Ph.D. dissertation, Massachusetts Institute of Technology.

McCloskey, J. (1997), 'Subjecthood and subject positions', in *Elements of Grammar*, ed. L. Haegeman, Dordrecht: Kluwer.

Merchant, J. (2000), 'Antecedent-contained deletion in negative polarity items', *Syntax*, 3.2, pp. 144–150.

Merchant, J. (2001), 'Why no(t)', Manuscript, University of Chicago.

Mitchell, E. (2004), 'Evidence from Finnish for Pollock's Theory of IP', *Lingua*, 116, pp. 228–244.

Mohammad, M. (1989), 'The sentence structure of Arabic', Ph.D. dissertation, University of Southern California.

Mohammad, M. (1997) 'A minimalist approach to verb movement in Standard Arabic', *Studia Linguistica*, 51.3, pp. 317–338.

Mohammad, M. (1998), 'The syntax of indefinite subjects in equative sentences in Palestinian Arabic', Manuscript, University of Florida, Gainsville.

Mohammad, M. (2000), *Word Order, Agreement, and Pronominalization in Standard and Palestinian Arabic*, Philadelphia: John Benjamins.

Moritz, L. and D. Valois (1994), 'LF pied-piping and specifier agreement', *Linguistic Inquiry*, 25.4, pp. 667–707.

Moutaouakil, A. (1991), 'Negative constructions in Arabic: towards a functionalist approach', *The Arabist, Budapest Studies in Arabic*, 3–4, pp. 263–296.

Moutaouakil, A. (1993), *al-wathiifa wa l-binya*, Casablanca: 'ocaadh.

Mughazy, M. (2003), 'Metalinguistic negation and truth functions: the case of Egyptian Arabic', *Journal of Pragmatics*, 35, pp. 1143–1160.

Nunes, J. (2004), *Linearization of Chains and Sideward Movement*, Cambridge, MA: The MIT Press.

Omar, Margaret (1967), *The Acquisition of Egyptian Arabic as a Native Language*, Washington, DC: Georgetown University Press. [Republished in 2007.]

Ouali, H. and C. Fortin (2007), 'The syntax of complex tense in Moroccan Arabic', in *Perspectives of Arabic Linguistics Vol. 19*, ed. E. Benmamoun, Amsterdam: John Benjamins, pp. 175–187.

Ouali, H. and U. Soltan (2014), 'On negative concord in Egyptian and Moroccan Arabic', in *Perspectives of Arabic Linguistics Vol. 25*, ed. S. Farwaneh and H. Ouali, Amsterdam: John Benjamins.

Ouhalla, J. (1990), 'Sentential negation, relativized minimality and the aspectual status of auxiliaries', *The Linguistic Review*, 7, pp. 183–231.

Ouhalla, J. (1991), *Functional Categories and Parametric Variation*, London/New York: Routledge.

Ouhalla, J. (1993), 'Negation, focus and tense: the Arabic "*ma*" and "*la*"', *Rivista di Linguistica*, 5, pp. 275–300.

Ouhalla, J. (1994a), 'Focus in Standard Arabic', *Linguistics in Potsdam*, 1, pp. 65–92.

Ouhalla, J. (1994b), 'Verb movement and word order in Arabic', in *Verb Movement*, ed. D. Lightfoot and N. Hornstein, Cambridge: Cambridge University Press.

Ouhalla, J. (2002), 'The structure and logical form of sentences in Arabic', in *Themes in Arabic and Hebrew Syntax*, ed. J. Ouhalla and U. Shlonsky, Dordrecht: Kluwer Academic Publishers, pp. 299–320.

Palmer, F. R. (1986), *Mood and Modality*, Cambridge: Cambridge University Press.

Parsons, T. (1990), *Events in the Semantics of English*, Cambridge, MA: The MIT Press.

Partee, B. H. (1973), 'Some structural analogies between tense and pronouns in English', *Journal of Philosophy*, 70, pp. 601–609.

Partee, B. H. (1984), 'Nominal and temporal anaphora', *Linguistics and Philosophy*, 7, pp. 243–286.

Pei, Mario A. and Frank Gaynor (1954), *A Dictionary of Linguistics*, New York: Philosophical Library.

Penka, D. (2011), *Negative Indefinites*, Oxford: Oxford University Press.

Pesetsky, D. (1992), 'Zero syntax II: an essay on infinitives', Manuscript, Massachusetts Institute of Technology, Cambridge, MA.

Plunkett, B. (1993), 'The positions of subjects in Modern Standard Arabic', in *Perspectives on Arabic Linguistics V*, ed. M. Eid and C. Holes, Philadelphia: John Benjamins, pp. 231–260.

Pollock, J.-Y. (1989), 'Verb movement, universal grammar, and the structure of IP', *Linguistic Inquiry*, 20, pp. 365–424.

Pollock, J.-Y. (1993), 'Notes on clause structure', Manuscript, Université de Picardie, Amiens.

Potsdam, C. (1997), 'NegP and subjunctive complements in English', *Linguistic Inquiry*, 28, pp. 533–541.

Potsdam, E. (1999), 'A syntax for adverbs', in *The Proceedings of the Twenty-seventh Western Conference on Linguistics*, ed. E. van Geldren and V. Samiin, Fresno, CA: Department of Linguistics, California State University, pp. 397–411.

Progovac, L. (1993), 'Negative polarity: entailment and binding', *Linguistics & Philosophy*, 16, pp. 149–180.

Radford, Andrew (1997), *Syntactic Theory and the Structure of English*, Cambridge: Cambridge University Press.

Ramchand, G. (2001), 'Tense and negation in Bengali', in *Linguistic Structure and Language Dynamics in South Asia: 'Papers from the Proceedings of the SALA XVIII Roundtable, MLBD Series in Linguistics 15'*, ed. A. Abbi, R. S. Gupta and A. Kidwai, Delhi: Motilal Banarsidass, pp. 308–326.

Ramchand, G. (2002), 'Two types of negation in Bengali', Manuscript, Oxford University.

Reinhart, T. (1976), 'The syntactic domain of anaphora', Ph.D. dissertation, Massachusetts Institute of Technology.

Richards, M. (2006), 'Week pronouns, object shift and multiple spell out: evidence for phase at the PF interface', in *Minimalist Essays*, ed. C. Boeckx, Netherlands: John Benjamins Publishing Company: Linguistik Aktuell.

Ritter, E. and M. Wiltschko (2004), 'The lack of tense as a syntactic category: evidence from Blackfoot and Halkomelem', Paper presented at the 39th International Conference on Salish and Neighbouring Languages, North Vancouver and the Canadian Linguistics Association Annual Meeting, University of Manitoba, Winnipeg.

Ritter, E. and M. Wiltschko (2005), 'Anchoring events to utterances without tense', *Proceedings of WCCFL 24*, Somerville, MA: Cascadilla Proceedings Project, Cascadilla Press, pp. 343–351.

Rizzi, L. (1982), *Issues in Italian Syntax*, Dordrecht: Foris.

Rizzi, L. (1989), *Relativised Minimality*, Cambridge, MA: The MIT Press.

Rizzi, L. (1997), 'The fine structure of the left periphery', in *Elements of Grammar*, ed. L. Haegeman, Dordrecht: Kluwer, pp. 281–337.

Roberts, I. (2010), *Agreement and Head Movement: Clitics, Incorporation, and Defective Goals*, Cambridge, MA: The MIT Press.

Roberts. I. and A. Roussou (2003), *Syntactic Change: A Minimalist Approach to Grammaticalization*, Cambridge: Cambridge University Press.

Rowlett, P. (1998), *Sentential Negation in French*, New York/Oxford: Oxford University Press.

Rowlett, P. (2007), *The Syntax of French*, Cambridge: Cambridge University Press.

Sauerland, U. (2004), 'The interpretation of traces', *Natural Language Semantics*, 12, pp. 63–127.

Schmidt, H. and P. Kahle (1918), *Volkserzälungen aus Palästina, v.1*, Göttingen: Vandenhoek und Ruprecht.

Schuchardt, H. (1885), *Über die Lautgesetze: Gegen die Junggrammatiker*, Berlin: Oppenheim.

Schutze, C. (1994), 'Serbo-Croatian second position clitic placement and the phonology-syntax interface', in *MIT Working Papers in Linguistics 21: Papers on Phonology and Morphology*, ed. A. Carnie and H. Harley with T. Bures, MITWPL, Cambridge, MA: The MIT Press, pp. 373–473.

Searle, John (1975), 'A taxonomy of illocutionary acts', in *Language. Mind and Knowledge. Minnesota Studies in the Philosophy of Science, Vol. VII*, ed. K. Gunderson, Minnesota: University of Minnesota Press, pp. 344–369.

Shlonsky, U. (1997), *Clause Structure and Word Order in Hebrew and Arabic: An Essay in Comparative Semitic Syntax*, New York: Oxford University Press.

Shlonsky, U. (2004), 'The form of Semitic noun phrases', *Lingua*, 114.12, pp. 1465–1526.

Shunnaq, A. (2000), *Dictionary of Rural Terms in the North of Jordan, (Arabic-Arabic)*. A project subsidized by the Deanship of Research and Graduate Studies, Yarmouk University.

Soltan, U. (2007), 'On formal feature licensing in minimalism: aspects of Standard Arabic morphosyntax', Ph.D. dissertation, University of Maryland.

Soltan, U. (2011), 'On issues of Arabic syntax: An essay in syntactic argumentation', *Brill's Annual of Afroasiatic Languages and Linguistics*, 3, pp. 236–280.

Soltan, U. (2012), 'Morphosyntactic effects of NPI-licensing in Cairene Egyptian Arabic: the puzzle of -š disappearance resolved', in *Proceedings of the 29th West Coast Conference on Formal Linguistics*, ed. J. Choi et al., Somerville, MA: Cascadilla Proceedings Project, pp. 241–249.

Soltan, U. (2014a), 'On the distribution and licensing of polarity-sensitive items in Egyptian Arabic: the cases of ?ayy and walaa', in *Perspectives on Arabic Linguistics XXIV–XXV*, ed. S. Farwaneh and H. Ouali, Amsterdam/Philadelphia: John Benjamins Publishing Company.

Soltan, U. (2014b), 'Splitting NEG: the morphosyntax of sentential negation in Cairene Egyptian Arabic revisited', in *Perspectives on Arabic Linguistics XXVI*, ed. R. Khamis-Dakwar and K. Froud, Amsterdam/Philadelphia: John Benjamins Publishing Company.

Speas, M. (1991), 'Functional heads and the mirror principle', *Lingua*, 84, pp. 181–214.

Sportiche, D. (1988), 'A theory of floating quantifiers and its corollaries for constituent structure', *Linguistic Inquiry*, 19.2, pp. 425–451.

Szabolcsi, A. (2004), 'Positive polarity-negative polarity', *Natural Language and Linguistic Theory*, 22, pp. 409–452.

Tieken-Boon van Ostade, I., G. Tottie and W. van der Wurff (eds) (1998), *Negation in the History of English*, Berlin: Mouton de Gruyter.

Travis, L. (1984), 'Parameters and effects of word order variation', Ph.D. dissertation, MIT University Press.

Vallduví, E. (1994), 'Polarity items, n-words and minimizers in Catalan and Spanish', *Probus*, 6, pp. 263–294.

Van Mol, M. (2000), *Modern Arabic Representative Corpus (MARC-)2000*, KU-Leuven: Leuven.

Van Mol, M. (2003), *Variation in Modern Standard Arabic in Radio News Broadcasts: A Synchronic Descriptive Investigation into the Use of Complementary Particles*, Leuven: Peeters Publishers.

Watanabe, A. (2004), 'The genesis of negative concord: syntax and morphology of negative doubling', *Linguistic Inquiry*, 4, pp. 559–612.

Wehr, H. (1953), 'Zur Funktion arabischer Negationen', *ZDM G*, 103, pp. 27–39.

Williams, E. (1981), 'On the notions "lexically related" and "head of a word"', *Linguistic Inquiry*, 12, pp. 245–274.

Wilmsen, D. (2014), *Arabic Indefinites, Interrogatives and Negators: A Linguistic History of Western Dialects*, Oxford: Oxford University Press.

Woidich, M. (1968), 'Negation und Negative Satze im Agyptisch Arabischen', dissertation, Munich, Ludwig Maximilians Universität München.

Wurmbrand, S. (2014), 'Tense and aspect in English infinitives', *Linguistic Inquiry*, 45.3, pp. 403–447.

Ya'qub, I. B. (1986), *Mawsuu'at Al-Nahuu wa-l-Sarf wa-l-'I'raab*, Beirut: Daar Al-Ilm lil-Malaayiin.

Zanuttini, R. (1989), 'Two strategies for negation: evidence from Romance', in *Proceedings of ESCOL V*, ed. J. Powers and K. de Jong, Columbus: Ohio State University, pp. 535–546.

Zanuttini, R. (1991), 'Syntactic properties of sentential negation', Ph.D. dissertation, University of Pennsylvania.

Zanuttini, R. (1996), 'On the relevance of tense for sentential negation', in *Parameters and Functional Heads. Essays in Comparative Syntax*, ed. A. Belletti and L. Rizzi, Oxford: Oxford University Press, pp. 181–207.

Zanuttini, R. (1997a), *Negation and Clausal Structure: A Comparative Study of Romance Languages*, Oxford: Oxford University Press.

Zanuttini, R. (1997b), 'Negation and verb movement', in *The New Comparative Syntax*, ed. L. Haegeman, London and New York: Longman, pp. 214–245.

Zanuttini, R. (1998), *Negation and Clausal Structure. A Comparative Study of Romance Languages*, Oxford Studies in Comparative Syntax, New York/Oxford: Oxford University Press.

Zanuttini, R. (2001), 'Sentential negation', in *The Handbook of Contemporary Syntactic Theory*, ed. M. Baltin and C. Collins, Oxford: Blackwell, pp. 511–535.

Zeijlstra, H. (2004), 'Sentential negation and negative concord', Ph.D. dissertation, University of Amsterdam.

Zeijlstra, H. (2008), 'Negative concord is syntactic agreement', Manuscript, University of Amsterdam.

Zeijlstra, H. (2010), 'On French negation', in *Proceedings of the 35th Annual Meeting of the Berkeley Linguistics Society*, ed. I. Kwon, H. Pritchertt and J. Specnce, Berkeley, CA: Berkeley Linguistic Society.

Index